The Legacy of Pluralism

JURISTS: PROFILES IN LEGAL THEORY

WILLIAM TWINING, GENERAL EDITOR

THE LEGACY OF PLURALISM

The Continental Jurisprudence of Santi Romano, Carl Schmitt, and Costantino Mortati

MARIANO CROCE
and MARCO GOLDONI

STANFORD UNIVERSITY PRESS
Stanford, California

STANFORD UNIVERSITY PRESS
Stanford, California

Printed and bound by CPI Group (UK) Ltd, Croydon, CR0 4YY

Cataloging in Publication Data is available on request.

Library of Congress Control Number: 2020937858

Cover design: Rob Ehle

Typeset by Newgen in Galliard Pro 10/15

Contents

The Legacy of Pluralism

Introduction

ALL DISCIPLINES ARE REPLETE with opposing intellectual forces voicing the richness of the human reflective attitude to who we are and how we organize our coexistence. All geohistorical contexts are traversed by more or less irreconcilable accounts of what their present is and what its characterizing traits are. The conceptual history we set out to explore is particularly remarkable for these oppositions and contradictions. Most of the plot of this book unfolds between the rise of late nineteenth-century radical pluralism and the post–World War I establishment of totalitarian regimes—a complex sociopolitical scenario in which national states were facing a lethal threat. Antiparliamentary, socialist, and Marxist movements; insurrectionary anarchism; irredentism; revolutionary syndicalism; and other antisystemic turbulences were challenging the authority of the state and the preeminence of state law over alternative forms of governing and, more profoundly, structuring the social world.

As early as 1909, leading Italian jurist Santi Romano—one of the three protagonists of this book—identified the *pluralist state* as the political form that would succeed to the (seemingly) more cohesive national state. In an essay called *Lo Stato moderno e la sua crisi* (The Modern State and Its Crisis) he maintained that such a political turmoil would change once and for all the shape of the state as a supreme authority endowed with exclusive legislative powers and the monopoly of coercion. The alleged unity of the state—which Romano regarded as a fictitious production of state public law—was confronted with "a set of organizations and associations . . . [that] are endowed with a blooming life and an effective power [and that] tend to join and to connect with each other."[1] Romano believed this process would be conducive to the gradual decline of the legislative state that emerged out of the French Revolution and to the complete reorganization of its apparatus as a much looser complex of semiautonomous substate bodies.

However realistic Romano's portrait may have seemed in the first decade of the twentieth century, it would soon be supplanted by the rise of totalitarian regimes intended to overcome the problem of pluralism with a drastic, brutal, and eventually disastrous solution. Despite this, the main claim we will make in the following chapters is that Romano, along with German jurist Carl Schmitt and Italian jurist Costantino Mortati, deployed accounts of the interplay between pluralism and the state that offered intriguing alternative solutions to the one which many Western states would soon adopt. A related claim is that these accounts were not only able to favor an alternative juridico-political scenario at the time—their considerations on how the state should cope with radical pluralism are particularly relevant to present-day politics as well.

Romano, Schmitt, and Mortati are leading figures of classic legal institutionalism, one of the most influential schools of thought in Western legal theory. It is between the end of the nineteenth century and the first half of the twentieth century that classic legal institutionalism developed as a counterhistory of law. It is describable as a "counterhistory" because most of its representatives never yielded to the common view that the law and the state coincide, and a fortiori the history of law and the history of the state. Nor did they accept that the destiny of law is formal constitutions. While some institutional theories were certainly more apt to shore up state-based political arrangements, most of them, even state-centered ones, made the case that law is a broader phenomenon than the political structures that give legal orders a context-specific shape. Not only was such a theoretical feat scarcely facetious—at the time it also sounded as somewhat sacrilegious. In effect, the nineteenth century had witnessed the rise and consolidation of powerful and cohesive states (including states that had lagged behind in terms of territorial unification, such as Germany and Italy), so much so that in the legal field debates mainly revolved around the foundational character of the sovereign will of the state, its legal personality, and the state's being the ethical shell of the national community.

Legal institutionalists took very seriously the series of unexpected fissures and breakpoints that at the end of the nineteenth century was threatening the state as the political form par excellence. In effect, a great many civil society associations, political organizations, and antisystemic movements were posing a lethal threat to the very idea of the state as the *destiny of politics.* These emerging social actors begun to depict the state as a corrupted and hegemonic construct that the dominant elites nurtured to sway civil society and the myriads of spontaneous, self-organizing forces at play within them. Within the polyvocal scene of European legal theorizing, legal institutionalists tried to decipher and handle the crisis to come—one that pitted the several claims to political autonomy and legal independence against the increasingly despotic power of the executive. For sure, other key legal and political paradigms, such as Otto von Gierke's law of associations, G. D. H. Cole's guild socialism, Harold Laski's political pluralism, Max Weber's sociological conception of law, Léon Duguit's sociolegal functionalism, Eugen Ehrlich's and Hermann Kantorowicz's Free Law Movement, were trying to pinpoint the difficult relationship between the centripetal attraction of a supreme political entity (the state) and the centrifugal plurality of social life (substate and suprastate movements, associations, and organizations).[2] However, legal institutionalists, and especially Romano, Schmitt, and Mortati, deployed a strikingly rich conceptual tapestry to explain why and how late nineteenth-century administrative state was ceasing to be the secure anchor for, and the linchpin of, speculation about the nature of law.

THE LEITMOTIV OF THIS BOOK

The recognized initiator of classic legal institutionalism[3] was French jurist Maurice Hauriou.[4] After him, many other institutional models were developed in France, Germany, Italy, and other countries. However, this book centers on the legal theories of Romano, Schmitt, and Mortati for one major reason. As we will elucidate in Chapter 5, they offered prototypical solutions to the problem of radical pluralism and how the state should deal with nonstate normative entities. In this context it would be certainly pointless to summarize these solutions and how these three scholars made their way to them. Accordingly, the aim of this Introduction is to illustrate how we plan to account for all this.

The leitmotiv of our exploration will be the double relation of *juristic* versus *political* conceptions of law and the interplay between *matter* and *nomic force*. Though these notions will become clearer as we go along, a few preliminary considerations will be of help. The opposition of juristic and political understandings is somehow inscribed in the history of Western law. Despite all attempts at singling out distinctive traits, from the Roman *ius civile* to medieval glossators' and postglossators' law through to modern state-based law, the legal phenomenon has taken many a shape depending on the sociopolitical arrangement. Doubtless, an important characteristic differentiating the various conformations of law is the relation between the legal and the political realms and thus the law's degree of autonomy or independence from politics. *Juristic conceptions* are those that tend to minimize the degree of dependence. Not only are the legal and the political separate realms (what also many advocates of political notions could easily acknowledge), but the law, its contents, and its procedures are never conditional on politics. Most juristic conceptions regard the law as a knowledge-based practice with a language and categories of its own, administered by trained experts. The law does not need political power either to be produced and amended or to be applied. The relation with politics, as it were, is extrinsic. Quite the opposite, *political conceptions* deem the law to be (to different degrees) conditional on the political structure of society. Depending on the particular theoretical paradigm, the law can be portrayed as the effect of a political decision or the outcome of struggles over the monopoly on political power. But the common element among the various political conceptions is that, whether or not law and politics are distinct organizational phenomena (and this varies according to the particular political conceptions one examines), the legal realm and its operators are granted limited autonomy. For the law to be produced, applied, and amended, political power and procedures are needed. The relation with politics is intrinsic.

It would be senseless to maintain that one of these views is wrong and the other correct. More appropriately, it could be argued that the juristic-political is a continuum with opposite ends. At one end, the law is largely casuistic, knowledge-based, administered by (more or less) autonomous elites. At the other end, the body of people who oversee legal procedures are subjected to political power, while legal rules and categories are produced and changed in compliance with politically implemented institutional mechanisms. Therefore, the continuum in question is able to capture the legal phenomenon at a particular stage in a particular geohistorical context—in the sense that the law of this or that context can find place in a particular section of the continuum. Without shreds of doubt, however, the law that emerged out of the multiple dynamics of codification and constitutionalization of the eighteenth century was decidedly political. Those dynamics inaugurated state legal orders as systems pivoted on a hierarchy of sources with the legislative power at its acme, while jurists (whether law professors, magistrates, or judges) became state officials. Needless to say, it is impossible in this context to offer a full account of such a historical process, nor is this among the focuses of the present book. Despite this, it is vital to keep in mind the distinction between the juristic and the political because it is at the heart of our account of Romano's, Schmitt's, and Mortati's theories. For the juxtaposition of these authors epitomizes the movement from one end to the other end of the continuum.

We will account for the relationship of the juristic to the political by exploring how these three jurists conceptualized pluralism. It is here that the issue of nomic power and its relation to materiality comes to surface. To put it shortly, *nomic power* is an entity's potential for producing normativity while *materiality* is the set of practical activities this entity engages in. A major focus of this book is the question of if, and to what extent, nomic power arises from materiality. Romano advanced a notion of institution as the interplay of nomic power and the material. In his juristic conception of law, law-producing practices always call for knowledge-production processes that give them legal shape. All entities that are organized regulate their practice through a form of knowledge that he had no qualms about defining "legal." The law, which is a structural property of all organized entities, is the process of organization itself as accompanied by a form of knowledge. On this account, the nomic and the material are not severable. While Romano held on to this view throughout his life, Schmitt had a striking turn of mind. Early in the 1920s he almost exclusively concentrated on the nomic power that the political sovereign confers on materiality with a decision, to the extent that materiality was portrayed as inert or even lifeless before this act of inception enlivened it. At the end of the 1920s, he gradually reconsidered the role of materiality. He attached more and more importance to the social practices that contribute to the normative life of a political community, and revised the role played by the political. The political power became a sieve rather than a dispenser of normativity. Finally, Mortati developed his political conception of law as he contended that the nomic is intrinsic to the material, in the sense that it is a peculiar conformation of the latter that triggers the former. More specifically, it is a certain aggregate of social forces that creates the conditions for the law to emerge and work effectively.

However unclear these quick indications might sound, what matters here is the collocation of law on the continuum and how this collocation affects the way these authors theorized pluralism. If the law is the interlacement of knowledge and practice, as Romano pointed out, law is a ubiquitous phenomenon and pluralism an inescapable feature of human normativity. Schmitt's understanding of pluralism changed as long as he revised his own position on nomic force—although his conviction that a political community must be socially and politically homogeneous remained unaltered through time. Mortati thought that pluralism is possible, and desirable, only once political forces have reached an agreement on a set of fundamental aims that join the groups of a political community together. It is evident that Romano's conception dwells in one end of the continuum and Mortati on the other, while Schmitt moved from the former to the latter. It is interesting to note, thus, that these authors' understanding of pluralism was significantly affected by the role they attributed to the juristic, and in particular to legal knowledge.

Romano thought that only juristic science can handle pluralism in a way that lessens the violence of social conflicts and creates the conditions for peaceful interaction among antagonistic entities. Juristic science, in fact, is something that does not belong to any particular legal entity. It exceeds the contingency of geohistorical contexts. On the contrary, Schmitt deemed legal thinking to reflect a particular, time- and context-specific juridico-political conformation. In other words, juristic thought is a reflective expression of the legal order in which it comes about. Mortati believed legal thought to be instrumental in the establishment of a particular political-constitutional setting, in the sense that it contributes to identifying those institutional facts that bring the legal order about. As we can see, the degree of autonomy of legal knowledge decreases as one moves from one to the other end of the continuum. To put it bluntly, the higher the autonomy of legal knowledge from politics, the more effective it turns out to be in the management of pluralism. Romano's legal institutionalism goes hand in hand with legal pluralism because he believed that juristic thinking does not exclusively belong to any particular legal entity. Schmitt and Mortati were skeptical of the autonomy of legal science from particular orders and posited a close connection between legal theorizing and the reinforcement of the political system. This does not mean that these two scholars had the same take on pluralism and its desirability. While Schmitt was radically averse to it, Mortati thought it was possible only within a constitutional order based on a previous consensus of social forces around basic principles and values.

In sum, this book will interrogate the role of legal theory in the production and understanding of law and its relationship with the political. At the same time, our analysis will unearth the relevance of the issue of pluralism to the legal theory of these three towering figures of Continental jurisprudence. The theories of Romano, Schmitt, and Mortati will reveal themselves as enlightening explorations of the issue of pluralism in a way that foregrounds the key role played by the relation between law and politics and how jurisprudence handles it. It is our conviction that our approach will prove particularly effective in reviving knowledge of three authors who have been largely neglected in the Anglophone tradition, with the exception of the "exceptionalist" Schmitt, who has attracted attention in recent years in the United States.[5]

THE STRUCTURE OF THE BOOK

The guideline we chose to analyze Romano's, Schmitt's, and Mortati's institutional theories is meant to illustrate how they came to muse on issues that would later prove key to the development of Western constitutional regimes and today are coming back to the fore. Well before US and

European future generations of lawyers, political theorists, sociologists, and legal anthropologists, Romano, Schmitt, and Mortati put to the test state-based legal paradigms by disentangling the legal phenomenon from the state. These authors tackled pressing issues that extant legal and political paradigms were unable to take up and raised questions that had vanished from contemporary legal theory. Why did the state come to be regarded as the only source of law? Why did the will of the state come to be portrayed as a living actor endowed with supreme power? Why and how did legal elites, jurists, and law professors progressively turn into an integral part of the state apparatus? How can the state-based political structure confront nonstate entities and their claim to legislative and jurisdictional autonomy?

No doubt—and this is what makes the juxtaposition of these authors particularly interesting—they reached different, and at times opposite, conclusions. As we indicated in the previous pages, one of the main differences lies in the role they assigned to legal knowledge and juristic science. This is why Chapter 1 will discuss the rise of legal theory as a discipline with an eye to identifying the "juristic point of view"—which is to say, a point of view on legal phenomena that does not attach preeminence to the law of the state. By doing so, the chapter will bring to light a fundamental division of theories that between the end of the nineteenth century and the beginning of the twentieth regarded the state as the source of legality and theories that believed legality to be detached from particular political forms. By investigating the trajectory of German and Italian jurisprudence, we will explain how the issue of pluralism emerged and the way legal scholars came to grips with it.

The discussion of the juristic point of view will pave the way for the analysis of Romano's legal theorizing in Chapter 2. We will focus on the conceptual line that joins his 1909 essay on the crisis of the modern state and his masterpiece, *The Legal Order*. The strong case he made for the juristic point of view could be summarized as follows: The law is a type of knowledge that provides a special language through which reality can be described in such a way that the very act of describing allows new compositions of legal entities. On Romano's account, all organized entities are legal by dint of being organized. The law then has a twofold nature, so to say. On one hand, it is the inner law of an organized entity; on the other, it is a language that belongs to all organized entities—the language of organization. The latter nature is that which allows all organized entities to interact *legally*. The juristic point of view is one that excludes all other points of view (typical of nonlegal approaches) and deals with conflicts between legal entities with exclusive recourse to the language of the law. While exploring this argument, the chapter accounts for Romano's groundbreaking notion of institution and his pioneering solutions to many of the most pressing issues of twentieth-century legal theory.

Chapter 3 will offer an alternative portrayal of Schmitt's theorizing. While he is notoriously known, discussed, and deprecated for his bold exceptionalism of the early 1920s, we will make the claim that the tangle of exception and decision characterized but a short phase in his thinking, one that Schmitt would jettison in the wake of Hauriou's and Romano's institutional theories. As early as the end of the 1920s, Schmitt laid the foundation of his concrete-order and formation thinking: a version of institutionalism that amended the conceptual flaws of his previous decisionism. While Schmitt's conclusions are mostly reactionary, and thus of little use to understand how the state should deal with pluralism, our concern will be with the reasons that led him to overhaul his position and the theoretical consequences of this move. His adhesion to institutionalism profoundly affected the whole structure of his thought. He deployed a more refined understanding of the roots of pluralism and its intrinsic relation to social practice. Thus, he completely reevaluated the role of social normativity—which he previously regarded as fully contingent on the political creation of the normal situation—and rethought the role of political power. So, it is the trajectory of Schmitt's institutionalist that will take center-stage in our analysis—one that will cast light on the theoretical risks of neglecting the nomic force of materiality.

Chapter 4 will examine the arguably most intriguing political conception of law ever produced in twentieth-century jurisprudence. Mortati's notion of the material constitution gets to the core of the relation between the political and the juristic in a way that truly reveals the alchemy of post–World War II constitutions. The dangers of dissolution inherent in pluralism can only be tamed by the congregation of social forces that reach consensus around a series of fundamental aims. These aims get entrenched in a formal constitution synthetizing the consensus and offering political direction for the attainment of the constitutional project. The material is therefore the genuine source of nomic force: the activity itself of social forces joining together and yielding a political project for the future triggers off a normative framework. Pluralism turns into a productive push as long as its centrifugal force decreases because of the constraining effect of the material constitution. This is in the starkest contrast to Romano's juristic conception. As the material spawns the nomic, juristic analysis is designed to identify those institutional facts that underpin the material constitution and to pinpoint their relevance to the formal constitution. No external vantage point is conceivable.

Chapter 5 will return to the double relation of juristic versus political conceptions of law and the interplay of matter and nomic force. It will clarify how the reassessment of these three leading figures of classic institutionalism is valuable not only in itself and for itself. Indeed, it brings to light the rich conceptual tapestry on which Western state legal orders are pivoted. At the same time, it highlights the tension between state constitutions and radical pluralism. These jurists' insights into the troubled relationship of order and pluralism are key to understanding the paradox of late-modern constitutionalism: the innate tendency to self-differentiation calls for a constraining force bringing order. Romano, Schmitt, and Mortati diverged on the degree of political direction that this tension requires. Romano thought that only the law ensures the composition of opposing forces, and therefore it should be as autonomous as possible from politics. Schmitt thought that political power should steer a complex machinery of social selection designed to rule out social practices that threaten political homogeneity. Mortati thought that only political law marks off the boundaries of a stable field where a reasonable degree of pluralism can serve as a vital source of political action. While it is not for us to determine who is right, we believe it is our intellectual duty to bring back to the fore the theoretical efforts of these three great protagonists of twentieth-century legal theory.

We would like to thank William Twining, who first brought up the idea of this book and supported us throughout the writing process, and Michelle M. Lipinski, who enthusiastically welcomed the project and provided constant help.[6]

CHAPTER ONE

Legal Theory as a Discipline and the Trouble with Pluralism

In the last decades the term *pluralism* has become the epitome of a social and political attitude based on the recognition of a seemingly innate trait of human sociality: no political community can be founded on one shared set of beliefs and lifestyles that is accepted as a common ground for the various individuals and groups who comprise it. For within liberal societies, pluralism appears to be a fate, an inescapable condition of humans' free exercise of their cognitive and practical capacities. John Rawls's seminal account of political liberalism is premised on the matter-of-fact nature of disagreements stemming from the "plurality of conflicting reasonable comprehensive doctrines, religious, philosophical, and moral" as the normal result of a liberal society's "culture of free institutions."[1] According to other authors pluralism is something more basic than a mere derivative of liberal institutions. It is an inherent feature of all human forms of life, as Richard Rorty's "polytheistic" view of pluralism holds: "To be a polytheist . . . all you need do is abandon the idea that we should try to find a way of making everything hang together, which will tell all human beings what to do with their lives, and tell all of them the same thing."[2] This latter view comes close to the version of deep pluralism that is often associated to towering figures of twentieth-century thinking such as Isaiah Berlin[3] or Max Weber, who claim that the intrinsic heterogeneity of value forbids any conceptions of the common good as well as any ways to settle disputes over value conflicts that do not engender further, even more serious conflicts.[4] On this account, the idea itself of a society grounded on a common conception of the good life "is not merely Utopian (which few deny), but intrinsically incoherent."[5]

In the last decades a good deal of academics have explored the conundrum of pluralism as one of the most pressing challenges after the fall of the Berlin wall. Influential scholarly strands such as multiculturalism and legal pluralism have emphasized not only the inconceivability of a society built around shared core values but also the potential harm associated to this monistic view. Communitarians regard substate contexts and relationships (e.g., family, neighborhood, civil society organizations, religious groups, political movements, and so on) as basic preconditions for the development of one's personal identity and the idea of plural citizenship. While people's pragmatic and social needs cannot be met by the macroapparatus of the administrative state, liberal institutions should foster substate practical sites where people can develop social bonds and a feel for the public. Even more radically, many advocates of legal pluralism advance the view of a society where semiautonomous normative regimes (especially religious and cultural ones) should be allowed to produce rules binding on their members and to exercise jurisdictional autonomy within limits set by the state.[6] These scholars give the lie to the late modern idea of the state as the ultimate normative context holding sway over the others. They maintain that constitutional statehood is the modern produce of violent struggles to dispossess nonstate normative regimes of their legislative, administrative, and jurisdictional competences.

Albeit topical today, the issue of pluralism is by no means new. It arose as a disconcerting historical phenomenon that at the dawn of the twentieth century was menacing to draw the modern state to an end. In most European countries, pluralism was both an explosive political issue and the object of a growing scholarly interest in many academic fields. Although this book does not center on pluralism as a historical fact, but on how Romano, Schmitt, and Mortati conceptualized it, it is no less important to offer a sketch of the sociohistorical and scholarly scenario they confronted. To achieve that, this chapter will not offer a conclusive analysis of pluralism in terms of the history of ideas. There are many good works about this topic, and we will mention most of them as we go along. Rather, what we do is track down the emergence of pluralism as a theoretical question of paramount importance so as to offer a glimpse of concrete historical events through the special (although hardly neutral) lens of scholars' reaction to it. Indeed the first step we intend to take is to foreground the relevance of pluralism to the birth and evolution of jurisprudence as an autonomous discipline. For we believe it is important to identify the link that existed between particular theoretical approaches to the state and the emergence of pluralism both as a concrete phenomenon and a conceptual paradigm. This somewhat implies that pluralism—especially the type of pluralism that was thriving between the end of the nineteenth century and the beginning of the twentieth century—cannot be disentangled from the history of modern statehood.

Thus, while this chapter maps the rise of legal theory as a discipline, it does that with the aim of identifying two attitudes to the study of the legal phenomenon. What we label the "jurisprudential point of view" qualifies a theoretical approach to law that emphasizes the distinctive nature of state law as separate from other forms of normativity, whereas the "juristic point of view" does not attach any special preeminence to the normativity of law. We will return to this distinction in more depth later on in this book. For now, what matters is that the division between "jurisprudential" and "juristic" brings to the surface a deeper division between theories that regarded the state as the source of legality and those that thought legality is an intrinsically social phenomenon. Within the former type of theories, law was painted as something special and specialized, whose understanding and management needed dedicated theoretical instruments. On the contrary, the latter type of theories deemed the insulation of law and legal knowledge to be the effect of the state's monopoly on the legal. While we are not concerned with this division per se, it proved particularly important when it came to conceptualizing pluralism in between the nineteenth and twentieth centuries. Jurisprudential conceptions that located the source of all law within the state were naturally inclined to view pluralism as a societal phenomenon requiring political treatment. Juristic conceptions that denied there being a separation between the social and the legal believed pluralism to the dire consequence of the state's grabbing legal power from sub- and suprastate entities.

Although arbitrary and cursory, the account of the rise of legal theory as a discipline offered in this chapter follows the path outlined above. We begin by expanding on how and why legal theorists felt the need to draw the borders of their discipline and what effects it had on the understanding of the relation between law, politics, and society. We then explore the most remarkable reactions to the outcome of legal theory becoming a specialized discipline, or rather, the identification of the general phenomenon of law with the law of the state. Based on this analysis, we go on to offer a short description of what pluralism looked like between the nineteenth and the twentieth centuries. The chapter concludes by explaining in what sense the relation between the specialization of legal theory and the conceptualization of pluralism provides the key to understanding Santi Romano's theorizing, which is the focus of the subsequent chapter.

THE CONTESTED NATURE OF JURISPRUDENCE IN GERMANY

While discussing Maurice Hauriou's institutional theory, Romano comments that one of Hauriou's main contributions to the conceptualization of institution (which, as we will see, is on a par with that of pluralism) is that he "suggested subsuming the general concept of institution—of which we had just a few, quite feeble traces in the terminology—under the legal world, rather than under political and sociological theorizing."[7] Here we are faced with Romano's fundamental contention that the theme of institution, and thus that of pluralism, is to be managed with the toolkit of legal science. While we will return to Romano's claim over the course of our discussion of his pluralist institutionalism, what matters here is that he reckoned that various academic disciplines were trying to grapple with the issue of pluralism and that he believed legal science was best equipped to deal with it properly. Before we discuss the phenomenon itself, we think it is worth taking up Romano's suggestion and try to pin down what kind of legal science he had in mind.

At the beginning of the nineteenth century, it is in Germany that legal scholars were more "preoccupied with the idea of law as a science" and "pursued it more consistently, debated it more intensely, and refined it more highly than any other contemporary legal culture."[8] In 1814 Friedrich Carl von Savigny (1779–1861) licensed his programmatic manifesto *Vom Beruf unserer Zeit für Gesetzgebung und Rechtswissenschaft*,[9] while *Zeitschrift für geschichtliche Rechtswissenschaft*, the journal that officially inaugurated the German Historical School of Jurisprudence, saw the light in 1815. In these two years, through an enormous scholarly effort, the basic tenets of the legal science as a discipline concerned with the sources of law and its historical nature were laid out. Gustav Hugo (1764–1844) had paved the way for such a momentous jurisprudential revolution as he had set forth a concept of legal science that recommended considering law from a historical standpoint: jurisprudence had to do with history. Savigny espoused Hugo's methodological concern, but at the same time believed legal knowledge should be of a systematic nature. Legal history cannot be uncoupled from the requirements of a systematic method.

This is particularly relevant for two, somewhat opposite reasons. First, certainly this ground-breaking juristic movement also started as a reaction to the conception of law and jurisprudence that had emerged out of the French Revolution and its Napoleonic aftermath. The French Revolutionists and their heirs were intent on severing the ties with old-age customary laws and were generally averse to the idea of law as a product of history. The monumental construction of legal codes that characterized postrevolutionary French legal life had two main characteristics. First, it was interpreted as a political, even bottom-up enterprise, one in which the political hovered over the legal authorities and their traditional claims to autonomy vis-à-vis political power. Second, such a hierarchical relation entailed the end of legal specialism, while the technicalities typical of the Ancien Régime's highly fragmented legal setting was presented as an unjustified anomaly, since codes should make legal rules easily accessible to every citizen. Savigny voiced German conservative skepticism about this understanding.[10] He thought that law parallels language in that it springs from the history and culture of a people. Second, the approach to law the Historical School advocated was not a form of static adoration, as history did not speak for itself. The production of laws based on the interpretation of legal sources required a circle of jurists well versed in the art of interpretation. In other words, Savigny's notion of legal history entailed the filtering activity of legal experts. The constitutional process that the French Revolution had conceived as a massive effort to build and codify the general will of the French nation was rejected in favor of a certainly more elitist conception of the legal character of history. For a people's life pivots on a rich texture of legal concepts and legal institutes that are valid not because of the political authority that issues or recognizes it, but because of their being entrenched in that people's history and are brought to light by the suitable interpreters.

In sum, the concept of law championed by Savigny centered on the shared historical experience of the members of the nation and placed emphasis on sedimented legal customs. Yet the system is conceivable only insofar law is lawyers' law (*Juristenrecht*) or even law professors' law (*Professorenrecht*). This scholarly stripe, which so remarkably contributed to the invention of modern legal science, never deemed this science to be a descriptive one, as only the juristic analysis of legal sources and legal consciousness is conducive to the legal institutes and legal relations that ensure systemic unity.[11] Such a productive contradiction between the popular element of traditional legal customs and the elitist element of legal specialism could hardly be overcome by Savigny and the other exponents of the Historical School. Indeed a substantial strand of this school, following Savigny, did not believe they could find the roots of German legal institutes and relations within Germanic customary law, but within Justinian's *Corpus Iuris Civilis* and other Roman sources. They saw Roman law as a basic presupposition of modern legal orders—a chameleonic source able to adapt to the mutable conditions of subsequent epochs. The main outcome of this scholarly effort was a highly systematic and extremely influential body of law called *Pandektenrecht*. Yet, philological interest eventually gained the upper hand. For although these scholars regarded law as the product of history, they ended up adopting an ahistorical and predominantly doctrinaire approach to the study of law. Roman law was exalted as an eternal, transhistorical source of law that should be taken as the steady basis for any future codification. The legislation inspired by this conception of law was characterized by heavy reliance on a technical and abstract lexicon and the abstraction of legal devices from their original contexts.[12]

This contradiction belied the reference to the *Volksgeist* (the spirit of the people) as "a rhetorical artifice, while, simultaneously, the unresolved issue of the 'material instance of law' came to the forefront."[13] The 1940s marked the end of the Historical School and the doctrinaire conception of law they had long defended. The Romanist and the Germanic branches of the School gradually drifted apart to the extent that Georg Beseler (1809–1888) could point his finger at Roman law as that which had caused the high degree of abstraction and formalization of German law and German jurisprudence. As a matter of fact, the popular element of the law envisaged by the Romanists had been ousted by the jurists' self-assigned monopoly on the art of interpreting a dead body of law.[14] Against spurious non-German sources used as a blanket justification for the legal interpreter, Beseler insisted that Germanic law was based on the interactions between enfranchised members of local and national associations. While, as we will see, this view will subsequently prove influential, in mid-nineteenth century another seminal conception of law was making its appearance: state legal positivism. For the erstwhile preeminence of private law, which was understood as the foundation of all law and legal relations, was about to give way to a renovated conception of state public power and consequently of public law. The mainstay of the new public law was the idea of legal person (*juristische Person*),[15] as a notion that promised to overcome the persisting antithesis between the public and the private. The state personality was wedded to the idea of the state as the holder of political sovereignty with that of the state as the source of the legal order. Therefore the state-person came to be considered as the condition of possibility for the relation between citizens and the state. It constituted a meta-order that turned the variety of diverging social forces and interests into a unity. In this way, the state was dogmatically represented as a "supersubject,"[16] in the sense that it was naturally endowed with an objectivity that bestowed legal subjectivity on those who were subject to it.

Evidently, such a jurisprudential view constructed around the idea of person fed off a mix of positivism and organicism. Carl Friedrich von

Gerber's (1823–1891) theorizing is telling in this sense. Although he abundantly drew from the methodology of Romanists, he rejected their penchant for fictions and abstractions. He believed that private law pivoted on "legal facts" and relationships that are constituted at a social level. This means that it reflected a specific culture. Gerber saw the science of private law as one that was designed to elucidate the "particular laws" of private law through the means of legal science. In this regard, he "moved on a fine line between pure positivist analysis and a more anthropological consideration of the relation between law and power."[17] Gerber held the same approach to public law. The person of the state was not an abstraction, as it was an ethical organism that is not so much moved by an external force as it moved because of a "vital principle" that lay within it.[18] The person these positivist scholars had in mind was an entity characterized by the self-conscious spiritual unity of a people.[19]

The subjectivity attached to the state personality evoked a mighty foundational power. In Gerber's graphic words: "The willpower [*Willensmacht*] of the state is a power to rule [*Macht zu herrschen*]; it is said 'state power.' The willpower of the state, the state power, is the law of the state. Public law is therefore the doctrine of the state power."[20] The state was thought to be a person with a supreme power, a supersubject endowed with a uniform power of domination. The requirement that this power be unifying and homogenizing was particularly important in a community, like the German one, that was still implanted on a corporatist social fabric. It should come as no surprise, then, that the new state positivism mobilized both the organicist notion of the state being a living body comprising substate organs and the positivist element of the state being at the origin of all positive law. However, reconciling these aspects was no facetious enterprise. For what was at stake was a fundamental hypothesis on the ultimate source of law. What is it that produces law? The vital forces creating connections between the state organs or the state's creational activity of issuing law? This scarcely reconcilable friction between positivism and organicism culminated in the contest between two eminent scholars, Paul Laband (1838–1918) and Otto von Gierke (1841–1921).[21] It was a contest about law as well as the theory of law. Law as statutory law emanating from the state's will versus law as the self-organization of associations within the broader state organism; legal theory as the interpretation of positive law based on purely jurisprudential methods versus legal theory as the philosophical, political, and juristic analysis of a living body.

The most influential illustration of state positivism, Laband's monumental work *Das Staatsrecht des Deutschen Reiches*, written between 1876 and 1914, can arguably be regarded as the complete systematization of the Second Reich public law. At the same time, it accomplished the positivization of legal theory. Laband conceived the legal order as a complete and gapless system, while jurisprudence should be tasked with producing a sound conceptual portrayal of it. To achieve that, jurisprudence should rid itself of contaminating elements appertaining to other nonlegal disciplines. This does not mean that Laband disregarded the sociohistorical and political conditions of his time. On the contrary, his conception of state law was particularly sensitive to the concrete developments of the German state,[22] but he thought any understandings of those conditions should not jeopardize jurisprudence's pureness. It was this particular awareness that led to such an epochal conceptual turn with respect to the foregoing legal scholarship. Indeed Laband did avail himself of the grand conceptual framework provided by decades of both the Romanist and Germanic members of the Historical School, especially in the field of private law. Yet he did that in such a way as to leave behind the polemics on the role of history, the nature of society, and the social sources of law. In this sense, Laband's insistence on the pureness of the theory was also a way to even the scores with preceding generations of legal scholars. However, pursuing theoretical pureness in the particular way Laband did meant introducing a burdensome presupposition, that is, the notion that the state holds a unifying power that surpasses (and enables) all nonstate ethical and cultural instances of normativity. In other words, Laband solved the persisting problem of the relationship between the social and the legal by juridifying state power and by taking this foundational legal power to be able to issue the social and its various fields (private life, the political sphere, the economic one, and so on).

Despite any claims to theoretical pureness, we defined Laband's as an epochal turn insofar as what had begun as the preeminence of legal experts over political officials ended up in the outright juridification of the state political preeminence over all manifestations of the social. On the one hand, the people and the territory of a state were nothing other than the natural bases of the Reich that could enter the sphere of legality by an act of state will. The matter-of-factness of all that is prelegal can be granted legal value only insofar as it becomes a manifestation of the legal order that emanates from the state. On this account, one's being a citizen is equivalent to one's being subject to the state, while one's civil and political rights as well as one's liberties are but reflections of the state legal order. From a more pragmatic standpoint, in consonance with Laband's political convictions, the Reich's sovereignty is at one with the Kaiser's. After all, the link between Laband's pure method and its political consequences are hardly deniable: "He was a convinced partisan of constitutional monarchy and not prone to self-doubt when it could be shown that the continuance of this form of government could be ensured with the help of legal-dogmatic truths."[23]

GIERKE'S THEORY: PLURALISM AND THE ORGANICIST DEADLOCK

It is worth devoting some attention to Laband's main opponent Otto von Gierke. He was the proponent of a theory of law that exerted unmatchable influence on subsequent conceptions of pluralism in many non-German areas. Gierke was a student of Beseler's and the exponent of what could be seen as the third generation of the Historical School. As we emphasized, the main subject of dispute with Gerber and Laband was how the law comes about and its relation to the social. The positivist school had come up with a conception of the state as the key legal subject that radiates legal value on otherwise factual, legally inert entities. On this view, the people was a construction that entirely hinged on the state-person and its supreme will. Yet Beseler and Gierke did not simply get back to Savigny's abstract notions of Volk and Germanic history. In particular Gierke prized the significant advances of jurisprudence as the members of various schools were trying to capture the essence of law. To some extent he also acknowledged the methodological requirement that jurisprudence be distinguished from other disciplines. What he refuted was positivism's tendency to reduce jurisprudence to the logical deduction of legal concepts. Gierke assigned jurisprudence the task of grasping positive law as a historical reality. He aimed to pinpoint the nexus between the legal and the social that made the law a living entity. This means that, methodologically, the theory of law could not do without the study of history and society, a study that was part and parcel of the legal method.

It is evident that Gierke's opposition to Laband concerned the nature of the social, that of the legal, and the study of both. While Laband's juridification of political power reduced the social to a legally indifferent substratum that needed subjection to the state to become legally relevant, Gierke espoused a much more nuanced conception of social phenomena. As we will illustrate below, it could be said that the genuine moot point was the relation between the legal and the social. Because of this, we would like to concentrate on one specific feature of Gierke's rich contribution to legal theory, although his opposition to the convergence between the traditional Romanist approach and legal positivism led to many theoretical innovations. For he excoriated the construct of legal personality based on Roman law as it projected onto the state the private law notion of personality that had no relation whatsoever with actual social interactions and thus was unserviceable when it came to harmonizing the two. He also lambasted positivists' reliance on a conceptual apparatus that unreflectively assigned private prerogatives to the state as a metaphysical entity. Still, however important these features of Gierke's thought might be, we believe that his main contribution is the seminal understanding of plural juristic orders he put forward.

According to renowned German historian Otto Hintze, the hallmark of the constitutional history of the Second Reich was an ongoing tension between *Herrschaft* and *Genossenschaft*.[24] The first concept referred to the state-centralized, almost authoritarian control over political and legal entities, while the second conjured the Germanic idea of free associations with autonomous rights and prerogatives of their own.[25] As we stressed, Laband took up Gerber's legacy but disposed of the organicist influence insofar as the Labandian state-person wielded an original and foundational authority. In Laband's public law theory, the relation between the various substate bodies was conditional upon the state radiating legal value on them through its *Herrschaft*. What Gierke found unsatisfying was positivist theory's incapacity to offer a better conceptualization of the relationship between the state and its organs, and thus to offer a solution to the Hobbesian problem of how individuals become members of the political community.[26] To find a way out of the conundrum that Laband had dissolved into an unquestionable subjection of all social entities to the state *Herrschaft*, Gierke had first and foremost to question the theoretical framework positivism worked with. For the logical-deductive mode of positivist thinking turned a blind eye to the basic constituents of the social and concealed them with an unjustified *persona ficta* deriving from Romanist private law conceptions. Instead, the state is a real (as opposed to fictional), living person arising from the connection among parts forming a totality based on *Genossenschaft* (fellowship).[27] The order of the state is nothing but the way these parts are connected and interact.

Conceptualizing the organic state required a theory based on disciplinary contamination rather than pureness. First, legal theory should be intimately connected to political theory. Second, this theory should stay sensitive to the contingencies of historical circumstances. Third, the theorist should be able to track down the interpenetration of juristic and moral conceptions of order.[28] It behooved legal theory to penetrate the reality of the state-person and capture its constitution, that is to say, the way the constitution worked—one that might reflect the state actual constitution, in its being composed of parts.

The first step of Gierke's reappraisal of organicism was the dissection and refusal of the modern idea of sovereignty. He criticized the use of sovereignty as "a magic wand, which can conjure up the whole sense and content of the State's general power."[29] He averred that sovereignty had come to denote the relation of the state to all that is under its omnipotent sway—a trait, said Gierke, that was upheld by the champions of absolute monarchy as well as by those of popular sovereignty. Such an undue sacralization of a legal concept took place as sovereignty came to be represented "as an *inherent and original* right of the State" that did not need to be explained "by any particular title of acquisition."[30] The identification of the sovereign with the state had led to a fracture that pitted the political against the populace, each of them holding a power that they claimed was superior to the power of the other. The supporters of state sovereignty, like Thomas Hobbes, the eminent father of modern absolutism, thought they could solve the riddle through an artifice. They envisioned "the artificial life (*vita artificialis*) of the great automaton (*homo artificialis*), an artificial person (*persona artificialis*) which, under the technical designation of *persona civitatis*, becomes the centre of public law."[31]

After dissecting and refuting the theory of sovereignty, Gierke moved on to examining how this theory affected the understanding of sub- and suprastate entities. He charged the modern theory of the state from Hobbes onward (with few exceptions, like Johannes Althusius and Daniel Nettelbladt) with unwarrantedly tying the knot between the fictional figure of the state-person and the contractual adhesion to the community represented by that person. In doing so, he counterposed the notion of mechanistic solidarity he called *Anstalt* (institution) to the organic interactions between enfranchised members of associations he called *Genossenschaft*. Based on this juxtaposition, Gierke made the claim that stable associations, which he referred to as corporations,[32] came to be considered institutions when modern thinkers "began to argue that the only force which could explain the existence of a corporation was a Ruling authority imposed from above and imposed from without."[33] Institutions, in Gierke's terminology, lack a spontaneous and cohesive integration as they are the authoritative products of a superentity. Certainly they were recognized as the bearers of an original desire to join together and form a union, and yet they were believed to be "able to will and act as such, by the addition of a representative Ruling authority."[34] On the contrary, the fellowship view of the corporation—what Gierke knew was a minority and finally defeated German reaction to corporations as institutions—drew its strength from the ties among members. This strength was not a merely solidaristic feature neglected by the theorists of institution. For it had an associational, hence normative, value. Gierke maintained that "a real Fellowship possessing the rights of a full corporation . . . became possible as soon as the action of subjects of a State, in concluding a contract between themselves, was admitted to have the power of producing a social authority," the basis of such authority being "the original contract for the formation of a society, which already brings into being a more or less comprehensive social authority."[35]

The fellowship view sheds light on the meaning of "juristic" and thus the normative status of corporations. As emphasized in the Introduction by Ernest Barker, who translated Gierke's *Natural Law and the Theory of Society*, although legal personality is a mental construction, it is no fiction. For a juristic creation is "a legally created capacity of sustaining rights and duties, which are also legal creations themselves; but it does not follow that it is not something real. In one sense it is artificial, as all things thought into being by us are artificial."[36] Far more enthusiastically, Maitland went so far as to wholeheartedly embrace the organicist metaphor:

> Our German Fellowship is no fiction, no symbol, no piece of the State's machinery, no collective name for individuals, but a living organism and a real person, with body and members and a will of its own. Itself can will, itself can act; it wills and acts by the men who are its organs as a man wills and acts by brain, mouth and hand.[37]

Importantly, "juristic" in this context takes a meaning of its own that distinguishes it from both "moral" and "legal." We will extensively dwell on this topic in discussing Romano's theory. But for now, suffice it to say that "juristic" can be interpreted as something that lies in between the social and the legal and cannot be reduced to either of them. On the one hand, a juristic order is certainly an expression of social normativity, and yet it surpasses the level of moral rules governing individual relationships. It is something that emerges out of people's stable interactions and acquires a particular identity as a *group-based practice*, one that is separable both in theory and in practice from the activity of the distinct members as individuals. On the other hand, this group-based practice sets up a regime of normativity that is not immediately legal, in the sense that is separable both in theory and in practice from the rules and institutes of official law. Introducing the juristic level does away with an understanding of legal normativity as the source of normativity par excellence—the source that confers normativity on the associational activities of private individuals. In other words, it brings the legal back to the broader level of normativity in general and puts all normative contexts on an equal footing. Gierke's "juristic orders" reclaimed social agents' capacity to bring about practical contexts whose normative power does not hinge on the state's power. Still, his most radical break with the modern theory of state sovereignty lies in his claim that it is the state's sovereignty that depends on those nonstate practical contexts. His onslaught on the state-based theory of public law came down to the apparently obvious but unprecedented conclusion that the state was conditional upon the normativity of nonstate group entities. In other words, while for the traditional state doctrine "the state is sovereign because other associations are its creation," for Gierke the obverse was true: the "state is created by other associations, and sovereign because it creates no other associations itself."[38]

Despite this, Gierke's discourse is obviously not framed as a conceptual analysis of social and legal normativity. Rather, his words were redolent with nostalgia for the "idea of the State as an organic whole . . . bequeathed by classical and medieval thought."[39] For example, while commenting on Althusius's conception of order, Gierke credited him for vindicating a normative sphere that is carved out by associations and only belongs to them—what, Gierke pointed out, was in line with medieval federalism.[40] Yet, Gierke thought that Althusius, despite his efforts, was still indebted to contractualism: "He derives all social unity from a process of association which proceeds, as it were, from the bottom upwards. He regards the contract of society . . . as the creator of the whole system of public law and order."[41] In the end, even Althusius failed to offer a conception of a group-based practice founded on a real group personality. Gierke's organicism, on the contrary, aspired to reconcile the part and the whole in such a way that the former might reflect the latter and the latter might share something with the former. This entails both that the part is a whole in its own right and that "the whole must share a purpose or end with the purposes or ends of each of its parts."[42] This view fed into the medieval imagery of an all-encompassing organization whereby an array of microuniverses comprise the macrouniverse in harmonic concordance.[43]

It is important to note that Gierke did not base the ties between the members of corporations on organic features, like blood or body traits, but on purely juristic connection. A *Genossenschaft* on his account was a real person: it was a person because it was a subject of rights and was real because it was not created by the legal order. Still, the juristic relations that existed within them were supposed to reflect the group as a whole, while the latter was supposed to be in harmony with the German society as a whole. This means that Gierke's conception of organicism moved away from naturalism and introduced an ethical-spiritual conception of the organism, whereby the parts are autonomous from the whole and contribute to making the whole what it is; and yet the parts have to coordinate harmoniously for the whole to continue to live. Gierke had in mind a *plurality in unity* within which the state is a totality composed of concordant autonomous parts. He thought that this could bridge the gap, engendered by positivist theories, between the state and the populace, between the social and the legal. The juristic is that sphere of the social in which people produce the material substance composing the body of the state. Nonetheless, the solution he put forward lived on a notion that was just as fictional as the state-person advocated by positivists and lapsed back into the metaphysical idea of *Volksgeist* propounded by the Historical School. For only within the framework of an imagined Germanic nation could German law be conceived as the expression of an organic whole, which reflected the juristic as well as the ethical, religious, and cultural attributes of a population.[44]

In sum, Gierke's pluralist state presupposed a far less pluralist understanding of how the various parts of the whole integrate. If for positivists like Laband the law was the technical machinery that solved social conflicts on account of an unjustified identification of state power and legal sovereignty, no less unjustified was the conciliatory role Gierke assigned to the law. All in all, Gierke presupposed a "pacified conception of society, with respect to which present turbulences are but a transitory deviation."[45] In other words, he failed to explain how pluralism could be theorized and tackled insofar as he harbored the imagining of a reconciled and harmonious plurality in unity.

ITALIAN PUBLIC LAW THEORY AND THE CHANGING SCENARIO

The founding father of Italian public law theory (and Romano's mentor) Vittorio Emanuele Orlando (1860–1952) joined the effort to mark the boundaries of legal theory. As early as the 1880s, he was striving to identify a specifically jurisprudential point of view to consider the state in a way that did not depend on political theories of the state.[46] On his part, he was at pains to set the stage for an Italian legal theory of the state and its sovereignty. He thought that only by laying out the toolkit of legal science could the state be appreciated as a legal product, and not as a biological or natural entity endowed with supreme but eventually despotic powers. What in the German scholarly and public debate had taken the form of a decided opposition between the state sovereign power and the associative inclinations of the social, in Orlando took the form of a just-as-decided opposition between the political and the legal. For the political was the realm of conflicts and divisions—Orlando was scarcely sympathetic to parties and the representative system as a way to reconcile conflicting interests—and the legal was the realm where a pacified composition of all societal elements could be pursued. It was in the national legal consciousness that the principle of social composition and pacification should be identified, while political approaches that emphasized the troubled relations between classes or between state power and the individual were destined to heighten conflicts.

In a way, Orlando's method paralleled the juridification of political power fostered by German positivists, as he regarded public law as the study of state law.[47] The state power could not be but legal power, while the same applied to its sovereignty. By the same token, Orlando drew from Gerber's and Laband's definition of sovereignty as a capacity of the state-person that had to be examined from a jurisprudential vantage point. Importantly, though, he rather agreed with Savigny that the law had to accord with the spirit of the people, so much so that the legislator did not create law. The parliament is called upon to draw out something that lied with the popular consciousness. His idea of sovereignty was tempered by his conception of a limited legislative power. Yet, Orlando was not so much concerned with the positivist notion of sovereignty as he was with the one that had emerged out of the French Revolution. In particular, he believed that the French Revolution had furthered an intrusive model of politics that had ushered in the view of a titanic legislator, one that had to be replaced with a jurisprudential understanding of state power. Indeed he thought that only such a jurisprudential understanding could resolve the perennial conflict between the social and the political. Politically, in Orlando's view, the conflict was hardly evitable. On one hand, legal production was the outcome of the slow-paced evolution of social customs and society's cultural mindset. On the other, the state was the sole holder of legislative sovereignty. The legislative power was easily tempted to regard itself as the absolute and limitless source of all law and legality. In the face of it, a jurisprudential understanding was capable of investigating and reinforcing the multiple links between the various social bodies and the legislative activity.[48]

Orlando's conviction was that positive state law and legal science should buttress one another. On one hand, there was no law other than the norms issued by the state. On the other, the state-person had to be organically constructed by and within legal science. This means that, while law was entirely reduced to state law, legal science could not be reduced to the analysis and interpretation of legal texts. Rather, legal science was instrumental in the construction of the state-person by emphasizing public law's proper end in order for it to be "considered, just like private law, as a complex of systematically coordinated legal principles. And here the antinomy between the two elements of theory and practice becomes harmony."[49] In other words, jurists are regarded as the only ones who can adopt a unifying point on view to (re)construct the symphonic development of the state's various bodies and powers for it to be captured as a systematic and coherent whole. Therefore it was legal science as a *technical device* for constructing the state that had to order systematically the various legal productions of the state. Orlando conceived legal science and the jurisprudential point of view as technical tools with foremost reality effects.

As Orlando was developing his theoretical system throughout the 1880s, an important conceptual distinction came to light, one to which we will return in many junctures in the next chapters. For him, society and the state were not distinct entities. Jurisprudentially, the state was at one with society. This means that society was alleged to be already-and-always unified through the state-person, which possessed ultimate authority. Obviously, this was a methodological presupposition meant to stress that concrete social conflicts revolving around competing interests within the social world should not be the jurist's concern. The discipline designed to study the state actions as manifestations of its supreme sovereignty was the science of administrative law.[50] But this science "can only deal with the *forms* and the *means* to actualize the state will, while it is prevented from investigating the *motivations* of its interventions; or rather, it should be alien to the cognition of the moment at which the state becomes *part* of the social processes under way by assigning priorities to the distinct—and often conflicting—social needs."[51] This is the gist of Orlando's *formalism*—a radical division between the state administrative mechanisms, which had to be studied scientifically in accordance with purely jurisprudential categories, and their material effects as party to an ongoing social struggle.

This is the main limit of Orlando's theory. He presupposed a methodological separation between the state as a legal entity and the state as a social actor that proved unable to pin down and face the serious social rifts that marked the end of the century and the subsequent decades. The reference to the spirit of the people was characterized by the same degree of abstractness that beset the *Volksgeist* of the German Historical School. Orlando built on the premise that the state-person could unify society and overcome its multiple divisions. He did not see this trait of the state's as the outcome of a political process, as he took it to be a fundamental presupposition of legal theorizing. This is why another prominent representative of the Italian culture of the late nineteenth century, Gaetano Mosca (1858–1941), who was Orlando's fellow student at the Law School of the University of Palermo, was so dissatisfied with this methodological distinction. As the initiator of Italian elite theory,[52] Mosca was particularly sensitive to a division in the field of constitutional study that spawned two opposed strands: those, like Orlando, who tried to set the study of public law apart from social conflicts, and those who thought public law was instrumental in settling those conflicts by establishing a juridical equilibrium among social forces. In line with the second strand, Mosca espoused a notion of public and constitutional law studies that departed from Orlando's equation of state law with administrative law. According to Mosca, constitutional law theory was intrinsically required to plunge into the material contexts where social conflicts came to pass. Public law scholars should not limit themselves to the study of existing positive law and institutions. They were called upon to identify the causes that triggered social change in order to help accommodate it. This was the dawn of political science as the scientific investigation of juridico-political phenomena—and thus as a much-needed complement for constitutional and public law studies.

In truth, both Orlando and Mosca were skeptical of traditional legal methods that centered on legal texts and legal sources. Orlando's formalism, as we pointed out, was a reaction to that which he regarded as a narrow conception of legal studies. These two writers parted ways on how the scholarly point of view should confront the social and its complex texture. What Mosca rejected was a conception of law as the investigation of the state machinery and its general purposes as a person—a conception that programmatically dismissed any considerations on how to impose these general purposes. Nonetheless, when it came to this latter issue, Mosca's view was no less simplifying and abstractive than Orlando's. Mosca's theory of the governing class held that in all societies there is a class of people who govern—basically, a minority who is more and better organized than the majority—and a class of people who are governed. The ruling class gathers around a particular purpose and becomes a minority group qualified to compete for leadership. Social change is nothing but the product of a change in the way a group becomes a ruling minority. The legitimacy of the ruling class is not based on purely factual power, as it is backed up by a "political formula," where the ruling class tries to "find a moral and legal basis for it, representing it as the logical and necessary consequence of doctrines and beliefs that are generally recognized and accepted."[53] Finally, a political organization should be measured against the type of relations it enables between the governing class and those who are governed and between the multiple levels the ruling class itself.

While it is not for this section to offer a general assessment of Mosca's conception of society and political science, it is undeniable that his insistence on grasping the connective tissues of the social did not eventually correspond to any serious engagement with the reality of late nineteenth-century Italian society. After all, *The Ruling Class* seems much more concerned with defending the institutional setting of the extant liberal-constitutional state than with understanding ongoing societal ferments. Mosca's theoretical proposal spoke to a society that was no longer structured along identifiable, vertical lines of authority and subjection. His simplistic division between the governing few and the governed many, if ever tenable, was inapplicable to a structure characterized by growing divisions and the emergence of fragmenting forces. In this sense, Orlando's and Mosca's attitudes to the newly minted disciplines of administrative law and political science were basically the same. Either of them strenuously opposed a kind of legal law that revolved around legal texts and constitutional charts and aimed to find the structural laws governing the development of society. Still, the inability of both models to face the rising social setting speaks volumes about the need for a truly novel theoretical approach to the fast-paced transformation that was dramatically changing Europe. If German state positivism was the reflection of a political state of things, Orlando's and Mosca's contributions were more alert to the morphing surroundings but failed to get to grips with them. They took refuge in a view of the social world that was redolent with nostalgia. In the end, like Gierke's organic imagery, the institutional models they envisaged were not well equipped to face the pluralistic uproars of the early twentieth century.

PLURALISM IN ACTION

Before we address the theories that tried to take issue with the centrifugal and fragmented scenario we hinted at above, it is worth exploring the destabilizing factors that led to it. As we have so far argued, the jurisprudential point of view was taking shape as a reaction to the massive change in European legal settings that occurred in between the eighteenth and the nineteenth century. As Raoul Van Caenegem has it, a fierce struggle took place between jurists, judges, and legislators as "the voices of certain groups of people expressing particular social and political forces in society."[54] What was at stake was the control over law making and the state administrative devices. In this regard, if for a moment we leave aside theoretical disputes, Savigny's opposition to codification, Laband's conceptualization of the state-person, and Orlando's theorization of administrative law were crucial phases in the production of a genuinely *jurisprudential point of view*—one that sought to make sense of the relationship between the social, the political, and the legal in a way that was instrumental in the construction of an autonomous discipline. At the same time, the search for theoretical purity turned into an impediment to a sounder understanding of the momentous societal transformations that were occurring at the run of the century.

As long as Gierke was less preoccupied with scientific purity (as he rather advocated an interdisciplinary approach to the study of Germanic law), he was more alert to the sinister breaks in the state structure. Although his idea of *Genossenschaft* was reminiscent of bygone times, he had come up with a theory of political authority that made room for the fragmented social setting jurists were faced with. As we illustrated, against the jurisprudential obsession with theoretical pureness, he elaborated on a *juristic point of view* for the study of the various organs comprising the state—what he considered as the genuine source of legal and political authority. The juristic point of view entailed greater openness to the autonomy of nonstate actors. At the same time, however, Gierke's system hinged on the idea of *Rechtsstaat* positing that "everything done by every individual and every group makes sense in dramatic terms" whereby "it is possible to identify the mask of the state with the actions performed by the state, as it will be possible to identify the mask of any other group or person with the actions that they perform—there is no need to identify the author, because where all persons are real, all masks authorise themselves."[55]

Gierke's symphonic notion of the state and its bodies was certainly an idealization, even if referred to the ancient Germanic tradition. Despite any evocative references to medieval ideals, the social scenario of the turn of the century was not the organic assemblage that he and his admirers prized so much. Rather, the state-person was threatened from many angles by a host of substate micro- and macro-actors that laid claim to autonomy and independence in a way that was hardly compatible with the mild and compromised parliamentarism of the liberal-constitutional state. Generally speaking, these movements contested the notion of a state able to condense the polychromy of the social. Factions, sections, groups, associations, parties, organizations felt dissatisfied with the parliament as it was unable to represent the diversity of interests. Importantly, these were inherently *collective* interests, in the sense that they were not broken down to the interests of individual members of those aggregations. What is more, at the end of the nineteenth century, radical ideologies infiltrated many of these aggregations. Ideals of corporatism, revolutionary syndicalism, socialism, and anarchism were putting the state under siege. Movements of different sorts set out to question the foundational divide between the public and the private in ways that resonate with today's scenario, but with two crucial differences. First, they were supported by remarkable social mobilization, as numerous constituencies were discontent with the liberal-constitutional state run by the elites. Second, they demonstrated a collective proclivity for violence.

Corporatism (from the Latin term *corpus*) is a sociopolitical and economic system dominated by professional, social, and economic groups that collaborate with the state as collectives. They are parts of a society that cannot be reduced to their members. Although a corporatist system usually refers to a governmental system, and is not necessarily at odds with state economic activity, the imaginings it feeds off are by and large disruptive of the state-individual division as well as the public-private one. Basically, it is grounded on corporations as interest groups working with the state on a political-economic agenda. In between the nineteenth and the twentieth centuries, many both from the right and the left expected corporatism to reduce conflicts between social parties as different organizations were created for each specific occupation or industry. The idea was to integrate these organizations within cooperative frameworks while government was but a mediator as well as the ultimate authority. Importantly, corporatism placed decision making in the hands of group leaders in that it coalesces individual interests into macro-actors. While the corporatist system offered, and would in due course be adopted as, a way to solve social conflicts and to avoid violent forms of protest, it certainly introduced an element of pluralism that unsettled the modern ideal of a political community only comprised of individuals.

As Philippe Schmitter points out, corporatism exhibits many pluralist nuances. It involves the active collaboration of associational units of representation; it recognizes that functionally differentiated and potentially conflicting interests cannot be eliminated by edict; it plays down territorial representation; it favors the interpenetration of the private and the public sectors.[56] At the same time, there are many differences between corporatism and pluralism. Unlike the latter, mostly on account of its romantic and nationalist origins, corporatism does not necessarily stimulate the emergence of multiple, semiautonomous formations organized along horizontal lines of authority and control. It rather relies on vertical integration and complementary interdependence. But state corporatism as the organization of the capitalist society into groups with a view to reducing class conflict and social upheavals was yet to come. In many European countries the atmosphere was saturated with a tendency to pluralistic fragmentation, and corporatism was one further way of asserting the primacy of groups over the feeble dyad state-individual.

Indeed the end of the nineteenth century was hallmarked by the explosion of a subversive political culture nurtured by socialists, communists, syndicalists, and anarchists. Among the most relevant, revolutionary or insurrectionary movements organized mass demonstrations and strikes on a regular basis both against the elitist state bodies and the reformist agenda. However, it would be mistaken to assume that these were negligible minorities, albeit violent and boisterous. For there were firm bonds and affinities between them and the high- and middle-class culture of the left: "In many respects underlying, unspoken common assumptions and similar social and educational backgrounds united the radical and reformist leadership who hailed from this socialism of the educated middle classes."[57] The myth of violence as a means to an end was not confined to radical factions. Intellectuals and professors, such as Arturo Labriola (1873–1959) and Enrico Leone (1875–1940), among the founders of revolutionary syndicalism in Italy, criticized anarchism but at the same time invoked a class war waged by the emerging industrial working class.[58] But the intransigence of these movements was met by just as firm an intransigence on the part of governing elites. Their response to popular outcries against oppression and economic hardship was particularly severe and most of the time involved the use of the army.[59]

In this framework, French theorist of revolutionary syndicalism George Sorel (1847–1922) had a profound impact on how to conduct social battles for the liberation of the proletariat.[60] Since the late 1890s he had followed the rise of the syndicalist movement, whose strategy pivoted on direct action on the part of the working class. Sorel's works exalted the potential of unions, as was the case with anarcho-syndicalist Fernand Pelloutier, who had turned the Bourses du Travail, a major French union, into an instrument of proletarian self-emancipation.[61] Society could be renewed only if the proletariat fought the bourgeoisie with all means and might. He thought that class struggle should be kept at a high pitch of intensity, whereas democratic forms of regulation were destined to erode the combative instinct of the oppressed. The instruments to revive and feed class struggle were not representation and mediation but violence and myth.[62] For Sorel, violence was not bare force, as it was a means to the destruction of political authority.[63] He was a fierce critic of all compromises between the socialists and the establishment, one that he deemed to be a kind of "system of diplomacy" between the Socialist Party and the state intended to tame social conflict.[64] The parliament was the theater of this system. Against the detrimental effects of compromise, Sorel thought class struggle should seize upon the spread of violence. Acts of violence, he wrote, "can only have historical value if they are *the brutal and clear expression of class struggle*: the bourgeoisie must not be allowed to imagine that, aided by cleverness, social science or noble sentiments, they might find a better welcome at the hands of the proletariat."[65]

Such a lethal combination of syndicalism and violence is not so much relevant per se as it is in that it foregrounds an element that is crucial in the present context. Indeed the unprecedented and polyvocal militant politics of pluralism we are dwelling on was destined to leave a mark on the subsequent decades, both in terms of state policies and in terms legal and political theory. Pluralism had gained momentum not only as a set of vehement political campaigns but also as a plurality of organized interests championing a radically alternative theory of political authority. What emerged out of these massive mobilizations was a comprehensive, though uneven, theory of groups with respect to the state: the institution of the social did not require any creative act of volition on the part of the state. Renowned exponent of British pluralist theory G. D. H. Cole (1889–1959) nicely summarized this view: society is not "a complete circle of social life, or a social group of human beings, but a resultant of the interaction and complementary character of the various functional associations and institutions."[66]

This casts light on the real import of the pluralist critique. For not only were associations of different types and nature asking for self-organizing powers with respect to an administrative apparatus they felt dissatisfied with. The battle was not, or not only, jurisdictional. Much more radically, these movements, as well as the scholars who theorized their dynamics, insisted that state ought not to interfere with their internal life because of the socio-ontological and genealogical preeminence of the group over the state. While pluralism doubtless arose as an attack on the monistic doctrine of the state-person we have analyzed in the preceding sections, and especially the idea of the state possessing foundational authority and absolute power, more than that, in their eyes, the state was unduly claiming binding authority over those groups that make it what it is.[67]

PLURALISM IN THEORY

As we argued so far, pluralism at the end of the nineteenth century was a far-reaching phenomenon that aimed to debunk the fictional nature of the state as a person that was able to put together the various elements of society. The turbulent, centrifugal onslaughts on the parliamentary system were a serious warning that the "concept of the state [did] not work as a unifying factor."[68] A vast array of micro- and macro-actors, more or less prepared to take up the armed struggle, had loosened the relationship between center and periphery. At the same time, the idea of a homogeneous state was foundering on the establishment of various mediatory organisms, whether from the right or from the left, but no less from the Catholic and Christian center. Legal theory could not ignore such momentous a change. British, French, German, and Italian authors were eager to push Gierke's legacy to its extreme and to contest the dominance of state positivism. Unlike Gierke, however, their attention was not focused on an alleged glorious past, but on how the present would shape the future. While this section does not, and could not, offer a satisfying outline of such crucial developments, the more modest aim it pursues is to show how legal theory changed as it begun to make room for a nonmonistic view of law.[69]

One of the main heroes in this surging reaction to state positivism was Léon Duguit (1859–1928), who brought Auguste Comte's and Émile Durkheim's influential sociological theories to bear on legal philosophy and legal sociology. His account of law as based on the inner functioning of groups was the stepping stone of one of the most remarkable attacks on the monist and potentially authoritarian nuances of positivist conceptions of the state. His wide-ranging critique of state-based theories of law was targeted both at French theories of popular sovereignty inspired by Rousseau and at German theories of the state will as the origin of law. Duguit believed that in one way or another these various paradigms fed off a dangerous combination of individualism and state monism. For subjective rights and state sovereignty were the two poles of an ongoing dialectic that had led to a sanctification of the state as both the guarantor of individual rights and the fabricator of the social. Most key modern philosophers, such as Rousseau, Kant, and Hegel, had nurtured a "metaphysical" understanding of the social and the state.[70] On one hand, they conceived individuals as free-floating, monadic rights bearers; on the other, the state was portrayed as a collective macro-actor possessing a will of its own. With the exception of Gierke's conception, individual autonomy and state sovereignty were intellectual constructs haunting the whole of modern thinking.[71] Unlike these theories, Duguit contended his view of objective law had purged itself of any mythical and metaphysical aspects, as it was based on the observation of social phenomena and the study of human psychology.

According to Duguit, law—what he calls "objective law"—is the bare fact that one who lives "in a given society is by that very fact subject to a rule of conduct whose violation involves a social reaction which can be organized."[72] By the same token, he denied there being such thing as a collective will of any macro-actors. The spirit of the people, the nation, or the state-person expresses nothing other than the need to detect a mythical source of law. The law's only source, Duguit thought, is humans' willful actions and the social rules that are required for these actions to be performed. Importantly, rules of this kind are not mandatory rules meant to constrain individual action. Instead, they are conditions of possibility for individuals to be part of a collective, that is to say, rules that confer membership and identity as group members: "Individuals who compose a social group are subject to the law of this group, a law which presides over its formation and development."[73] To put it otherwise, these are rules coordinating the actions of members within a group and, by doing so, shape the group identity. If this is the case, according to Duguit, obligations in the eyes of group members should not appear as genuine obligations, in the sense that there should be no real conflict between their deliberate actions and the rules governing their conducts. Insofar as people are members of a particular group, their purposeful conducts require the existence of rules governing and organizing them. If one fails to comply with a social rule, this infringement will meet with social censorship. In fact, there is no social coordination that can do without social rules, so much so that interaction breaks down if people contravene them. In short, Duguit's notion of objective law rested on a functionalist conception of a rule as that which enables coordination within social collectives, is spontaneously followed by their members, and is backed up by generalized social pressure.

Certainly, Duguit's account of law was highly affected by the developments of public law services in the late nineteenth century.[74] The state was involved in the massive organization and provision of such services as education, social security, and utility services regulated by a system of public law. In other words, he was particularly interested in the function public law had come to play. However, he applied his view of objective law to all social groups: all group members have social duties—that is, not merely moral—to contribute to the existence of their group and, at the same time, these members are by and large aware that these duties are what allows them to enjoy their group identity and the very group to exist. In doing so, he clearly blurred the dividing line between social and legal normativity as he traced the emergence of law back to the internal regulation of groups. For he rejected not only command- and personality-based conceptions of law but also differentiation theories. The law cannot be described as the materialization of a second layer of control, whereby a particular population issue and change rules. In Duguit's words:

> There exist, in fact, certain societies where no differentiation has yet arisen between governors and governed. Do rules of law exist in such societies? . . . They compose what I have already called a social discipline, which must exist. Without it, there would be no permanent group. The sanction of the rule is indeed still unorganized; but it exists none the less: it consists in the spontaneous reaction of the entire group against the authors of a violation.[75]

State bodies, Duguit claimed, can and do serve as jurisdictional devices, but it is not this type of state intervention that makes a rule legal. The legality of a particular rule rests entirely with its being a coordination mechanism in the eyes of the members of the various groups that are present in a given community. He called these rules "standardizing rules," in that they standardize behavior and behavioral expectations. While these rules correspond to what in today's jurisprudential parlance are rules of conduct, Duguit acknowledged the existence of rules conferring powers that he called "constructive" or "technical rules." This latter type of rules make sure that standardizing rules are complied with and to this end establish competences and create procedural standards. Interestingly, though, it was Duguit's conviction that not even technical rules acquire their validity from the state. The state cannot itself issue any commands, as the latter "emanate from an individual or from a group of individuals, whose wills cannot be wills commanding other individual wills which are subordinate and obedient. This hierarchy of wills does not exist and cannot exist."[76] Rather, the validity of technical rules hinges on them being instrumental to the application of standardizing rules. In short, the validity of all rules of the state legal system pivots on there being social rules that are developed by people within the groups they are member of. Legal normativity is ancillary to social normativity. The binding force of complex modern legal systems, comprised of a host of technical rules conferring powers, "can only be explained if it is admitted that they have to support them the standardizing rule whose application they tend to guarantee."[77]

It is here that an important conceptual conundrum emerges—one to which this book will return in detail at a later stage. A view that makes legal normativity entirely conditional on social normativity is also called upon to explain how come certain social rules make their way into the legal system while others remain outside of it (and are regarded as nonlegal, extralegal, or illegal). Duguit's solution to this conundrum built on a specific conception of human sociality that he simply took to be obvious. Drawing from Aristotle's and Aquinas's social anthropology, he conceived human beings as social beings who share basic principles of justice and are more or less aware of the fact that generalized noncompliance eventuates in chaos.[78] Based on this view, he concluded that a rule is legal when "the mass of individuals composing a given society understand that the interdependence which unites them would be gravely compromised if this rule were not given a sanction."[79] This generalized view of an undeviatingly socialized human being, however, was not accompanied with an idea of society as one homogeneous collective founded on one shared conception of justice. Nor did Duguit think that objective law springs from a common societal nucleus. In line with the fragmented and polarized structure of his surroundings, he regarded society as a set of narrow groupings, each giving rise to its own objective law. Societies are composed of an undefined variety of normative frameworks developing rules of their own and giving rise to a condition of normative pluralism.

Still, this begs a further question that, as we will show, is woven into the conundrum we are discussing: How can diverse and potentially competing groups share the basic principles of justice enshrined in law? How can they converge on one legal system and give rise to an organized macrostructure? While some claim that Duguit's answer to this question lay in an unstated "harmonism" whereby different normative frameworks end up converging on a basic view of objective law,[80] others place emphasis on Duguit's eventual rehabilitation of the state.[81] A chaotic condition of potential conflict between social groups could be avoided only on account of social interdependence attained through the use of governmental force. Duguit's treatment of the potential risks of pluralism epitomizes the conjunction of corporatism and pluralism we discussed above. On one hand, he welcomed the revived function of corporations as a way out of the double metaphysics of individualism and state personification. The reviviscence of alternative forms of representation marked the end of modern statehood, while the pluralist legislation that was being implemented beckoned the progressive pluralization of the state. On the other, though, he maintained that associationism and syndicalism should not aim for armed revolt. They should get rid of revolutionary urges so as to become part of a pluralist state within the framework of *functional representation*, one in which representation is not based on territorial distribution but mirrors the occupational composition of society and the groups of social functions to be performed.[82] According to Duguit, the reform of the representation system would make sure that the state always act in the interest of the groups it encompassed.

The truth is that Duguit harbored an idealized view of syndicalism as entirely consistent with state government: "The reason why Duguit was so commendatory about syndicalism (and thus was sometimes mistaken for a revolutionary syndicalist) was because he saw in it what he wished to see."[83] He was so convinced about the requirement that unions express the organic unity of the nation that he was against the right to strike even in the private sector. In his view, functional representation would integrate unions into the state and domesticate the subversive push on more combative groups. Simultaneously, labor relations should be pacified in the name of the natural interdependence of social parties. Duguit tasked the state with legally integrating the self-organization of employers and employees through mixed unions and to recognize the conventions elaborated by professions. He saw these tasks as a superior end that the state was called on to pursue on the community's behalf. Such a state-based integration between social groupings would eventually restore the executive's full power and authority. The tendency to social disintegration would be tamed through the peaceful integration of those societal forces and movements that were trying to attain preeminence over traditional state bodies. This public service-oriented state would finally overcome the individualistic proclivity of French law as individuals would be able to pursue their ends as members of functional groups fully integrated into public law.

As the trajectory of Duguit's thinking illustrates, theoretical efforts were being made to reconcile the centripetal action of state law with the centrifugal force of pluralism. His mix of pluralism and corporatism, as we pointed out, hinged on a substantive notion of the human being and an idealized notion of functional integration that reinstated the state preeminence over social groups. More importantly for our purposes, though, is the jurisprudential portrayal Duguit put forward. While the law of the state is but the outcome of the functional integration of groups, standardizing rules—that is to say, rules of conduct—are produced by groups' members at the level of everyday interaction. Although established in the narrower context of a particular group, some standardizing rules are borrowed into the legal system when the bulk of the population recognizes their importance to social coordination. As we noted earlier, from a legal-theoretical viewpoint, this is a reductionist view of law whereby legal normativity can be traced back to social normativity—the law being nothing but the selection of those standardizing rules that are deemed to be vital to generalized social interaction. Needless to say, this account demotes both the legislator and the jurist to "readers" of the social, as the latter comes across as a text requiring accurate interpretation for those who issue law to identify those rules that people's legal consciousness regards as crucial to social integration. At the same time, the judge is an official who plays a technical role governed by technical rules of state law.

In the same years, the animators of the influential Freirechtsschule, known in English as the Free Law Movement, came to the same conclusion as to the social origin of law, but in a way that never restated the role of the state as the social pivot. While this movement provided an innovative and somewhat disruptive theory of law, though loose and unsystematic, most of its members were primarily concerned with the issue of legal uncertainty. They questioned the conventional jurisprudential answer to the problem of how judges draw the rules or principles that justify their decisions. In a way, the Free Law Movement broke both with the Historical School and state positivism. For both strands of legal thought ended up supporting codification. The exponents of the former thought that the *Juristenrecht* could be written down insofar as the jurists' sophisticated conceptual apparatus enabled them to draw legal rules out of the spirit of the people. Positivists regarded legal codes as the sedimentation of the state sovereign will that gave life to private relationships between individuals. None of these legal currents truly questioned the completeness of legal texts and the function of legal officials as appliers of unambiguous rules. The Free Law Movement got underway as a challenge to this widespread doxa. However, we will deal with this question insofar as it is relevant to the issue of pluralism, especially in that it was formulated by one of the leading figures of this movement, Eugen Ehrlich (1862–1922).[84]

Although the inspirer of this jurisprudential strand was Duguit's colleague and friend French lawyer François Gény (1861–1959),[85] the Free Law Movement arose at the blossoming of legal codification. Indeed in 1900, after two decades of polemics and compromises, the German civil code (Bürgerliches Gesetzbuch) went into effect. The members of the Free Law Movement challenged the widespread conception of judges as neutral appliers of definite, finite rules written down in the code. Against the grain of a seemingly coherent, homogeneous, and self-contained list of commands, the code and its textual guidelines left much room for judicial discretion. Yet they did not see this as a flaw, but rather as a virtue. They thought that only socially responsive judges were able to fill the unbridgeable gap between the bloodless legal text and the uncodifiable nuances of social reality. Thus, their point did not so much have to do with the substance of law as with the judges' approach to it. As Ehrlich put it: "The principle of free decision is really not concerned with the substance of the law, but with the proper selection of judges; in other words, it is the problem of how to organize the judiciary so as to give plenty of scope to strong personalities."[86] They reckoned with the artificiality of legal rules vis-à-vis the practical file of social rules in the realm of everyday life.

Like other members of the Free Law Movement, Ehrlich's main preoccupation was not with how to conceive law, as he rather took issue with what is central and peripheral to it.[87] For he thought that legal codes and statutory law could capture but a small fraction of the legal phenomenon. At the same time, like Duguit, he insisted on law being a technical device that is the acme of the broader phenomenon of social normativity. Ehrlich claimed that "norms for decision" (i.e., legal rules applied by state officials within courts) must be distinguished from the "rules of conduct" governing people's everyday life: the former regulate nothing other than a minute portion of social life, whereas rules of conduct are the normative guidelines on which people rely to conduct their life and to settle conflicts on a daily basis within informal dispute-settling arenas. This distinction squares with the further distinction between *Rechtssatz* (legal proposition) and *Rechtslebe* (life of the law, generally rendered as "living law").[88] The core of legal life does not reside in codified state laws but consists of the rules produced and applied by the various associations of human beings present in a given community. According to Ehrlich, the main mistake of legal science is its myopia to the nonofficial dimension of law, that is to say, how law works on a daily basis in informal settings. Mainstream jurisprudence confined the life of law to the cramped sphere of state legal texts and courtrooms and hence looked at law from "the point of view of the judge" as "a rule according to which the judge must decide the legal disputes that are brought before him."[89] In other words, his point was that approaching law through the conceptual grid of state-based jurisprudence impaired knowledge of the law practiced by ordinary people in their ordinary life.

The substance of living law is people's interactions taking place in those practical spheres that Ehrlich called "associations." By drawing from Gierke, he defined an association as "a plurality of human beings who, in their relations with one another, recognize certain rules of conduct as binding, and, generally at least, actually regulate their conduct according to them. These rules are of various kinds: rules of law, of morals, of religion, of ethical custom, of honor, of decorum, of tact, of etiquette, of fashion."[90] On this view, associations are the sites where most of people's legal life occurs and develops, while their recourse to official state law is much more sporadic. For within associations people develop and implement *rules of conduct* that govern the life of individuals as association members. The genuine core of the legal phenomenon is people's self-organizing activities by means of rules of conduct that turns a group of humans into a stable association: "A group of human beings becomes an association through organization."[91] To the contrary, official law is composed of *norms for decision*, which are rules of conduct specifically addressed to the courts.

Ehrlich's point was that the idea of law expounded by contemporary legal science was instrumental in nurturing the national states of late modernity. According to him, modern states were ideological abstractions that claimed to have disrupted and replaced all the previous forms of substate identity and ties. Correspondingly, the state-centered view of a self-contained and self-sufficient law was unserviceable and unrealistic, as the grounds on which judges make their decisions often exceed the legal text. It is the intellectual flaw that alleges law to be entirely reducible to official law that hampers proper understanding of how law works. Legislators, judges, jurists, and legal experts ought to admit what they learn from their everyday experience, to wit, that the true heart of legal life is the complex web of associations, whose rules of conduct assign "to each individual his position and his function."[92] The intellectual flaw of contemporary legal science, in Ehrlich's view, would end up increasing the distance between formal law, encapsulated in codes and statutes, and the concrete organizational dynamics of associations. This would in the long run reduce the vivacity of legal life and then harm its vital flux: "The water that is put in the pond is no longer a living stream but a stagnant pool, and but little water can be put in the pond."[93] State criminal and civil codes and public statutes, when too insensitive to the requirements of associations, can exert disruptive influence, not only on them, but on the political community as a whole. In fact, Ehrlich's claim was that an effective legal order rests on an effective functioning of the internal law of associations, in that individuals conduct their life as members of associations and in compliance with their rules.[94] What it thus requires is that legal propositions reflect the rules of the living law that generally individuals comply with "quite voluntarily" as well as the "innumerable legal relations" they enjoy as members of their associations.

To lay proper foundations for the argument that this book sets out to make, it is imperative to emphasize some distinctive features of Ehrlich's influential paradigm. Unlike Duguit's, Ehrlich's concern was mainly theoretical, in the sense that he wanted to advance a concept of law that reconciled the theory and the practice of law. He was at pains to bring out the inconsistencies and instrumentality of the widespread conception that equated law with the propositions of official state law. In reality, these propositions were more the overt basis of legal judgement than their substantive grounds. A more accurate analysis of how law worked on a daily basis provided evidence that legislators and judges continually referred to the living law of associations. This is particularly relevant in light of what we pointed out at the beginning of this chapter. From the early nineteenth century, legal scholars were seeking to draw the borders of jurisprudence with two, interlaced goals. First, they wanted to produce a theoretical toolkit suited to capture state-based law as it was taking shape. Second, this seemingly neutral and purely scientific enterprise was unsurprisingly coupled with furthering a particular understanding of the law, be it the jurists' law or the law of the sovereign state-person. Ehrlich thought that describing the law as an insulated sphere pertaining to the state machinery was in fact part and parcel of a political agenda. The legal practice showed that the phenomenon of law was so broad as to include the rules that people produced and obeyed within substate normative contexts.

While discussing the interactions between official law and the various laws of associations, Ehrlich mainly thought of the customs and practice-based regulations of the countless ethnicities living within the borders of the Austro-Hungarian Empire. Hardly could one coherent legal text do justice to such a variety of forms of life. Therefore courts would often be forced to look into the rules that people informally applied to administer quotidian matters, such as contracts, trade, or marriage. Customary rules were prevalent also in the legal practice of state officials notwithstanding the widespread jurisprudential view that law is only that which is written down in official legal codes. Therefore like Duguit and, to a lesser extent, Gierke, Ehrlich made the point that law is nothing but the summit of a normative phenomenon that encompasses the social as a whole. He claimed that it is very difficult to identify a distinguishing line between social and legal normativity. Obviously, he could not accept the source theory that law is only that which the state commands, in that legal practice was highly abundant in references to nonstate forms of normativity. Unlike Duguit and Gierke, however, Ehrlich did not rely either on a substantive organicist theory of the state or on a functionalist view of public law. He never introduced theoretical hypotheses presupposing the harmonious composition of different normative regimes. This is why it is of some interest to discuss how he solved the problem that we emphasized above while speaking of Duguit—which is to say, how come certain rules make their way into the legal system while others remain outside of it?

To address the issue of where social normativity ends and legal normativity begins, Ehrlich advanced a solution that interpreters found "not altogether happy"[95] especially because it "is difficult to apply and is incapable of providing a reliable distinction between legal and non-legal norms."[96] In other words, the criterion to distinguish legal rules from the myriad of social rules one can come across in the social realm is a practical one, viz., people's psychological attitude to the rule at issue:

> The question as to the difference between the legal and the non-legal norm is a question not of social science but of social psychology. The various classes of norms release various overtones of feeling, and we react to the transgression of different norms with different feelings. Compare the feeling of revolt that follows a violation of law with the indignation at a violation of the law of morality, with the feeling of disgust occasioned by an indecency, with the disapproval of faithlessness, the ridiculousness of an offence against etiquette and lastly with the critical feeling of superiority with which a votary of fashion looks down upon those who have not attained the heights which he has scaled.[97]

Those who defend Ehrlich's characterization of legal rules argue that it was meant to be neither a technical description of the features of legality nor the indication of a clear-cut line between the legal and the social. Rather, it is but a hint at the fact that, whether or not there are features that distinguish law from other types of normativities, these features are not reducible to the activity of the state.[98] And Ehrlich himself acknowledged that the criteria he offered to distinguish between legal and nonlegal rules do not identify any differentiating features, mainly because he was convinced that such features can hardly be identified at a theoretical level: "The sociological science of law . . . will not be able to state the difference between law and morality in a brief, simple formula in the manner of the juristic science that has hitherto been current."[99] The question of what law is and how it can be distinguished by other normative systems can only be solved by a praxiological approach.[100] In the end, Ehrlich's idea that legislators and judges should be sensitive to the living law of associations did not mean to set forth a full-fledged theory of law. It was more "a demand of political prudence that the norms for decision which are prescribed to the judges by the lawmakers conform to the value judgments held by the people whose controversies the judges decide."[101]

Despite the ambiguities of Duguit's and Ehrlich's conceptions of law, the present section mainly wanted to lay stress on the topicality of this theoretical struggle. They were the spearheads of a growing reaction to the idea that law is a creation of the state and that social normativity depends on legal normativity. Both of them claimed their theories were more faithful to the reality of everyday legal practice as the positivist theories they criticized were far more concerned with conceptual clarification of recent legal construct of state sovereignty—one that was subservient to the state as the only holder of legal power. Duguit and Ehrlich denied there being a clear, recognizable line separating the special normativity of state law from the more general normativity of the various social orderings. As we will discuss later in this book, much as they tried to explain what law is in respect of the internal law of social orderings, Duguit and Ehrlich came to the conclusion that it was impossible to provide an irrefutable answer on this problem. Their treatment of this issue was rather meant to advance two major claims as to the nature of law and its relation to the social. First, the law is an inherently social phenomenon on a continuum that runs from the informal rules of more or less transitory practices to the formal rules of legal texts. Second, as to the administration of ordinary life, the unofficial ordering of substate associations were more relevant than the formal laws that were used and applied in official courts.

CONCLUDING REMARKS

Throughout this chapter we sought to isolate two perspectives that in various areas scholars had been developing since the first decades of the nineteenth century: the *jurisprudential* and the *juristic* point of view. Although these labels are our own, they identify two opposite attitudes to the law. The jurisprudential point of view originated from the awareness that the development of law as a technical device in the hands of the state government required an analogous development of the legal science as a specialized body of knowledge. The possession and management of this knowledge, as we illustrated, was a contested issue. It was unclear whether those who can gain access to the mystery of legal phenomena were jurists, legal professors, or legislators. Despite this, all those who adopted a jurisprudential point of view in a way or another were adamant that law is something special and had to be cognized through special conceptual devices. This obviously entailed a sharp separation between various forms of social regulation and the law as a technical device and a specialized knowledge. Quite the reverse, the juristic point of view was born as a reaction to the gap that the jurisprudential point of view introduced between different normativities. Theorists who adopted this perspective decried the ideological nature of demoting social normativity to a negligible epiphenomenon or even a by-product of state law. The juristic point of view implied that neither law nor legal science had anything special. Law was but the visible acme of the wide-ranging dynamics of social organization, and therefore legal science needed to incorporate insights from other disciplines to get to the core of such a multilayered social phenomenon.

Be that as it may, both points of view were faced with a fragmented and potentially explosive reality, where associations and organizations of different sorts claimed autonomy from the state while others championed a complete overturning of the capitalist system. Movements from the left and from the right advanced perilous recipes to free society of (what they regarded as) the decaying ideology of state sovereignty. While this chapter did not aim to provide a conclusive portrayal of nineteenth-century legal theory as a response to specific challenges, it intended to pave the way for the analysis of Santi Romano's seminal contribution to the conceptualization of this pluralist scenario. Our contention will be that his oeuvre should be read against the background of the set of issues we have brought up in the preceding pages. Romano's theory can be pithily summarized as an admirable attempt at reconciling the jurisprudential and the juristic points of view with an eye to taming pluralism.

CHAPTER TWO

Santi Romano and the Juristic Point of View

THE PRECEDING CHAPTER PROVIDED a sketch of pluralism as a serious societal predicament and the ways in which it affected the conceptualization of law and its relation to the social. The liberal-constitutional state of the late nineteenth century was under siege. A growing number of nonstate actors was claiming autonomy from the state in an unprecedented manner. They challenged the role of the state as the source of legality and denounced parliamentary representation as an elitist system that neglected most sectional interests and needs. In the face of these societal ferments, theorists of various strands felt dissatisfied with both state positivism and organicism. They thus set out to advance new conceptual vocabularies that might overcome the inadequacies of state-based conceptions of law. While Gierke's seminal contribution to reconsidering the role of substate associations in the life of the state was still indebted to an irenic conception of the state body, Duguit and Ehrlich, to different degrees, propounded a theory of law in which the state figured as a marginal, residual meta-entity. These alternative conceptions of law and the state paved the way for the proliferation of pluralist theories of the state as a political apparatus that did not possess either creative power or overriding authority. In France, Germany, Italy, the United Kingdom, the United States, and other countries, a great deal of pluralist thinkers came to consider law as something that could hardly be confined to official legal texts or official courtrooms. The idea that law originated from the self-organizing activity of social groups was destined to upturn the consolidated view that the state is the pivot of a community's political life.

As we go along in this chapter, we will see that Santi Romano's whole oeuvre was deeply concerned with such a complicated interplay between available jurisprudential categories and the morphing social landscape. Various interpreters hold the opinion that Romano epitomizes the difficulties jurisprudence had in keeping up with the changing scenario. On one hand, he was the first to grasp the genuinely *legal* import of those momentous changes as he struggled to produce a *jurisprudential* account of what was about to change the state in an unmatched manner. On the other, Romano, they argue, fell victim of the mismatch that existed between the traditional legal-theoretical apparatus and the emerging configuration of the social world.[1] This chapter offers a portrayal of Romano's capital contribution to legal theory by advancing an interpretive hypothesis—one that questions the majority view of Romano being torn between two equal and opposite forces: *theoretical* pluralism and *institutional* monism. Although he was the champion of a pluralist version of legal institutionalism and thought that legal pluralism is the natural outcome of consistent legal theorizing, according to the bulk of the extensive literature on his work (especially in Italy, where Romano's impact is impressive), he fell short of the goal of harmonizing institutionalism and pluralism. While in the preceding chapter we presented Duguit's and Ehrlich's as somehow opposite versions of pluralism, like the former, Romano is generally believed to reassert a de facto primacy of state law and thus to weaken severely his sensitivity to pluralism.

Against the grain of this majority view, this chapter addresses the gist of Romano's overall theory by elaborating on a hypothesis that presents institutionalism and pluralism as coherently glued together. His overall contribution comes down to the conclusion that the only way to make social and political pluralism work is to provide a *jurisprudential account of it*—one that remains within the boundaries of the juristic practice and never exceeds it. This is what we will call the "juristic point of view." If this is the case, it makes sense to say that Romano intended to put forward a conception of legal theory as a *technique of description* that is capable of engendering particular social outcomes—as well as effects of domestication and compatibility insofar as social pluralism is concerned.

In the first chapter we tracked down the rise of jurisprudence as a discipline developing specific conceptual tools and pursuing particular aims. Although the various theories we mentioned hinged on largely incompatible views of the law and its relation to statehood, most authors agreed that legal theory is a distinctive, privileged approach to the legal phenomenon. There is no doubt that Romano's formation was highly influenced by this stance. He was born in Palermo, Sicily, on January 31, 1875. At the time Palermo was the cradle of a host of renewed legal studies that deeply changed the way of conceptualizing public law in Italy. His teacher and mentor was Vittorio Emanuele Orlando, who, unlike Romano, enjoyed a successful career as a leading statesman. Solicited by Orlando, the young Romano contributed to a seminal collection of volumes devoted to Italian administrative law, *Primo trattato completo di diritto amministrativo italiano* (First complete treatise on Italian administrative law), published between 1900 and 1915. Yet, he would soon part ways with his mentor (though they remained good friends, with the inevitable ebb and flow of pre- and postwar times) and developed a new, seminal approach to the legal phenomenon.

Unlike Orlando, Romano devoted all his life to legal studies and legal teaching. He taught in Camerino (1897–1902), Modena (1902–1907), Pisa (1908–1923), and Milan (1924–1928). His unconditional scholarly commitment, however, drew to a close on January 1, 1929, when he had to resign as a professor as he was appointed by Benito Mussolini as the president of the Council of State,[2] the court of last resort in administrative matters. Although his judicial activity took most of his time, Romano continued to teach and to give lectures as an adjunct professor at the University of Rome "La Sapienza." He first taught administrative law and then constitutional law, as Orlando, who had hitherto held the chair of constitutional law at La Sapienza, nominated him as his successor. Romano resigned from the presidency of the Council of State in 1944, a few months after the Allied powers liberated Rome from Nazi occupation. Romano died in Rome on November 3, 1947.[3]

This chapter will look into those that are commonly considered as Romano's signature works, a small but seminal essay produced in 1909, "Lo Stato moderno e la sua crisi" (The modern state and its crisis), which was the inaugural lecture for the academic year at the University of Pisa, and *The Legal Order*,[4] one of the most influential writings in Continental jurisprudence. This does not imply that his preceding works are unimportant. However, while interesting interpretations have recently tried to cast light on the *fil rouge* joining his early reflection on public and constitutional law with his more mature texts, we will look into those works of Romano's that cast light on the convergences and divergences with Mortati's and Schmitt's.[5]

WHAT TO DO WITH THE STATE? ROMANO'S "THE MODERN STATE AND ITS CRISIS"

One of the main issues debated in the rich Italian literature on Romano's oeuvre is the degree of continuity between *The Legal Order* and his preceding work. As we mentioned, this question begs the further question of Romano's attachment to the *state* legal order and his (allegedly) ambiguous approach to legal pluralism. Albeit very young, Romano contributed to Orlando's collection on Italian administrative law, and interpreters disagree on whether there is a link with subsequent theoretical developments. Most of them agree, however, on the significant connection between *The Legal Order* and the germinal 1909 essay, "The Modern State and Its Crisis."[6] The title of this essay signals his deep awareness of a set of epochal transitions that would rapidly change the nature and practice of the liberal-constitutional state. While some writers regard this text as a proof of Romano's unquenched passion for the marvelous machinery of the state,[7] others stress that his fine-grained analysis of the gaps of the state order gestures towards a new way of conceiving the state and its tasks.[8] While both readings capture important points, it is our claim that a different interpretation of this text offers a first glimpse into the particular way law was changing *through* Romano's theorizing.

To commence, we would first like to examine the reasons why Romano is believed to reassert a conventional idea of the state endowed with a legal personality that makes it a truly self-sufficient entity, one that is not reducible either to its sovereign or to its subjects.[9] "The Modern State and its Crisis" begins by claiming that the state—a "magnificent creation of the law"[10]—is able to assemble "the various elements that comprise it" on account of its personality. Its power is rooted in its own nature and force, that is, the force of law. Because of this, the state "goes beyond the individuals' transient existence . . . and rises above, and balances, particular interests."[11] Although he did not disavow the origin of the state, which he traced back to the French Revolution, he averred that that particular form of state had a major flaw. Romano did not lambaste the establishment of the new political structure at the expense of the Ancien Régime. For if it is true that the Revolution drew to an end the traditional pluralist order unfolded throughout the Middle Ages, this happened because other institutions and forms of government had been emerging in the interstices and fissures of society. In short, the Revolution brought to light and sped up a much slower process of sociopolitical, cultural, and economic transformation that was eroding the status quo. However, he thought that the French revolutionaries made the serious mistake of disregarding those institutions and forms of government. The new order's "original sin" was to believe that "it could afford to neglect a host of social forces," which it ingenuously believed "would collapse . . . in that they were considered as mere historical remnants destined to wither away shortly."[12]

In other words, the revolutionary state was unable to profit from the emergence of other, nonstate institutional entities, and sought to efface them once and for all through the implementation of an extensive and powerful administrative apparatus. At the same time, the newly minted state forcefully imposed its all-encompassing ideology based on the dyad state-individual: if all administrative entities are subjected to state authority, there remains no filter between the citizens and the state other than the political system of representation. While there were numerous forms of collective organizations, the state that emerged out of the French Revolution acted as if state agencies, on one side, and the individual, on the other, were the only political actors at play. As a complement to this state-centered ideology, the state fostered an abstract notion of the individual as an isolated legal subject who is vested with "an infinity of rights emphatically proclaimed and conferred with costless generosity."[13] In this way, such a mix of state-centrism and individualism made the revolutionary state blind to the existence of nonstate aggregates—though in practice these could hardly be completely obliterated with recourse to brute force. Romano went on to say that those institutions and forms of government in reality continued to exist and to nurture the aversion and resentment against the new state order. Based on these considerations, "The Modern State and Its Crisis" offers an analysis of the rise of turbulent nonstate formations that were threatening the state.

Needless to say, one's interpretation of Romano's diagnosis of the new ferments depends on whether one views him as an advocate of the traditional state-person. But let us have a dispassionate look at what he wrote. Like the authors we discussed at the end of the preceding chapter, Romano's attention was drawn to the host of substate and suprastate associations and organizations that, whether peacefully or not, were laying the claim that the state was unable to organize and regulate social life and were developing alternative forms of self-government. These substate and suprastate associations and organizations "tend[ed] to join together" and, although they "pursue[d] diverse ends, they share[d] a common trait."[14] They fostered a regulatory framework that, according to many scholars, was irreconcilable with the state legal order. These were labor-based organizations, such as workers' federations and various kinds of trade unions, whose imaginings about social organization evoked a patrimonial, status-based, and corporatist political structure. As we pointed out in Chapter 1, Duguit was elaborating on the notion of functional representation as a way to reform the Senate. This would be elected through indirect suffrage to represent these associations and organizations. Yet, in the concluding pages of "The Modern State and Its Crisis," Romano argued that the emphasis on labor-based and profession-based criteria should never wipe out traditional features of the state, such as territory and population. In his view, the tension between the nation-state and the corporatist state was perilously increasing to the detriment of social stability.

Apparently, the main argument of "The Modern State and Its Crisis" was that the state should not be jettisoned, as it is the only organizational form that secures justice and equality. Romano recognized that the state could not continue to be blind to aggregates that are neither official state bodies nor individuals. The state should be able to accommodate the various substate and suprastate self-organized entities that the French revolutionary state adamantly ignored. Yet, he concluded by saying that less extremist associations and organizations should break their ties with seditious ones to contribute to a far-reaching state reform. If this were the correct exegesis of Romano's view of the matter, it would doubtless be difficult to reconcile this position with the clear-cut passages of *The Legal Order* where it is stated that "the idea that the state system has become the only system in the legal world is to be most decidedly rejected" and that "the state is nothing other than a species of the genus 'law.'"[15] But the reason we used the distancing expression "apparently" at the beginning of this paragraph is that we believe these junctures of *The Legal Order* gesture to an alternative interpretation of Romano's view of the matter in "The Modern State and Its Crisis"—one that centers not so much on the factual circumstances he discussed but on the distinctive nature of law and legal theory.

Indeed, it is very significant that "The Modern State and Its Crisis" opens with the following sentence:

> Every science finds in its own nature and the procedures that appertain to it some particular and specific causes for mistakes. But possibly no sphere of human knowledge lumps together so many and perennial sources of delusions as the one that deals with the study of political institutions. These are phenomena of which it is even difficult to provide a description, because their form often conceals and distorts their substance and also because they take multiple and at the same time elusive appearances, as they stem from the continuous and never reconciled struggle between irreconcilable principles.[16]

In this juncture Romano had in mind (what he deemed to be) a spurious kind of sociological realism coupled with legal reductionism. Immediately after this opening, he conjured Savigny's idea of a law as something that arises out of a people's spirit. He commented that, however abstract

Savigny's view might be, it is no more unrealistic than conceptions depicting the legal system as the upshot of a battle for power. Romano's argument revolves around the relation between history and law, and yet it does not entail any historicism or history of ideas. As we will illustrate in more detail, his attention was focused on the time that is required for legal formations to take shape. Against theories contending that the law "derives from a struggle, whose outcome is only determined by material force,"[17] Romano thought that there is an important truth to Savigny's intuition of law's gradual, barely visible development through time. For modern public law is nothing other than a series of legal devices evolved through time in order to bring about unity among the host of social groupings that comprise society and the divergent and potentially conflicting interests they pursue. This is a first important clue to Romano's take on the relation between pluralism and institutionalism. While the fractures of the social world cannot be recomposed without there being a concrete legal order that harmonizes the various social parties, this concrete legal order is neither an act of fabrication nor a compromise between social forces. As Savigny intuited, what had led to the construction of the formidable machinery of the modern state was the time-consuming elaboration of conceptual categories that gave shape to the development of political forms. This is what Romano meant when he wrote that the state is a "magnificent creation of the law"—and this is no facetious remark, as it was not the state that brought about the law but the law that gave life to the state through a slow, steady, progressive historical evolution.

This is evidence that he was more concerned with the legal framing of the issue of social change than with the issue of social change itself. Pluralist scholars' almost exclusive interest in societal ferments and movement politics drew attention away from accurate legal conceptualization. While criticizing the pluralist theories of the state that we briefly touched upon at the end of the preceding chapter, Romano was careful enough to separate the conclusions he endorsed from those that he refuted. He concurred with pluralist theorists that the dyad state-individual neglected the activity of intermediary bodies that played a significant organizational role. Also in this context, though, Romano made his case with the instruments of legal analysis, as he averred that "there is no genuine law that does not reflect an actual social condition."[18] In fact, the sociological method that pluralist theorists embraced downplayed the genuinely *legal* concern with how the law affects social reality. It is worth noting that, for Romano, the misleading assumption that the state was doomed to crash under the weight of social movements stemmed from a flawed understanding of state law. A lengthy quotation from "The Modern State and Its Crisis" will help unpack this point. The problem does not lie with

> creating institutions that are contrary to the new requirements and needs, but only the illusion of having given life to full-fledged legal institutions, while in reality these institutions were nothing but contentless forms, schemes that needed, and still need, filling. Modern constitutions claimed that their text consecrated all fundamental principles of public law. Yet most of the time they did nothing but hint at institutions [*istituti*] that they failed to regulate. . . . As a consequence, they are full of gaps bigger than we are inclined to believe. That was and is good, since in this way the battle that at the moment seems to target them can take a different shape, once we realize that [this battle] takes place in a field where there are no trenches to pull down but only shelters to erect. . . . Probably the new edifices will not be at odds with the solid and severe architecture of the modern state, but will rest on its bases and will become part of it.[19]

The gist of Romano's argument is that there is no real clash between emerging social formations and the constitutional state, as it is the law-nature of the latter that structurally makes room for continuous amendments. However, unlike theorists who repudiated the whole edifice of modern statehood, this argument draws upon a thorough jurisprudential analysis that rejected naïve sociological realism and legal reductionism. If this is the case, then it makes sense to say that Romano's main concern was with the particular approach to reality that jurists have to take qua jurists and, consequently, with the distinction between legal and nonlegal concerns. In other words, Romano thought that a nuanced *legal* inquiry into contemporary sociopolitical phenomena that does not yield to hasty oppositions led to a view of public law as something that operates and oversees social change—and clearly this is a methodological statement concerning the boundaries and methods of legal analysis.

The interpretation we are putting forward rests on Romano's two main claims. Although not fully and explicitly articulated by him, they help clarify his overall stance on pluralism and the state in "The Modern State and Its Crisis." First, not only did he believe jurists should be able to identify the elements of social phenomena that are relevant to *legal* inquiry, but he also thought jurists should avoid polluting the *juristic point of view* with non-legal concepts and research methods. Second, and more importantly, this methodological pureness is not so much meant to help understand social reality as it is meant to *affect* social reality in a very particular way. In sum, although unlike Hans Kelsen, Romano never explicitly theorized the separation between legal theory and other disciplines, the specificity of jurisprudential devices seems to be a main presupposition of his conceptualization. At the same time, he thought the juristic point of view is the only one that, by *describing reality through the prism of law*, is likely to exert particular effects on reality.[20] For the juristic point of view makes the coexistence of different institutions and organizations possible as it captures their common element, that is, the capacity to self-organize.

This reading of "The Modern State and Its Crisis" presents the book as a first insight into a conception of law that Romano perfected between 1909 and 1917. On his view, legal theory is a technique that is capable of engendering specific social outcomes. As we will explain in detail below, the law is not a stable body of norms and principles that is created as the outcome of a process of organization but *the process of organization itself.* Accordingly, legal theory is the point of view that identifies this process as law. If this is so, then legal theory can significantly contribute to the transformation of public law as it morphs to accommodate social change. While we will expand on this conception in the following pages, our analysis so far aims to illustrate why "The Modern State and Its Crisis" cannot be charged with being a conventional defense of a notion of law as coinciding with state law. Romano's critique of pluralist theories in this valuable essay was not intended to reinstate the liberal constitutional state of the nineteenth century but to show how legal theory was expected to contribute to its adjustment. What jurists had to do was to show that it is not altogether necessary to get outside of the legal field to change the existing state of things. Rather, it is part of the nature of the legal field to lend itself as a site where reality can be renegotiated and reframed. Accordingly, individuals and groups that were dissatisfied with the liberal-constitutional state could erect new shelters to be granted protection. If this is the case, Romano's main theoretical argument in 1909 was that it is not the state itself which is likely (or unlikely) to enable the peaceful coexistence of nonstate associations and organizations and the liberal-constitutional state. Instead, it is the juristic (i.e., nonphilosophical, nonsociological, and so on) description of the state and its relation to nonstate associations and organizations.

LAW AS AN INTELLIGIBILITY CONDITION: THE ORDERING FUNCTION IN *THE LEGAL ORDER*

Although *The Legal Order* is one of the most influential books in Continental legal theory, its translation into English only appeared one hundred years after the publication of the first chapter as a journal article in 1917.[21] Jan Paulsson, who drew on Romano's theorizing for the elaboration of his influential theory of arbitration, commented that "it is a major scandal of intellectual history that this seminal monograph has never been translated into English."[22] In the same vein, Martin Loughlin praised it as a book that "remains unsurpassed to this day as a study of the essential elements of institutional jurisprudence."[23] *The Legal Order* offers one of the most robust institutional theories of law that fascinatingly glues together legal institutionalism and legal pluralism. In the sociopolitical context we described in the first chapter, it should not surprise anyone that Romano's major concern was with the various conflicts between state law and other forms of ordering. Moreover, the key to interpreting his thinking provided in the previous section suggests that there is no conflict between his defense of state law and his pluralist understanding of the legal phenomenon. Since

The Legal Order is a rich and dense book that can hardly be summarized in a few pages, we will take this as the main thread of the present analysis of Romano's book.

The Legal Order aspires to provide what today we refer to as a "grand theory" of law. Although unsystematically, it scrutinizes the most relevant legal paradigms of the time to come up with a conception of law that solves the riddles they left unsolved. The book is divided into two parts that lay the foundations for Romano's pluralist version of legal institutionalism. "Part I. The Concept of a Legal Order" makes the case for a concept of law that does justice to law's institutional character, well beyond law's comprising rules and procedures. "Part II. The Plurality of Legal Orders" explores the relation between state law and other nonstate types of law. It is no coincidence that the original version of Part I, first published in 1917, bore the subtitle "Studies on the Concept, the Sources and the Characteristics of Law." This is evidence that Romano regarded the 1917 text as the first contribution to an ongoing, much wider project delving into the nature of law and its various branches. In reality, he completed *The Legal Order* the year after with Part II and never returned to it until 1946, when he produced a second edition with important integrations (in the form of footnotes) to take into account the enormous deal of debates and criticisms *The Legal Order* had stirred up thus far.

The first sections of Part I betray Romano's ambition to lay out a new jurisprudential paradigm as they take issue with widespread definitions of law that he believed to be flawed. The opening lines of Part I read:

> All the definitions of law that have been advanced so far have, without exception, a common element, that is to say, the *genus proximum* to which that concept is reduced. Specifically, they agree that the law is a rule of conduct, although they to a greater or lesser extent disagree when it comes to defining the *differentia specifica* by which the legal norm should be distinguished from the others.[24]

Romano's approach is not only conceptual-analytical, but also methodological. He lamented that all available paradigms were unfit to capture the nature of public law as they had been formulated to explain and increase knowledge of private law. Not only did he want to set forth a novel theory of law, but also aspired to mark off a whole new field of legal theorizing. To this end, he went on by examining those elements that had so far been identified as the distinguishing marks of law. Romano was highly unsatisfied with notions such as coercion and norm not because he thought they are irrelevant. Rather, they are elements of a more comprehensive picture that is obscured if one only concentrates on one of them: "To define a whole legal order, one cannot only consider its distinct parts . . . ; rather, one needs to pinpoint the characterizing feature, the nature of this collection or this whole."[25] In Romano's view, law's characterizing features are to be discovered somewhere else, and specifically in the element that qualifies the legal order as *a self-standing entity*. However, before we elucidate this point, it is worth exploring why and how he denied norm and coercion being what makes law. It is interesting to note that, in doing so, he advanced lines of reasoning that remarkably resonate with the landmark conception that H. L. A. Hart advanced a few decades later in *The Concept of Law*.

Like Hart, Romano questioned the idea that the legal norm is the quintessence of law because norms are but elements of a broader practice that makes them legal. Although he did not distinguish between primary and secondary norms, norms do not owe the trait of legality to the fact of being norms. In *The Concept of Law* Hart argued this case by subsuming legal norms under the general category of social norms that make "certain types of behaviour a standard" as they are "a combination of regular conduct with a distinctive attitude to that conduct as a standard."[26] In short, it is only by means of a complex interplay of norms, reflection, and conduct that norms acquire the characteristic of legality. Throughout the years, Hart reduced the scope of his analysis of social norms to make the claim that it was only intended to capture legal officials' attitude to the rule of recognition and other legal norms[27]—and as we will discuss below, this is a major sticking point with Romano. Despite this, the fact remains that in Hart's view a legal norm is legal because it is encompassed in a comprehensive practice involving officials' reflective (though mostly tacit) acceptance of the norms by which they recognize and administer other norms.

Analogously, Romano anticipated Hart's forceful critique of sanction-based theories of law. In *The Concept of Law*, Hart censured former positivists' "itch for uniformity" as it had led them to identify coercion as the common feature of all types of legal norms. To give them the lie, he dwelled on the different nature of the different disadvantages that different types of norms entail. While actions contravening secondary power-conferring norms are not followed by a sanction but are voided, primary norms mandating or prohibiting particular conducts are met with specific punishment. However, Hart continued, it is not this punishment that creates the norm or makes it binding. For it is "logically possible and might be desirable" that there be such norms of conduct "even though no punishment or other evil were threatened." In other words, primary legal norms incorporate norms that are already binding whether or not a legal sanction is there to threaten disadvantage. Regardless of whether this argument truly defies the conceptions that Hart was criticizing, what matters here is that he questioned the idea that a norm is legal because another norm threatening sanction is attached to it and makes it legal.

In § 8 of *The Legal Order* Romano offered a critique of sanction-based models that strikingly parallels Hart's. He first argued that most legal theories espoused a narrow concept of sanction. They neglect that the consequences of complying with, or breaking, norms can be "a simple guarantee, whether direct or indirect, immediate or mediated, preemptive or repressive, certain or merely probable, and thus uncertain, provided that it is, in a sense, preordered and organized within the framework itself of the legal order."[28] But a more conclusive criticism is that the claim that sanction makes a norm legal is caught in an infinite regress:

> According to the dominant view, a precept can be said to be legal only when it is accompanied by another norm that, by granting a right of coercion, is able to protect the right created by the former. Formally, these different precepts can be coupled, but essentially are to be regarded as uncoupled. They bring about two rights, of which the one is primary or principal, while the other secondary and ancillary; hence, they do not stem from the same norm. At the same time, for the sec-

> ond precept to be deemed legal, it should be accompanied by a third one, and the third by a fourth one, and so on and so forth; in this way, we necessarily come to a point where this precept is not available at all, and we are left with a norm without sanction. In truth, this line of reasoning, which is right *in se*, and has been used to deny sanction being a necessary feature of law, in my opinion simply demonstrates that its premise is groundless, and hence can well be utilized.[29]

As was the case with norms being law's distinctive trait, both Romano and Hart insisted that sanctions are not the hallmark of legality. They are elements of a more comprehensive practice. It is at this point, however, that a first noticeable difference with Hart surfaces. While Hart held onto a notion of sanction as penalty, and coercion as the use of force on the part of official state agencies, Romano worked with a broader notion that fitted his pluralist understanding of law. For he remarked that not always are sanctions specific punishments attached to prohibited behaviors, as most often they are "immanent and latent" in the mechanisms of the law. He went so far as to say that admitting that sanction is an element of the legal order is further evidence that the legal order does not only comprise norms: "Saying that the sanction is a feature of law implies saying, whether intentionally or not, that the law comprises elements other than legal norms, and that these are bound up with, or even hung up on, other elements from which their force derives."[30] Based on this train of thought, Romano emphasized the practice nature of law as an organizational activity including a variety of elements: "In this way, the sanction or, rather, those other elements, far from being complementary or ancillary to the norms, actually pre-exists them: they form the base on which norms are constructed, their root, and, while defining law, it is necessary to take them into account ahead of the norms."[31]

THE FORMAL STRUCTURE OF INSTITUTIONS

If Romano's criticisms to existing jurisprudential paradigms are pretty clear, his constructive arguments on what law is are less so. Part I of *The Legal Order* intends to justify an institutional theory that drew on, but significantly departed from, Maurice Hauriou's. This key French jurist was appointed to a chair in administrative law at the University of Toulouse in 1888, and remained there until the end of his career. His series of leading treatises on public law made him a world-renowned legal scholar and one of France's leading legal philosophers. He published his first relevant sociological text, *Cours de science sociale. La science sociale traditionnelle*, in 1896. Other seminal works are the first edition of *Principes de droit public* (1910), *Précis de droit constitutionnel* (1923), and "La théorie de l'institution et de la foundation" (1925)—the last one being the only text specifically devoted to the concept of institution.[32]

Hauriou developed an influential state-centered institutional theory of law that portrayed the state as the institution of institutions. Although his position changed significantly over time, the state to various degrees is presented as the quintessential form of institution as well as the highest and most perfect social formation. Hauriou's was a reaction to the conception of law advanced by Duguit, as he advocated the antivoluntarist idea that positive rules are ancillary, derivative aspects of the legal order, while the main elements of the legal practice are the creative power of individuals and the organizational potentialities they possess. Influenced by Henri Bergson's vitalism, Hauriou aimed to explain how psychical elements permeate social reality and mold it. His notion of institution postulated that any institution comprises three constitutive features: First, a directing idea (*idée directrice*) of social action, that is, a foundational idea that leads a social group to carry out its enterprise. Second, the formation of a structuring power that determines what the steps are to be taken in order to achieve this end. Third, the widespread acceptance of the directing idea, that is, a visible agreement within the association around the aim they pursue and the means to accomplish it. Based on this analysis, Hauriou came up with a path-breaking definition of institution as

> an idea of a work or enterprise that is realized and endures juridically in a social context; for the realization of this idea, an organized power equips it with organs; on the other hand, among the members of the social group interested in the realization of the idea, manifestations

of communion occur and are directed by the organs of the power and regulated by procedures.[33]

Although this definition appears to cover all social formations that are structured by an ordering principle, its unstated assumption is that institutions are characterized by the powers and functions that are generally considered as basic features of the state. Put otherwise, only apparently do many social formations qualify as institutions, whereas in fact the state is the sole institution that meets the requirements of Hauriou's conceptual description. Romano's critical remark on this aspect is blunt: "Hauriou was carried away with the idea of modelling his institutions on the broadest among them, that is, the state, even the modern state, while it behoved him to delineate a very general figure, whose contingent characteristics can vary, and actually vary indefinitely."[34] It is of particular importance that the disagreement between these two leading fathers of legal institutionalism revolved around the *legal* nature of institutions. Hauriou considered institutions as types of associations that are "manifestations of communion" among the group members, but these do not qualify as legal in themselves—they carry out an organizational task through the law. In this sense, law is nothing other than a regulative structure that supervenes at one point in time to sustain an institution. According to Romano, this conception objectifies the institution and unjustifiably separates it from its regulative structure. Whereas Hauriou intended to isolate institutions' objective character, the result is that institutions are portrayed as *prelegal* entities that at one point develop a legal structure. Against such an abstractive separation between institutions and their legal structure, Romano advanced his most provoking idea: as the organizational activity of a social entity *is* its law, any "institution is an objective legal order."[35]

This contrast between Hauriou and Romano is key to understanding what an institution is in the latter's view.[36] In line with the methodological attitude of "The Modern State and Its Crisis," he rejected all nonjurisprudential (especially philosophical and sociological) accounts of institution. While he thought that law is synonymous with organization, and organization is synonymous with institution, he was adamant that legal theorists have to remain within the boundaries of legal science to avoid any contaminations with vocabularies that appertain to other disciplines: "The concept of organization cannot be of any help to jurists unless it is turned into a legal concept." More generally, Romano was on the lookout for an "uncontaminated" terminology that could fit his jurisprudential inquiry:

> Insofar as one speaks of "corpus mysticum," structure or edifice or social system, or even mechanism to differentiate the organization from a natural organism, the terminology in use might well be correct, it might well serve to make the idea imaginative and plastic, but it is not legal. Therefore, it might help jurists but it does not discharge them from the duty to replace it with another word, one that has both the form and the substance that are needed to draw this concept in their own realm, which is not that of sociology.[37]

He went so far as to speak of a "duty" to identify the correct terminology, one that might unveil the identity between law and institution as an organizational phenomenon. Consequently, insofar as the term *organization* is employed to refer to a group of people who work together in pursuit of collective goals and deploy some sort of rule-making and decision-making procedures, however elementary these may be, this is *not* a legal concept. If it is true that—as many of his detractors remarked—it is not easy to pin down the notion of institution in Romano's book, this is because he often oscillated between focusing on the characteristics of institutions and focusing on the process that turns a collective into an institution. Without a doubt, when he spoke of "things and energies" and "permanent and general ends" along with "guarantees, powers, subjections, liberties, checks," he seemed to be thinking of the observable traits of organizations. An approach of this sort rests on an empirical survey of the steps that are necessary to deploy a specific structure that, as Romano himself underlined, "consecrates the principle of the coexistence of individuals, but above all takes it upon itself to overcome the weakness and limitedness of their forces, to exceed their feebleness, to perpetuate particular goals beyond their natural life, by creating social entities that are more powerful and durable than individuals."[38] Yet, this was not Romano's main concern, as these are recurring features of all institutions, not that which brings them about.

For the sake of the argument, let us distinguish the institution's *formal structure*—that is to say, the process whereby it comes to life—from its *substantive characteristics*. Our contention is that, while the latter are obviously central to there being institutional phenomena, Romano concerned himself with their formal structure in the first place. More in particular, his main argument was that an institution is a normative structure that allows a particular ensemble of individuals to conceive themselves, and to be conceived by others, as the members of a stable and durable collective. In § 10, he went so far as to say that "society" simply stands for "institution." While expanding on this, he singled out three main features of institutions that are not substantive characteristics but elements of a formal structure. First, within institutions the connections that tie people together must be objective, stable, and permanent, in the sense that they are sheltered from the potentially variable will of individual members: "A class or a group of people that is not organized as such, but is only determined by mere affinities between people themselves, is not society proper."[39] Second, these connections are ordered in a way that powers and competences are internally allocated among members, whether formally or informally. In other words, "social order" simply stands for "institution." Third, the order (or the "internal law of the institution," as Romano often called it) is not a collection of norms—which may well be essential parts of the institution—but "an organization, a structure, a position of the very society in which it develops and that this very law constitutes as a unity, as an entity in its own right."[40]

In doing so, Romano coalesced the notions of institution, law, legal order, internal ordering, organizational structure: these terms are nothing but different words denoting the same phenomenon. Interestingly, the theoretical distinction of formal structure and substantive characteristics gives away his take on the interplay of matter and nomic force, in the sense that we elucidated in the Introduction. The practical life of an institution, and especially its organizational activities, are never severable from an internal attitude drawing out their nomic force. These material activities are not nomic on their own but insofar as agents develop a knowledge about them. This also explains why all institutions are deemed to possess a law of their own. When the substantive activities of organization are coupled with a reflective attitude, this ipso facto brings about a law. For the exercise of this attitude separates these activities from the agents who concretely perform them, and hence they come to form an autonomous structure, although formal. This spells out the meaning of Romano's term "position": the progressive separation of a set of actions from the knowledge that unfolds around them. Therefore, the nomic force of an institution emerges out of the knowledge production process that organizes its material practices.

This is a first key aspect of Romano's unique blend of institutionalism and pluralism. For if it is the "position" of a formal structure that establishes whether an ensemble of people forms an institution, then all ensembles of people can in principle qualify as legal orders. In other words, it does not matter whether the purpose of an institution (one of its key substantive characteristics) has to do with religion, politics, morality, economics, or other areas of social life: "The celebrated contention that the law represents the ethical *minimum* is partly true and partly seriously mistaken. The law not only represents an amount of morality, but also of economy, customs, technique, etc. And this amount, which cannot be circumscribed and measured *a priori*, might not be a minimum."[41] Put otherwise, the law can be the internal normative structure of a collective regardless of its religious, moral, political, or other types of nature. All institutions that stably tie people together and are ordered in a way that powers and competences are internally allocated, along with a knowledge unfolding around them, are legal orders.

Romano's conclusion that all institutions are legal orders regardless of the associative purpose serves as a conclusive rejection of the idea that there is an essential connection between law and morality. Although Romano cannot be listed in the tradition of legal positivism, he sided with positivists as to the potentially indefinite contents of law. He did recognize that there can be a potential tie between a given legal order and the widespread morality of a community. Yet, he hardly considered this tie as an essential feature of law. As we will discuss later on, this is key to Romano's legal-pluralist notion that also the legal orders that, in the eyes of the state, are deemed to be unlawful are perfectly legal. For now, however, let us stick to the conceptual discussion of the formal structure of institutions. As far as the latter is concerned, it might be the case that morality is a substantive characteristic of a legal order, but this is by no means a necessary condition for there being a law. In other words, while institutions (viz. legal orders) are of different types, it might be the case that, under some circumstances, the internal normative structure of some of them exhibits a special connection with the morality shared by the group members. Romano added that it might at times be the case that the state legal order is explicitly designed to implement particular moral principles. But in this case, too, the connection between law and morality is accidental and contingent.

This analysis sheds some more light on Romano's notion of institution. In one of the footnotes from the second edition of *The Legal Order*, in which he took issue with a variety of criticisms, he lamented that many of his commentators failed to realize that his jurisprudential investigation had nothing to do with the sociological method: "These observations and the subsequent ones have been overlooked, or even misinterpreted, by those who contended that my inquiry is not jurisprudential, but pre-jurisprudential, and thus sociological, that it fails to identify the difference between the fact of social order and the legal order that it brings about, and so on."[42] As we mentioned, critics were not always uncharitable or mistaken, because at times Romano's formulations are confusing and obscure. Yet he was right in insisting that his discussion mainly revolved around the formal process whereby an institution comes into life. It is a structure that turns an ensemble of people into a stable organization with an inner legal order. Therefore, it is not this or that substantive characteristic, but something that transforms a population into an institution. When we say that a formal process transforms a population into an institution, however, it is important not to give the impression that Romano's view is beset by a sort of genetic fallacy. By underlining that his analysis was not sociological, he was remarking that legal scholars should not address the emergence of institutions as factual events. The nomic force of these events does not spring from their bare existence but from the fact that they are reflectively taken to be part of a formal structure. For it is evident that institutions arise and collapse at specific times and places, but legal analysis is not called upon to identify a point in time at which a given ensemble of people factually turns into an institution. Rather Romano insisted on the *point of view* from which one can determine whether something is an institution, regardless of the time-specific and context-specific events that generate institutions. This point of view, and the reflective attitude one can take from there, are crucial to the emergence of the formal structure. Accordingly, for Romano, jurisprudential enquiry serves the purpose of identifying the intercourse of material practice and knowledge production that is the source of an order's nomic force.

In substance, to overcome the limits of Hauriou's dominant theory, Romano advanced a notion of institution that identifies its distinguishing mark with its formal structure. Yet, the latter is not something objectively and ostensibly visible, as it is a perspective on institutions, one that allows grasping their legal nature. This is what we dub "the juristic point of view." § 15 nicely summarizes it:

> If law only can materialize and take shape within the institution, and if, conversely, all that is socially organized and is subsumed under the institution as one of its elements takes on a legal character, we obtain the following corollary: the law is the vital principle of any institution, that which animates and holds together the various elements that compose it, which determines, fixes and preserves the structure of immaterial entities. In its turn, the institution is always a legal regime.[43]

According to Romano, the notion of the juristic point of view unravels many of the puzzles that were tormenting legal and political theorizing of the time—for example, the question of whether the establishment of the state precedes the creation of its legal order, or whether the state is an ethical entity with the mission of protecting and implementing particular principles and rules. Importantly, Romano's point of view *dissolves* these and other questions: within a given geohistorical context, there are at one and the same time myriads of institutions that interact and overlap, so much so that it makes no sense to question the moral nature of an institutional entity. It is worth exploring this Romano's insight more in depth.

THE OBJECTIVE CONCEPTION OF INSTITUTION

To understand how Romano dissolved the issue of the relation between an entity and its internal order, we need to make our way into his conception of legal pluralism. As we discussed, Romano rejected views that defined either morality or coercion as the distinguishing mark of law. More generally, he claimed that no individual trait of an entity can determine if this entity has a legal character. Instead, it is this entity's being internally ordered and organized that makes it legal. Further reference to Hart's theory will be of help. According to Hart, secondary norms are designed to establish how primary norms can be recognized, laid down, and amended. The legal system is a combination of primary and secondary norms. In other words, the law is a normative context in which there are two distinct types of norms (primary and secondary) generally addressed to distinct groups of individuals (respectively, lay people and officials), one of which is called upon to administer primary norms in compliance with secondary ones. In this definition, prominent features are the formalization of norms and the specialization of roles.

It should come as no surprise that one of the milestones in legal-pluralist scholarship, Marc Galanter's "Justice in Many Rooms," points to a plethora of nonstate orderings that have this structure. By distinguishing between indigenous and exogenous orderings, he rejected any dichotomous view that straightforwardly opposes official state law to indigenous orderings. He suggested understanding the legal universe as an imaginary normative continuum with pure types at the ends. Official "exogenous" law comprises formal written norms, remote from everyday life, enunciated and enforced by specialized agencies. At its "indigenous" end there are norms variously applied by nonspecialized individuals and backed up by social pressure. In between these pure types there are multiple forms of law that approximate to them to a smaller or greater degree. With reference to Hart's legal theory,

Galanter commented that a clearer distinction between types of law can be obtained by identifying a "differentium," that is "the introduction of a second layer of control—of norms about application of norms."[44] In effect, exogenous laws often rely on more explicit normative standards, more deliberation about their application, and clear-cut norm-making and norm-applying procedures, whereas indigenous laws are norm-based practices in which the means to coerce compliance are rarely governed by secondary norms and there are no specialized roles.

However, according to Galanter, this remains a provisional distinction serving specific heuristic purposes, as most of the time the line between laws and nonlaws is far from firm and unequivocal. He continued by arguing that "the distinction of law from customs or morality carries in its train a history of conceptual struggles over the meaning of law."[45] In doing so, Galanter mixes together a factual-historical thesis and a theoretical one. On the first, his claim is that, as a matter of fact, in all geohistorical contexts many groups, associations, institutions, organizations, and fields produce their own norms, possess their own mechanisms for coercing compliance, and develop dispute-settling procedures. What people define as law in the here and now is the result of a struggle over meaning. Western national legal systems are nothing other than "institutional-intellectual complexes" that claim "to encompass and control all the other institutions in the society and to subject them to a regime of general rules."[46] Setting the stage for the modern state-centered scenario required that many normative orderings be reduced to a "subordinate and interstitial status." On the second, theoretical thesis, Galanter's point is that most theories that fail to accommodate this sociohistorical fact are just as unsuccessful when they seek to arrive at a conceptual criterion whereby state law can be unmistakably distinguished from other types of orderings. Since all definitions of law have to take those facts into account, no purely theoretical criterion based on the specialization of norms and roles can explain how to distinguish state law from most organizations where such a specialization obtains.

These two claims nicely summarize Romano's pluralism. At the same time, however, Romano thought it is vital to distinguish the factual-historical claim from the theoretical one. As far as historical facts are concerned, legal pluralism "in certain periods and especially in ancient times" was an unquestionable fact and a conceptual commonplace. "The Romans had the *ius gentium* or *naturale* alongside the *ius civile*," while "in the Middle Ages—because of the constitution itself of a society that was divided, riven with many and diverse communities often independent from, or loosely connected to, each other—the phenomenon of the plurality of legal orders manifested itself with such an evidence and force that it would be impossible not to reckon with it." In short, history teems with examples of diverse legal orders coexisting—whether harmoniously or not—in the same geohistorical scenario. Still, Romano was convinced that this awareness was programmatically removed from legal consciousness because of the triumph of the ideology of the state as the only source of law and the guarantor of social peace. As Galanter maintained that legal centralism impaired knowledge of "indigenous laws," so did Romano when he wrote that "the rise of the so-called modern state, and the consequent expansion of its force and its dominance over other communities that had so far been independent and sometimes antagonistic to it, nurtured the illusion that there was a unified legal order. . . . This fostered the theory that deems the state to be the lord and the arbiter not only of its law, but of all law."[47]

While Romano was conscious that a chain of historical events had led to the erasure of nonstate forms of law, he was also convinced that legal pluralism as a theory was "relatively recent, at least as a conception that advances a theoretical principle."[48] This is why Romano was concerned with furthering legal pluralism as a theory that does need not be based on historical observations to prove true. As is the case with Galanter and other legal pluralists decades after Romano—we will return to this below—the main issue at stake was how to set the threshold, as it were, of pluralism. Galanter's problematization closely reflects Romano's take on this issue. In the latter's view, the gist of the legal phenomenon is the transformation of a set of individuals transitorily doing things together into a stable collective, an organized institutional practice. If this is so, it goes without saying that institutions go through various developing stages over time. Hence, in all societies the normative structure of some institutions is more informal and loose, while that of others is more stable and specialized. Evidently, the idea of a continuum squares with Romano's view of the legal universe as composed of less organized and more organized institutions. In addition, he concurred with Galanter that the *differentium* is the presence of a second layer of control. Romano's opinion becomes manifest in the passage where he discussed the position of Italian legal philosopher Widar Cesarini Sforza, who had proposed a distinction between organizations *at a diffuse state* (such as informal social practices) and organizations *at a solid state* (more formal institutions).

In a book called *Il diritto dei privati* (The law of private subjects), first published in 1929, Cesarini Sforza censured Romano's institutionalism in that it undervalued the role played by individual agents in the process of institution making. In his reading, Romano's approach is objectifying in as much it portrays the law as an objective superstructure that encompasses and transcends the position of institutions' individual members. On the contrary, Cesarini Sforza insisted that legal orders are nothing but the set of *jural relationships* that bring them into existence.[49] In short, Cesarini Sforza thought of the social world as the cradle of many forms of interaction, some of which are jural in the sense that they are characterized by an *interdependence* between two agents, "such that one of them is the bearer of a right in relation to the other, while the latter has a duty towards the former."[50] Put otherwise, jural relationships are types of shared practices that are intelligible only with reference to the norms that structure them. The attribute "jural" denotes all interactions that are governed by a shared norm. But the picture is more complicated than that. Cesarini Sforza argued that not all jural relations give life to a law. Rather, all jural relationships possess nomic force of their own for the simple fact of giving life to norms. He thought that the nomic force of an order does not derive from the superstructure that Romano had in mind. All jural relationships possess that nomic value which is the seed of legality. It is a matter of bare power whether they are selected as official normative standards of the state legal order.

In the series of footnotes where he dwelled on his critics' comments, Romano reiterated his conviction that views of law such as Cesarini Sforza's were overinclusive. He wrote:

> It is not always easy to determine when we are faced with an institution that possesses the characters I delineated in the text. There are

borderline cases: for example, when we are faced with very rudimentary organizations such as, for example, people standing in queue at a bank counter or waiting to enter a club, or those less embryonic organizations but "at a diffuse state," which ideally put together compliance with customs or other shared rules, games and sports lovers, and the so-called chivalry, those who obey particular worldly customs.[51]

Romano referred to an example of Cesarini Sforza's as the latter tried to explain that a queue in a post office gets institutionalized when there is a distribution of numbers, so that each new arrival may take a consecutive number and wait for it to be called. Cesarini Sforza's argument was meant to indicate that every rule-based activity, though loose and improvised, can develop into an organized practice by means of institutionalization. Understandably, Romano conceded that these are borderline cases because, after all, this type of institutionalization is characterized by the rise of a second layer of control with some form of agency, although ephemeral, supervising the activities undertaken in a particular area of interaction: from transitory activities (such as a queue) to more permanent practices (among the examples provided by Cesarini Sforza, social manners, chivalry, sports). Yet Romano was adamant that "however large the criteria may be for identifying the characters of institution in very simple and scarcely developed forms of society, I do not think we can go so far as to say that that the legal phenomenon can be found in 'all states of human coexistence.'"[52] In brief, Romano could agree with Cesarini Sforza that embryonic organizations are borderline cases, not because they institutionalize jural relationships, but because jural relationships in those contexts undergo a structural process whereby an institutional structure comes into being. Put otherwise, for Romano, as illustrated above, the institution coincides with the formal structure that organizes relationships, while for Cesarini Sforza it amounts to these relationships. Romano was crystal-clear on this matter:

The institution can never be reduced to one or more specific legal relationships (§ 10). The legal relationship has to do with the subjective conception of law, as it presupposes at least two terms as points

> of reference. . . . The relationship is not an entity in its own right, but a relation among different entities, this word being used in a broad sense. The institution, instead, is objective law, and is objective law because it is an entity, a social body, which, within the legal domain, enjoys an effective, concrete and objective existence. It implies relationships but cannot be reduced to them. Rather, it is foundational to them, in the sense that it represents the organization or structure that is necessary for relationships, if and when they occur within its orbit, to be qualified as legal. The institution is unity; the relationship, whether legal or not, presupposes plurality. This is why, for example, the conception that the state is a simple legal relationship proves not only insufficient but also erroneous—such a conception has to be rejected also in the case of states that lack legal personality.[53]

THE NOTION OF ORDER

The last juncture reveals a further, central concern in Romano's theoretical framework: the institution is an ordering principle conferring unity on the elements it orders. He was not against the idea of jural relationships on account of any anti-individualist or objectivist biases. Instead, he was interested in the dynamic whereby an institution affects the identity of its members, to the extent that they come to be considered, and to consider themselves, as members. If it is true that jural relationships produce norms of their own—as Romano recognizes—it is also true that a multiplicity of jural relationships could give rise to a multiplicity of norms, to such an extent that apparently similar jural relationships might not be describable as the same institution. Romano hinted at this while discussing the difference between a couple and a married couple:

> It is impossible to envisage an institution only composed of two physical persons; for these will remain two individualities, unable to morph into one. This, importantly, does not imply that there cannot be institutions where the personal element is represented by two persons only; yet, in this case, this element has to be integrated with some

> other elements with a cohesive and unifying efficacy, which would otherwise be lacking. Accordingly, the conjugal society, which if considered in itself and for itself is but a relationship, can and usually does adopt the legal figure of family, or rather, an institution.[54]

One might rephrase Romano's example as follows. The social practice of romantic coupledom can be actualized in a variety of ways that develop and obey norms of their own—norms that are only valid for the two individuals who are involved in the distinct couple-formation. These are certainly norms in Cesarini Sforza's sense. On the pragmatic side, they create mutual expectations and corresponding obligations; on the epistemic side, they provide an intelligibility scheme to understand the behavior of these individuals. However, the norms of romantic coupledom can be actualized by social actors in so different a way that one would be hard pressed to bring them under the same normative scheme. Things change when individuals decide to get married. In this case, the element with "cohesive and unifying efficacy," which marriage as a legal institution is, brings the various couple-formations under the same normative umbrella. Norms can no longer be flexibly remolded by individual members, as the norms of the institution of marriage are no longer amenable to transformation unless specific procedures are followed. While in noninstitutionalized romantic coupledom the second layer of control is represented by those who perform the practice, who can change and apply norms as they see fit, a legally regulated conjugal relationship allows no such identity between norm-abiders and norm-makers/appliers. Although the individuals are the same, and although romantic coupledom continues to subsist, the individuals' norm-making capacity is superseded by the normative preeminence of the legal category of family.

It was this *normative metamorphosis* that interested Romano—one that the notion of jural relationships failed to capture. He wanted to emphasize the presence of a structure that makes it impossible for an institution's individual members to modify its normative configuration. This casts light on a passage that was fundamentally misinterpreted by Schmitt in 1934. Even though we will have to return to this subject while discussing Schmitt's institutionalism, it is worth saying a few words in this context to pave the way for the future discussion. At the end of the first chapter of *On the Three Types of Juristic Thought*, Schmitt gnawed at normativist conceptions of law that put norms at the heart of the legal phenomenon. In a way that clearly bespoke an important theoretical amendment to his prior decisionism (see Chapter 3 of this book), his argument was that legality is pivoted on social normality in the sense that all norms that aspire to regulate the factual circumstances they are referred to emerge from those very same factual circumstances. In other words, norms stem from the generalization and the standardization of normal, widespread situations that become standards to assess similar situations. If this is the case, Schmitt continued, the law is not so much a set of norms as it is an institutional complex providing actual figures and categories that are drawn from the concreteness of a political community's daily experience. The law is a substantive body of concrete standards that, as a whole, protects a shared form of life. At this point, he quoted Romano as follows: "The legal order . . . is a uniform essence, an entity that moves to some extent according to rules, but most of all itself moves the rules like figures on a gameboard—the rules represent, therefore, mostly the instrument of the legal order and not so much an element of its structure."[55]

There is little point here in considering the remarkable differences between Romano's original text and Schmitt's translation—we will take up this issue in Chapter 3. What matters for now is the divergence between the idea of unity held by Romano and the one that Schmitt believed he had found in *The Legal Order*. Schmitt mistook Romano to say that the legal order confers unity on norms, in that those norms can only be recognized as norms qua elements of that order; on the contrary, norms can be changed without that order changing in any essential features. According to Schmitt, this occurs because the legal order is nothing but the shelter of a concrete form of life. Not only does it confer unity on norms, but it also produces them as the generalization of a set of exemplar conducts. In other words, the order secures a substantive, ethical, even ethnic unity. Pace Schmitt, this is not what Romano meant. The unity he spoke of is an entity's membership in an institutional complex, one that at one and the same time makes room for a multiplicity of memberships in other complexes. In this sense, membership is not tantamount to exclusive belonging, as Schmitt's notion of a concrete order implies. For example, while making the point that international law is just as legal as the state legal order, Romano wrote: "For now, we can disregard the question of whether such a community [the international community] should be understood in a broad sense, or rather, if it is cohesive and if the bulk of states partake in it, or whether there are as many communities as the groups of states, which then intersect in many ways and give life to a particular international law."[56]

All of the exemplary cases discussed in *The Legal Order* involve institutions that overlap, while their members are at one and the same time members of other institutions. A household, a factory, a civil society association, a political party, a church, the state, and the international community are of course not examples of enclosed, sealed-off, homogeneous entities. It is highly likely that a member of one institution also belongs to others and acquires plural identities accordingly. Evidently, the unity that Romano had in mind is something that accommodates a multiplicity of identities for the same individual: a type of nonexclusive membership. Thus, it is this conferral of institution-dependent, nonexclusive identities that interested Romano as long as it triggers a normative metamorphosis. What he called "unity" allows the members of an entity to conceive themselves as members as long as they belong to an institution. Members acquire an identity that is institution-dependent. Individuals are describable as members of the institutions and their set of expectations, obligations, rights, prerogatives, liabilities varies in a way that is no longer depended on distinct individuals and their relationships to one another, because these relationships depend on the secondary norms of the institution.

The fact is that the notion of jural relationships as the cornerstone of institutions misses that point. The norms that jural relationships generate most of the time depend on rule-abiders and can be changed regardless of formal procedures. This does not apply to those institutions that Cesarini Sforza defined as organizations at a solid state. Yet, as both organizations at a diffuse state and organizations at a solid state share the basic phenomenon of jural relationships, Romano was dissatisfied with Cesarini Sforza's amendment as it failed to account for the normative metamorphosis discussed above as the genuine core of institutional phenomena. This is why Romano insisted that a legal order "is not a sum of parts but a unity in itself—and a unity, it is worth stressing, not artificial or obtained through a process of abstraction, but a concrete and effective unity . . . different from the distinct material elements that comprise it."[57] And also when he claimed that "society is an entity constituting a concrete unity . . . that is distinguished from the individuals who comprise it. And this has to be an effectively constituted unity."[58] If, as we specified above, "society" stands for "institution," it is clear that Romano was thinking of a set of intertwined and overlapping institutions where physical individuals acquire an identity whose normative status is not conditional on them.

At the same time, however, there is no substantive, objective superstructure that encompasses individuals' whole life and all instantiations of their practical activities. Romano's pluralism entailed an idea of individuals as members of a variety of legal orders simultaneously.

THE ORGANIZATIONAL FUNCTION

Romano's notion of institution leads to a conception of law that easily accommodates premodern and non-Western instances of the legal practice. Although the bulk of this conception was deployed in *The Legal Order*, he returned to the issue of what a legal order is in an important collection of small essays called *Frammenti di un dizionario giuridico* (Fragments of a legal dictionary—hereinafter *Frammenti*), first published in 1947. Although *Frammenti* touches upon a variety of legal topics, such as the notions of individual right, duty, interpretation, legal body, authority, and so on, it should be read in counterpoint to the second edition of *The Legal Order* (published in 1946)—and especially the footnotes in which Romano took issue with the host of criticisms and comments he had received in the course of three decades. For he clarified many questions that in 1917–1918 were underdeveloped and perfected a rich conceptual tapestry that helps interpret *The Legal Order*.

In the entry "Legal Norms (addressees of)" Romano tackled a few questions that were destined to haunt twentieth-century jurisprudence. He began by saying that the notion that the legal system is a set of commands issued by an authority was instrumental in fostering the idea that the only legitimate source of law is the state authority. This conception gave rise to the problem of who the addressees of these commands are—whether they are the citizens of the state or the officials who operate the state's various bodies. In reality, Romano commented, neither the legal order as a whole nor its distinct norms have any addressees. A provisional definition that obviates this conceptual mistake is the following: "The legal norm is objective insofar as, in any case and whoever the author may be, it resides in a higher sphere or level than that of the subjects who have to, or can, comply with it, and in which the various figures and subjective manifestations it regulates are outlined."[59]

Importantly, this position of superiority that the norm enjoys is not due to the authority that issues it. Rather, it depends on the norm being an element of the normative metamorphosis whereby subjects acquire an institution-dependent identity that comes with a set of powers, rights, obligations, and so on. To clarify this point, in another entry Romano addressed the question of customs as the source of law. While—especially in civil law systems—customs are demoted to reiterated practices endowed with a normative value that requires state recognition to be considered as legally binding, Romano assigned customs the role of "normative facts." They are effective practices that incorporate an "anonymous, involuntary, unwitting"[60] normative force. In other words, the law does not require any will that consciously operates to bring order, as most of the time it is an anonym and involuntary process of self-organization of a practice or context. As he did in *The Legal Order*, Romano equated law and organization so that the institution is presented as a process more than as a set of substantive characteristics. The institution alters an already existing normative contexts by "gathering together, assembling, and ordering the various elements that comprise them."[61] The law should not be mistaken for those elements—in that, again, the law is the process, not the substance—as it is that which confers on them "an individuality of their own and an essence of their own."[62] In the entry entitled "Law (Function of)," Romano insisted that "the law determines, stabilizes, immobilizes, crystallizes . . . the manifestations of social life."[63] In this frame, norms

> supervene upon the will of those who are subject to them, dominate them with their authority, . . . override the will [*arbitrio*] of the distinct individuals by replacing it with criteria and principles that are stable and clarified once and for all . . . and thus manage to stabilize particular instantiations of activities and the effects of these activities which would otherwise be extremely variable.[64]

Romano's recourse to the notion of functions helps unravel the puzzle of law as an organizational process. This of course does not qualify him as a functionalist—if by functionalism in sociology we mean a theory and a research method that interprets actions and social processes in the light of its functional effects on the broader social unit where they occur. Rather, Romano's is a kind of "thin functionalism"[65] that strikingly resonates with Karl Llewellyn's concept of law-jobs. In the article "Law and the Social Sciences" Llewellyn treated the concepts of institution and institutionalization as the correct framework where the law and how it operates on social reality become clear. The way he spoke of these concepts does recall Romano's idea of institution as an organizational activity that is necessary for a group to exist and acquire (and maintain) an identity as a group. Llewellyn wrote:

> It is the job for any group, for any community, for any political entity, for any society, of becoming and remaining and operating as *enough* as a unity, with *enough* team-work, to be and remain recognizable *as* a group or *as* a political entity or *as* a society. . . . Groupness does not just happen, without machinery and without work. It does not just continue, without machinery and without work. Neither does it just operate, without machinery and without work.[66]

Interestingly, Llewellyn's understanding of institution is as pluralist as Romano's. For he contended that these processes have to be analyzed in the context where they take place: "The whole vast job of team-work or groupness is too broad for easy study all-at-once. I have found the actual operations to cluster conveniently around certain sub-problems or -jobs (well described as the major 'law-jobs')."[67] Llewellyn had already clarified this point in his seminal article "The Normative, the Legal and the Law-Jobs," where he underlined that the processes the article centered on were not confined to the legal world, as they extended "through all group-living, in any type of group."[68] Inspired by sociological realism, Llewellyn's view reads that the existence of groups should not be a taken-for-granted object of social theory, as it is that which needs explaining. All groups—"from a group of two persons on up"[69]—are exposed to the permanent risk of centrifugal tendencies that are fended off by a certain number of jobs. At the same time, Llewellyn's pluralism gestures to differentiation theory as groups that become too big to be handled as comprehensive units tend to split into separate subunits that give life to the same types of law-jobs. The jobs he thought of relate to the disposition of trouble-cases, the preventive channeling and the reorientation of conduct and expectations, the legitimate allocation of authority, and the net organization of the group to provide direction and incentive.

Whether or not Llewellyn's theory of law-jobs provides an effective portrayal of institutionalization as a process of group making, group repair, and group maintenance,[70] it is a significant complement to Romano's functionalism as it centers the actual processes that are required to bring about groups. For there is no doubt that Romano tended to neglect the dynamics that are involved in the establishment of an order. In this sense, his functionalism was slightly thicker than Llewellyn's, as it portrayed the emergence of institutional settings as the sedimentation of norms and the definition of roles marked off by an objective set of obligations, rights, prerogatives, and so on. On the contrary, Llewellyn concentrated on the missing link between legal relationships and institutional dynamics, as he spoke of generalization and the creation of patterns. Despite this, while there is no doubt that the theoretical background they had was different—especially in terms of behaviorist nuances that were totally absent in Romano's theory—Llewellyn's observation that norms emerge as generalization of behaviors that are made binding unravels some of the mysteries that surround the process of institutionalization. Norms are standards of rightness that are applied to similar cases. They establish that "action like this is out of line with what action ought to be *in general*."[71] However, this widespread understanding that cases alike should be dealt with alike is the effect of a creative act whereby standards are projected on reality in such a way that reality should fit them.

In this latter respect, Llewellyn's realist thin functionalism also comes close to Cesarini Sforza's notion of how an institution emerges out of an activity of selection. Cesarini Sforza thought that the norms of the state legal order are nothing but generalizations of the jural relationships that the state decides to select as generally binding legal standards. For the state

> does not create jurality but only determines to what [jural] instances it is willing to lend its own force in order for them to be realized—in other words, for example, it does not create the jurality of contracts, which the parties may conclude and execute even when they have an unlawful cause.[72]

Put otherwise, Cesarini Sforza maintained that the various codes that comprise state law are the result of a selection whereby state agencies collect the sets of behaviors that they believe to be beneficial to the community and attach sanction to those that are detrimental. In this sense, institutional orders simply perform a jurisdictional function based on the standards selected from potentially countless jural relationships. Also in this case, this insight aligns with Llewellyn's as he wrote that "the possibilities of normative generalization are limitless; the idiosyncratic actualities are almost so."[73] Accordingly, the generalization of norms, whether in smaller social groups or wider political communities, pursue a set of goals that recall Llewellyn's law-jobs. First, orders are jurisdictional devices pursuing the end "of reducing as far as possible the breach of peace."[74] Second, groupness has the "capacity to override the litigants,"[75] to implement decisions and therefore to settle conflicts. All institutional contexts that solidify as orders hold a factual supremacy over jural relationship as particular rules are selected and are turned into compulsory imperatives. In other words, all official institutions and in particular official legal orders in actual fact correspond "to an infinite array of organizations having quite different goals and quite different forms, mutually coordinated by means of a relation of hierarchy and contiguity; and each organization, or coordinated group of organizations, represents an organic system—i.e., an order—of jural relationships."[76]

This is a question that we will have to return to while illustrating Schmitt's conception of institution and the decisionist activity of selection that he considered as necessary to bring about order. For now, our aim was to emphasize the convergences between Romano's idea of institutionalization and Llewellyn's thin functionalism and how the latter brings out the limits of the former. Indeed, Romano never clarified how institutions concretely come about. Arguably, he thought analyses like Llewellyn's exceed a juristic account of the institution, in that they involve sociological consideration of how certain norms emerge as generalized standards. However—Romano would presumably argue—legal theory is not called on to explain why certain norms become norms, but has to be concerned with the general process whereby norms do their institutional job. Similarly, he also never explained what the normative gap is between the various "states of human coexistence." There seems to exist a chasm between what he called a "subjective" and an "objective" conception of law:

> The legal relationship has to do with the subjective conception of law, as it presupposes at least two terms as points of reference. I believe one of them is constituted by a person considered either as in its entirety or with reference to one of its specific aspects, or even (if it is a legal person) with reference to one of its bodies; the other term is either this very person—when its aspect or body faces another aspect or body—or finally the object of one of its rights or obligations. Thus the relationship is not an entity in its own right, but a relation among different entities, this word being used in a broad sense. The institution, instead, is objective law, and is objective law because it is

> an entity, a social body, which, within the legal domain, enjoys an effective, concrete and objective existence. It implies relationships but cannot be reduced to them.[77]

While, as we commented above, it is clear that institutions cannot be dissected into relationships, it is less clear whether relationships precede institutions or whether they only exist because of there being institutions where they can unfold. Unfortunately, Romano never clarified this problem. As we will see, this ambiguity also hampers understanding of his pluralist conception, which is time for us to scrutinize more closely.

THE PANLEGALIST PREDICAMENT AND THE NOTION OF RELEVANCE

As Julius Stone remarked in his short but penetrating analysis of Romano's institutionalism, this Italian key jurist rejected "the solution of giving supremacy to the state legal order in case of conflict, on historical, theoretical, and positive grounds."[78] Stone referred to many junctures of *The Legal Order* where Romano criticized the identification of law with state law. While he was convinced that his theory of institution would conclusively debunk state-centered conceptions from a theoretical point of view, he also strove to show that those conceptions had been elaborated on as a statecraft strategy to support the state-form as the only form of political organization. Romano made the point time and again that state-centered conceptions of law were not only historically aberrant but also and above all detrimental to the construction of the liberal-constitutional state. For the idea that the state only comprises its citizens and its agencies drew attention away from the host of substate and suprastate associations and organizations that concretely made up the state body. However, these theoretical and historical considerations were also shored up by considerations based on positive law, which in Romano's view left much leeway for an understanding of law in a pluralist sense.

In effect, one of the most interesting traits of Romano's legal pluralism is that it remains within the boundaries of positive legal inquiry. Based on the argument—developed in Part I—that all orders are legal for the simple fact of being ordered, he ruled out the existence of meta-orders establishing how orders should interact with each other. If the qualifiers "legal" and "institutional" come to merge, to such an extent that all orders are equally legal, there is evidently no metalegal way to handle the relations between orders. At the same time, as we illustrated above, Romano rejected the view that relations among orders are a matter of bare power—let alone something that can be sorted with recourse to the principles of morality. How, then, can relations between orders be handled legally when there are no meta-orders laying down higher criteria of legality? In Part II of *The Legal Order* Romano addressed this question by introducing the notion of "relevance," which is to say, a legal technique for appraising and governing the effects of orders on one another. *Legal* relevance

> should not be confused with the *de facto* importance that an order could have to another; nor should it be confused with the material uniformity of more orders which is pursued or determined not by a legal need, but by political convenience or opportunity. . . . To condense my thinking into a quick formula, I can say that in order for legal relevance to obtain, the *existence* or the *content* or the *effectiveness* of an order has to be conditional on another order on the grounds of a legal *title*.[79]

Romano's move is ingenious. In light of the concept of relevance, the question is no longer "which legal order is *the* legal order but what are the relations between the various legal orders, so that we can better understand the problems thrown up from the viewpoint of one order or another."[80] Legal relevance can be defined as a *perspectival technique* that allows describing the effects of the *existence* or the *content* or the *effectiveness* of one order on another. Romano singled out five prototypical circumstances in which an order can be relevant to another. First, an order can be subordinated to a superior one, as is the case with an institution that "is included into another and contributes to constituting it in such a way that the former's order is, in some respects, surrounded by the latter's more comprehensive order." Second, an order could be the presupposition of a more complex institution, also when the former is subordinated to the latter—for example, "the international community presupposes the states that belong to it." Third, two orders independent from one another could depend on a superior one. Fourth, an order could spontaneously subordinate some features of its content or of its effectiveness to another order from which it is totally independent but that in this way becomes relevant to it. Fifth and finally, an order can merge into another and cease to exist.

Without delving further into the various cases that fall under one or the other of these categories, Romano's approach has three main advantages. First, relevance does not entail any privilege to this or that order, and thus circumvents the vexed question of recognition: if every institutional entity is recognized as possessing a legal order of its own, no order is called upon to recognize, or to be recognized by, any other order (unless the former's existence depends on the latter's, as is the case with the state agencies or substate territorial administrations that are state bodies in the first place). Second, the conflictual potential that lies in the relations between legal orders is mitigated in so far as they are transformed into purely *legal* relations—in other words, political conflicts morph into legal matters administrated with recourse to a specialized set of norms and principles. Third, the law that is supposed to solve this legal conflict is not the law of one particular order, but the outcome of the efforts of legal experts who, by adopting the juristic point of view, analyze the conflict at hand to find a legal solution to it.

While we will have to return in some detail on the third point, it is worth giving emphasis to Romano's "translation" (also see Chapter 5)—the genuinely political issue of what legal order has precedence over the others is transposed into the issue of what the legal effects are of one order on the another. As we noted, this translation hinges on a legal perspectivism that permits looking at the relations of subordination and superiority between orders as a matter of *effects* on one another. Thus, as Stone pointed out, one major strength of Romano's legal pluralism is that it evades the question of who is authorized to establish what is legal and what is not. This is doubtless a form of panlegalism, in the sense that the attribution of the label "law" to one specific kind of orders turns out to be utterly arbitrary, as all organized entities are ipso facto legal. At the same time, this panlegalist conception triggers the problem that William Twining dubbed "definitional stop":

> If one opens the door to some examples of non-state law, then we are left with no clear basis for differentiating legal norms from other social norms, legal institutions and practices from other social institutions and practices, legal traditions from religious or other general intellectual traditions and so on.[81]

Based on our preceding analysis, it is evident that Romano thought this problem was the outcome of a historical misconception. Never before the modern era was the term *legal* exclusively attributed to states—if only because states, as we know them today, had yet to come about. Historically, the designation of the state order as *the* legal order results from the factual imposition of a set of administrative mechanisms on other nonstate organizations, which were demoted to the nonlegal, extralegal, or illegal sphere. But if this is a conclusion Romano shares with present-day legal pluralists, it is interesting to juxtapose his theory of relevance with more recent pluralist paradigms.

In the second half of the twentieth century—quite a different sociopolitical scenario than Romano's—legal anthropology and sociolegal studies began to pave the way for an alternative understanding of law as conceptually and (at least in some geohistorical contexts) practically independent of the state. As early as the late 1920s Bronisław Malinowski advanced the theory that the legal body of the "savages" was not composed of rules prohibiting specific conducts, as other colleagues of his had suggested.[82] He argued that primitive law (or, more precisely, the law of the Trobriand Islanders he was studying) should be described as of a "civil law" type, understood as a "body of binding obligations, regarded as a right by one party and acknowledged as a duty by the other, kept in force by a specific mechanism of reciprocity and publicity inherent to the structure of their society."[83] His all-embracing definition of law minimized the relevance of "Western" notions such as coercion and authority for the analysis of non-Western normative contexts.[84] Malinowski believed that the mechanism meant to ensure compliance was the publicness of rules and the reciprocity among community members. The image of law that emerged was that of an internal mechanism of social life, inscribed in the web of interactions developed by social agents.

In her seminal article on semiautonomous social fields, Sally Falk Moore seized on Malinowski's sensitivity to nonstate laws to extend its heuristic scope, and proposed a methodological amendment to it.[85] Whereas Malinowski explored a community's organizational system as a unified whole, Moore, by drawing on Max Weber and Leopold Pospisil, questioned the unity of the anthropological "subject of study." In a way that echoed Romano's "The Modern State and Its Crisis" and *The Legal Order*, she commented that "it is well established that between the body politic and the individual, there are interposed various smaller organized social fields to which the individual 'belongs.'"[86] Social fields are contexts having rule-making capacities and the means to induce or coerce compliance—in short, said Moore, they have a legal order of their own. On this account, state rules can still be distinguished from nonstate rules in terms of reflective, emancipative, transformative, but also artificial and technological character; yet these characteristics are a matter of degree, unable to determine either a conceptual or an ontological difference.[87]

Although the stream of pluralist studies that sprang from those sources is vast and heterogeneous,[88] most legal scholars took up the cue from them. Legal pluralism ceased to be only a method for the anthropological study of legal phenomena outside the West and began to be used as a conceptual toolkit for investigating the legal phenomenon within Western states. A ground-breaking article that revived the study of pluralism in this sense is John Griffiths's "What Is Legal Pluralism?" where he characterized legal pluralism as the aversion to the "ideology of legal centralism." This ideology, Griffiths wrote, states that "law is and should be the law of the state, uniform for all people, exclusive of all other law, and administered by a single set of state institutions," while all other social orderings present in society "ought to be and in fact are hierarchically subordinate to the law and institutions of the state."[89] Despite widespread aversion to it, the rebuttal of legal centralism has given rise to an ambiguity within the legal-pluralist field of study, or better, two alternative perspectives on what should be considered as a genuine condition of legal pluralism.

For example, Gordon Woodman distinguishes two circumstances.[90] "Deep legal pluralism" occurs when distinct sets of laws with their own different sources of authority and separate jurisdictions coexist in the same geohistorical context. "State law pluralism" occurs when given state law makes room for distinct bodies of norms that have their origin in nonstate normative contexts. Some advocates of legal pluralism claim that it is not altogether clear whether state law pluralism can be categorized as a type of legal pluralism. Griffiths influentially classified it as "weak" legal pluralism, a spurious type that should be distinguished from cases where there is no superior, recognizing source.[91] In his opinion, when the state incorporates a norm that belongs to another type of law, the latter can no longer be considered as a type of law. State law retains his supremacy over other normative nonlegal orderings. From a descriptive point of view, Griffiths pointed out, it would make no sense to account for state law pluralism as the coexistence of two laws. The misleading view that state law pluralism amounts to a genuine condition of legal plurality is the result of a state-centered interpretation of the relationship between official law and nonlegal orderings.

Many debates on legal pluralism have largely revolved around state law pluralism without any clear distinction from deep legal pluralism. We concluded Chapter 1 by discussing theories that, in line with Ehrlich's take on state law, more or less agreed that "the inner order of the associations of human beings is not only the original, but also, down to the present time, the basic form of law."[92] As we briefly illustrated in Chapter 1, Ehrlich excoriated (what he regarded as) the fictitious idea of a common national state[93] issuing rules valid for everyone, because it widened the gap between the life of associations and the activities of official courts. He thought that legislators, jurists, and judges should realize that the core of social life was the complex web of associations, whose rules of conduct assign to each individual their position in the world and the role they had to play as association members.[94] State criminal and civil codes and public statutes, when too insensitive to the requirements of associations, could exert disruptive influence, not only on them, but on the whole political community. In short, the law could not be shrunk and confined to the cramped space of official codes and statutes, as this would seriously jeopardize the vitality of associations and the contribution they gave to the broader community. Ehrlich maintained that an effective state legal order always rested on the effective functioning of associations. In fact individuals plan their lives as members of associations and in compliance with their rules: whereas they in general perform by and large voluntarily the duties assigned to them by the legal relations they have as members of their associations, state law is eventually dependent on these spontaneously dutiful conducts, which formal legal propositions cannot produce, but have to support and promote.[95]

Although Ehrlich's is an iconic representation of law as a *self-organizing activity*, it does not amount to an instance of deep legal pluralism. For the idea that human sociality is innately plural is not necessarily tied up to the idea that societal pluralism entails a plurality of legal orders. Many nonpluralist scholars have no qualms about recognizing that society is characterized by a multitude of substate entities that comply with rules and regulations of their own. In this sense, many (though of course not all) pluralist theories are in actual fact theories of *social* pluralism.[96] On the contrary, Romano is not concerned with social pluralism. As "social" (in the sense of "organized") and "legal" are synonymous with each other, pluralism is already and always legal. But even more importantly, he put panlegalism to work as a theoretical conundrum that should be intensified. As we illustrated above, the main conclusion of Romano's legal pluralism is that historically, conceptually, and positively it is pointless to deny there being a plurality of legal orders in the same geohistorical context where there is more than one group or association. However, this conclusion of Romano's does not entail any political and/or moral statements about conflicts between orders. From the conceptual thesis of a basic equality between orders, no pragmatic conclusions can be derived.

As we pointed out at the outset, many critical interpreters hold the opinion that Romano's lip service to pluralism foundered on the factual preeminence he gave state law. For when he mused on the various cases of relevance, he always stuck with the legal point of view of state officials. However, we believe this is a misreading that speaks volumes about Romano's dissolution of the problem—one that turns the problem into a strength. As we discussed, Romano was concerned with a *perspectival* matter: What is the point of view from where the "matter-of-factness" of the conflict between institutions can be reframed in legal terms? Can *practical* conflicts be transformed and tamed as they are turned into *legal* ones? If this is the question Romano was trying to answer, then he never pitted the law of the state against the law of other institutions. Instead, he intended to task jurists with providing an account of social reality that might find a route to make the various legal orders compatible with each other. At the same time, calling jurists on to play this role did not make Romano lapse back into a state-centered perspective. For while it is true that state *officials* are *state* officials, it is also true that the law is not the production of the state. Legal officials qua law experts deal with something that exceeds the state by far. What they do as legal officials always has to be performed from a *juristic point of view*.

It is worth referring again to Llewellyn's theory of law-jobs. He spoke of the juristic as a method in the sense that it is something that goes hand in hand with the emergence of specialized personnel. It is how legal tools are handled to law-job ends and how these tools have to be administered. Certainly, this gestures to the emergence of a second layer of control that we mentioned while introducing Galanter's view—a layer that, as also Llewellyn specified, can be more or less visible and more or less specialized. But while in the former sections we pointed to this aspect to foreground the formal structure of institutions and their normative metamorphosis, in this context it is important to stress that the juristic method is not a merely inward-oriented mechanism (in the sense that it only contributes to the identity of an institution and to its upkeep). The juristic transcends a group's legal repertoire at least in one important respect. As Llewellyn put it:

> The conflicts which emerge . . . on matters involving questions of what is right, and then, what is the imperative, and then, what is the Legal answer—these conflicts open the fascinating tasks of juristic method. For juristic method has as its task the use of the available

> law-stuff, or the creation of new, to choose between conflicting needs, to choose between good needs to fill and worse ones, to invent as well as to choose—and to do all this, somehow, in tune with the net requirements of the Entirety, as those requirements shape up in terms of getting the law-jobs done and their questing aspects furthered.[97]

In other words, the juristic method presents the law not as an entity or a body of rules, but as a process. The law from the juristic point of view is the process of finding the *legal* answer to both recurrent and emerging problems, whether normal or exceptional ones. If this is the case, the law has no specific boundaries. It is an activity carried out by a dedicated personnel (whether specialized or not: the wise old man, the peacemaker, the judge, the priest, the Ifugao combination of advocate and mediator, or the sorcerer, to draw from Llewellyn's own examples) with an eye to making the law-stuff go places. This echoes Romano's proposal. Within his theoretical framework, the juristic point of view is a way of describing reality through the prism of law that, by dint of this legal description, exerts particular effects on reality. Needless to say, this is not how Romano put it, primarily because of the cultural milieu and the technical jargon of the time. And yet, we believe this is the gist of his understanding of law as a process that deals with pluralism. Pluralism is not an intrasystemic problem of, say, how to accommodate other normative sources within the legal order. As such, it does not pose any direct threat to one order or the other. For legal pluralism is positioned in the ongoing activity of assessing, measuring, and handling the effects of relevance.

The law then becomes a matter of legal perspective. By adopting the notion of relevance as a guideline, jurists can move back and forth from intrasystemic to extrasystemic considerations and develop a shared juridical lexicon that allows speaking of the relation between orders as *legal* relations—"legal" insofar as they always concern legal entities potentially capable of affecting each other. Considerations of different nature are not admitted when looking at these relations from the vantage point of relevance: neither power, nor interests, nor morality may contaminate the purely juristic inquiry that is required to address relations among orders legally. This attitude marks off a semiotic space of pure legality that turns all potentially nonlegal relations into legal ones. This is why law, in a Romanian sense, has more to do with translation than regulation. And this is also why, in the end, panlegalism is a resource more than a problem. The intercourse between orders makes the law a lexical circuit that jurists dwell in as they perform their jurisprudential practice of finding the legal answer through the juristic method.

CONCLUDING REMARKS

All in all, the core of Romano's theory is that jurists should stay alert to the train of history that the legal doctrine of a particular order carries with itself. Law is always something more than the bordered area of one legal order and its knowledge apparatus. The law exhibits a natural inclination to panlegalism, as it is that without which no entity could settle and reproduce. No doubt, Romano was aware that legal conflict cannot supersede political conflicts, as we can see from the *Frammenti* section where he addressed the relation between law and revolution. Here he tried to deal with such a delicate matter from the juristic point of view. "Any revolution implies various institutions, connected to each other in a unified organization, which, when considered in itself and for itself, independently of the evaluation of the state law in force, has all the characteristics of a legal order."[98] Even more effectively:

> As long as it lives and operates, [a revolution] is an order that cannot but be taken into account as such. A revolution is an antilegal fact in the eyes of the state positive law against which it is carried out. However, this does not exclude that, from the quite different point of view from which it qualifies itself, it is a movement ordered and regulated by its own law. . . . The revolution is violence, but legally regulated violence.[99]

Yet it is exactly when he discussed how the revolution can become a permanent, nonrevolutionary order that Romano gave away his view that legal orders need specialized personnel performing their law-job with the juristic method. Indeed, what most hampers the stabilization of the revolutionary order is

> the conviction that legal formalisms are useless, even disadvantageous. . . . And this is quite a serious mistake, in that the difficulties [that all revolutions meet require] competences that are way higher than the normal ones. . . . Those are orders that have to penetrate the extant institutions, as they could not work otherwise and would remain isolated, with no support.[100]

It is evident that Romano addressed the question of revolution as a matter of legal pluralism. In such an extreme case, too, jurists are required to adopt the juristic point of view. First, they have to acknowledge that the revolution is the confrontation of two orders. Second, the effects of this confrontation are to be dealt with legally. Only in this way can the far-reaching sociopolitical outcomes of revolutions be lessened. It is a radical depoliticization of conflicts that tasks jurists with safeguarding the internal order and handling the relations with other orders. What they do as they embrace the juristic point of view is likely to produce a revision of the order in the sense of its compatibility with other orders and the normative frameworks these orders are knotted into. As we will see, this depoliticization of conflict through the juristic point of view could not be farther from Schmitt's institutionalism—while ironically Schmitt somewhat regarded his own institutionalism as the continuation and the overhaul of Hauriou's and Romano's institutional theories. Therefore, moving on to Schmitt's conception of law will also be of help in better understanding Romano's pluralist institutionalism.

CHAPTER THREE

Carl Schmitt and the Concrete Order

THE NOTION OF ORDER LENDS itself as a counterpoint to the notion of system: the whole legal debate of the first three decades of the twentieth century can be read through the prism of the dialectic between these alternative modes of the legal. An idea of law as an organized normative complex that brings order to society through the production and implementation of statutory rules (system) rivals an idea of law as something that arises out of people's practices and gets incorporated into state-based institutional categories, figures, and models (order). "Order" gestures to something that can be neither created ex nihilo nor exhaustively verbalized, as it escapes human beings' limited law-making faculty and can only be interpreted—albeit partially—as it gets discovered. While "system" gives a sense of something that is artificially laid down to provide guidance for action—as people perform practical activities and try to foresee what others will do—"order" conveys a sense of material intertwinement of social life and the law. Accordingly, a system belongs to a higher order of normativity with respect to social normativity, in the sense that the former claims to guide, mold, constrain, regulate, govern the latter from outside and from above. Quite the reverse, the order is not severable from the practice of daily life, in the sense that it springs from it and never claims to hover over it. The order is a normative force that governs by gathering motivational resources from the very practices it regulates. Therefore, the forms of observance that system and order imply are antithetical to each other. While the system always makes room for frictions between the reasons for action it provides (mainly in terms of action planning, threat of punishment, and reward) and rule-abiders' private reasons, the order's main reason for action is that it is internal to the practice it governs from within.

This prism is the guideline we chose to follow in exploring Carl Schmitt's influential theorizing. It is our claim that Schmitt's overall theory was profoundly affected by his thoroughgoing revision of the role of the order in the creation and maintenance of a political community. Needless to say, at no point was he a supporter of the idea of a system, as he fiercely chastised the systematic idea of law advocated by his fiercest intellectual adversary, Hans Kelsen. However, Schmitt's critical take on the concept of a system changed significantly at the end of the 1920s, as he gave an institutional twist to his theory of law and politics. This chapter will investigate this major theoretical change whereby Schmitt dispensed with his famed theory of the exception and put forward a theory of the concrete order. The scrutiny of the different types of criticisms he leveled at the normativity of the system will allow us to show that his main concern was with pluralism as an *ongoing threat of dissolution*. While Schmitt's persisting obsession was with the homogeneity of the political community, he importantly changed his mind as to how it can be attained and how it should be preserved. This analysis will also shine a light on the difference with Santi Romano's idea of order, especially as to how their disagreeing conceptions of it led to disagreeing conceptions of pluralism. As will also become clearer in Chapter 5, Schmitt's revision of his own theory, juxtaposed to Romano's firm conceptualization of the juristic point of view, teases out what is at stake in the opposition between juristic and political conceptions of law.

THE TRACES OF INSTITUTIONALISM

The name of Carl Schmitt has long been associated with the notions of exception and decision and the corresponding paradigms of exceptionalism and decisionism.[1] While this is obviously not mistaken, we believe this interpretation omits remarkable variations in his intellectual biography and the productive tensions between the multiple facets of his work as a whole.

Certainly, in this context it is impossible to retrace his voluminous work to sketch the complete trajectory. What we set out to do instead is foreground Schmitt's moving away from decisionism and the conceptual reasons for his eventual adhesion to his own version of legal institutionalism, which he dubbed "konkretes Ordnungs- und Gestaltungsdenken" (concrete order and formation thinking). This short section aims to pinpoint a few, sparse traces of an institutional inflection before the 1930s, while the subsequent one will discuss a possible interpretation of Schmitt's decisionism that, though partly mistaken, ferrets out significant conceptual tools that will prove useful to the understanding of his thinking. This will pave the way for a more nuanced analysis of Schmitt's progressive inclusion of the institutional elements that severed the ties with his previous exceptionalism.

As early as 1910 Schmitt licensed his dissertation on criminal law titled *Über Schuld und Schuldarten* (On guilt and types of guilt). The dissertation was supervised by Fritz von Calker, who was professor of criminal law at Kaiser-Wilhelm-Universität in Strasbourg and was a member of the National Liberal Party. In this text, Schmitt sought to clarify conceptually the notion of guilt in order to put forward an *entirely juristic* definition of it. In an antisubjectivistic fashion, he claimed that the concept of guilt cannot rest on subjectivistic motives, such as dispositions, impulses, or inclinations, but has to be founded on legal categories that thoroughly integrate it into the legal order. Guilt is not something pertaining to subjective reasons that are external to the legal order, nor does it merely have to do with the infringement of legal norms. Rather, it is a disposition to act in such a way that the order itself *objectively qualifies the performed action as inadmissible.* Importantly, in this context Schmitt explained that not only legal rules but the whole legal order can be assigned specific and concrete ends; which is to say, a sort of normative guidance illustrating what it is that guilt is directed against. Guilt is never an individual act, but a hindrance to the general ends of the legal order. A crime is a conduct that is objectively antithetical to the norms reflecting the order's ends and the guidance it offers. While this original though minor text could be interpreted as an early manifestation of Schmitt's subsequent decisionism,[2] Andrea Salvatore rightly avers that Schmitt offered us two main cues to an alternative reading. First, as we already remarked, the existence of specific ends that the legal order pursues as such. Second, the fact that these ends are encapsulated by institutional instances that the order encompasses and makes legal. In this light, the conflict between the legal order and the criminal is a conflict between two types of ends and therefore between the instances of two rival orders.[3]

Schmitt's subsequent book, *Gesetz und Urteil* (Statute and judgment) (1912), went down the same path. It marked a clear departure from Laband's conclusion that judges are the "viva vox legis" as they apply statutory law—nothing other than logical operations and subsumptions. While what is at stake in this writing is the judicial decision, the term *decision* in this context bears no resemblance to the notion that Schmitt adopted a few years later as the cornerstone of his 1920s decisionism. For he criticized Laband's idealization of a gapless legal order that leaves no elements of individual discretion. Still, it is worth noting that the *judge's* decision is not a *sovereign*, *political* decision, but a *judicial* one, which does not institute a legal order—as is the case with the sovereign decision Schmitt's later decisionism centers on. This decision plays off of the indeterminacy that every legal norm entails. No doubt, also in this case one would be justified in detecting a decisionist tinge in this book. The idea that all that counts is the judge's making a decision appears to "foreshadow Schmitt's major themes of the 1920s: orientation towards the exception, the emphasis on the value of the act of deciding, and the distinction between legality and legitimacy, which he plays off against one another."[4] However, as Salvatore notes, Schmitt is particularly concerned with the far less decisionistic notion of judicial *normality* as something that provides the ground for a stable decisional practice among judges. The judge is called upon to adjudicate in a way that *conforms to the current practice* with a view to *making it uniform and consistent.* According to Schmitt, a judge's decision is correct when another judge could in principle arrive at the same decision. It is the *normal* judge, the *normal* legal expert. Not an *ideal* judge, but the *average* judge.

> However, at no point in the decision may the judge follow an absolutely free discretion, his particular subjectivity, his personal belief as such; the "other judge" is the normal, legally cultivated judge, where

the word "normal" is used in a quantitative-average sense, not describing an ideal type, not qualitative and teleological.[5]

Interestingly, the normal judge is entrusted with safeguarding the order as a whole by reiterating a practice that incarnates a standard. In this sense, it is evidently at odds with any variation of exceptionalism. The fact that this is Schmitt's main concern before the 1920s supports Martin Loughlin's (2016) argument that Schmitt's overall oeuvre should be read as an exercise in *political jurisprudence*, that is, a type of jurisprudential inquiry that aims to capture the character of the basic laws of the political. These basic laws can hardly be discovered in the unstable circumstances where normality is suspended and the law awaits a sovereign decision to be brought into life. Rather, Loughlin continues, one fails to latch on Schmitt's key concerns unless one pays due heed to the texts in which he came to elaborate on his concrete-order thinking. We believe this interpretation does justice both to Schmitt's self-understanding as well as the efforts he put into solving the puzzles his previous decisionism had generated.

While Schmitt's espousal of institutionalism as well as the theoretical path that led him to it have been abundantly debated in the last few years,[6] what we set out to do in the successive sections is to identify the frictions between Schmitt's exceptionalism and his later institutionalism. As we will clarify, we will not go so far as to argue, as some have done, that exceptionalism was merely apparent and that he was always concerned with the concreteness of the order. We believe it is more likely that early in the 1920s he genuinely thought the exception could convincingly explain what law is and that he progressively became conscious of the limits of this conception. He was certainly always sensitive to how the conditions of normal, everyday life is produced, as attested by the early writings we have briefly examined. However, in his decisionist phase he was genuinely inclined to believe that the intervention of a sovereign decider was foundational to the political community and that a sovereign decision is needed to set the possibility conditions for normality. It was not until the end of the 1920s that, he came to realize he had underestimated the vital role of concrete, institutional, daily practices in the production of the legal order. Based on this, he broke with exceptionalism and overhauled decisionism by introducing elements of an institutional theory of law. The subsequent sections home in on this transition.

THE EXCEPTIONALIST READING

As one thinks of Schmitt, two books spring to mind: *Political Theology*, published in 1922, and *The Concept of the Political*, first published in 1928. In the course of a few years, Schmitt deployed an influential theory of the legal order as the creation ex nihilo of legal normality through a decision that cuts out that which a sovereign decider identifies as a lethal threat to the political community. In light of this conception of the legal order and how it emerges, it comes as no surprise that most interpreters postulated a link between these two books. This section intends to make the claim that this exceptionalist reading does justice to *Political Theology* but severely misreads *The Concept of the Political* and misses out on Schmitt's main preoccupations in this latter text.

In *Political Theology* Schmitt developed two conceptual devices that are commonly known as "decisionism" and "exceptionalism." It should not be neglected that he elaborated on them as a response to the normativism of positivist thinkers. For from the very beginning the exception plays out as a "borderline concept," that is, a concept that permits testing the tenability of a general theory of sovereignty and the state. He reasoned that no general theory can be premised on the normal case, because the latter is always parasitic on the "borderline case." Normality is a by-product of a decision. To make this point, Schmitt presented the legal order as the interplay between two elements: norm and decision. Importantly, in *Political Theology* he only took into consideration these two elements, and as we will see later on, this is key to untangling Schmitt's subsequent revision of his own theory. For now, however, let us concentrate on the reasons for the exceptionalist reading. The initial pages of *Political Theology* set the stage for a harangue against the normality of everyday life where the law carries out its tasks of regulation and coordination. Schmitt insisted that the contribution of jurisprudence cannot be limited to the study of the "recognizable" (12), namely, that which ensures the regularity and predictability of people's behavior. Such an undue separation between jurisprudence and sociology prevents positivism from getting to the core of the legal phenomenon.

Schmitt was by and large right in insisting that legal positivists believed the legal order is intelligible and can be accounted for by scrutinizing its *formal structure*. For example, Kelsen's influential version of legal positivism, known as "pure theory of law,"[7] claimed that legal scientists can make sense of the unity of the legal system only insofar as they postulate the existence of a "basic norm," whereby all norms appear as linked to each other and finally anchored to the constitution in force. By preserving the boundaries of such a "pure" methodology, Kelsen intended to expunge all extralegal (that is, political and/or moral) considerations from the conceptual toolkit of legal science. All that is required for legal scientists to produce a workable and consistent description of the legal system is contained in the theoretical toolkit of legal science. The study of law does not and should not accommodate any extralegal notions—such as justice, sovereignty, will, power, and others—that are not reducible to the concepts of legal norm and legal sanction.

Schmitt's main preoccupation in his analysis of legal positivism is that the (alleged) self-sufficiency of the positivist theoretical toolkit omits to consider *the source of the legal order* and exclusively places emphasis on the normal case. He averred that legal positivists took the state for granted and only contemplated the legal order when it is already up and running. Positivism deliberately ignored how the state came about, as if this formative process were not part of the law and hence were not of the legal scientist's concern (and importantly, Schmitt viewed this as a *conceptual* flaw). However, he went on to say, the state, its existence, and its jurisgenerative force can hardly be taken for granted. He wrote: "The existence of the state is undoubted proof of its superiority over the validity of the legal norm."[8] If this reading makes sense, chapter 1 of *Political Theology* should be interpreted as a *conceptual* critique of legal positivism by which Schmitt reintroduced the issue of the law's origin as a key jurisprudential concern and depreciated normality as ancillary. The overemphasis on normality made legal positivists blind to the foundational nature of the exception as a foremost jurisprudential concept. The exception is a circumstance where the normality of everyday life is suspended because a novel, emerging configuration of social life has grown so pervasively that the law cannot be complied with and the normal status quo is subverted.

It deserves attention that, on this account, the state of exception in Schmitt *does not signify the primacy of politics over law*, but *the conceptual relevance of the original moment* when the law is brought into life along with the normality of social life in which the legal order can work properly. Moreover, Schmitt's insistence on the origin of law was instrumental in disproving the identification of law and the state. Pace Kelsen and prior authors, in Schmitt's view paying heed to the exception demonstrated that the law *does not* coincide with the state. Importantly, as he pointed out, what he was concerned with was not a "causal or psychological" origin of law.[9] Rather, he was concerned with a conceptual definition of law in the light of how it comes to life. He wanted to pinpoint not the legal order's *factual* conditions of existence but the *conceptual* ones—that is to say, the element without which no defensible conceptualization of law can be advanced. This is why he attached the utmost importance to the sovereign decider who makes the decision that creates the order without any previous power-conferring norm.

Schmitt's sovereign is not a predefined institutional figure (although in some circumstances it can be, when the constitution provides for special prerogatives of the executive in circumstances of extreme peril). Rather, the sovereign is the one who decides on the state of exception; which is to say, the person or group who effectively and successfully imposes an order after suspending the order. On this account, the exceptionalist reading of *The Concept of the Political* might appear to be correct to such an extent that the connection between this book and *Political Theology* turns out to be decisive. It is this connection that makes it clear that the sovereign's decision coincides with an *act of identification of the enemy* and that this decisional activity *creates the friend*. In effect, *The Concept of the Political* portrays the friend as contingent on the enemy because of a *polemical* and *polemogenic* process that is required to bring about the order.[10] This is the gist of Schmitt's incipit in *Political Theology* where he says that the "exception in jurisprudence is analogous to the miracle in theology."[11] The creation of an order requires the intervention of a supreme entity that generates it, while this entity carries out this creational task by identifying an enemy that stirs the friend's willingness to stick together and to fend off the enemy. On one hand, the sovereign fulfils her duty if and only if she brings the friend to believe that the enemy is posing a lethal threat to them, one that menaces to wipe out their form of life. On the other, the friend turns into a self-conscious political entity if and only if people are disposed to give their life and take the life of their enemy, if such an extreme step needs to be taken.

Based on the connection between *Political Theology* and *The Concept of the Political*, two enlightening notions come to the fore: the *formal metamorphosis* of nonpolitical conflicts and the *performative conception* of the enemy. First, in *The Concept of the Political* Schmitt clarifies that the political is not so much a field as it is the effect of an ultimate distinction "to which all action with a specifically political meaning can be traced."[12] Famously, as we mentioned above, this ultimate distinction is the friend-enemy criterion. It signifies "the utmost degree of intensity of a union or separation"[13] of an association or dissociation of humans "whose motives can be religious, national (in the ethnic or cultural sense), economic, or of another kind and can effect at different times different coalitions and separations."[14] This implies that any opposition, whatever the realm in which it occurs, can potentially escalate into a political conflict. As soon as this metamorphosis comes about, the conflict becomes a political one and the friend-enemy distinction takes over. The opposition between the opponents ceases to be moral, religious, or economic and turns into a genuinely political conflict. This means that it can no longer be accounted for as moral, religious, or economic, but as *quintessentially political.* This implies that the distinctive trait of *political* antagonism is the fact that the stake of the conflict undergoes an essential transformation: it no longer concerns the material substance around which it orbits (e.g., moral disagreement or economic competition), but the existential menace it poses to both parties. People no longer dispute over the stake, but associate their existence and their subsistence (as a group) with this stake to the extent that they are ready to kill and to be killed when it comes to disputing over it. We defined this metamorphosis "formal" because the content can well stay the same, whereas the group's disposition to stand up for it intensifies so much so that they are ready to kill and die.

This leads to the second notion we mentioned above. If the political is the utmost degree of intensity, and not a socially observable field or a specific type of conflict, it is arguable that it serves as the *performative condition* for a group to come into life. The formal metamorphosis of a conflict urges the members of a group to *conceive of* themselves as parties to the same entity. In a way, this could be likened to an activity of "performative citation" whereby the talk over something brings this something into existence by dint of being mentioned as something.[15] On this reading, the degree of intensity that marks the political prompts a group to verbalize their condition in such a way that a new entity becomes the pivot of their verbalizations. This *citational performance* parallels the creational activity Schmitt mulls over in *Political Theology*, whereby one's pointing the finger at the menace posed by the enemy performatively *constitutes* the group of friends as the latter look at the situation *as a group* and conceive of themselves as such.[16] If this is the case, despite Schmitt's emphasis on the *concrete* and *existential* nature of the conflict, the friend-enemy antithesis is first and foremost a *conceptual device*; or better, it is essentially hallmarked by the *virtual possibility* of an existential conflict. The insistence on the virtual and the possible means that it is not the actual conflict as such that counts, but *its bare likelihood*, that is, the group's tendency to conceive of a conflict—regardless of its stake—as something that involves the disposition to kill and to die.

This means that more than the *polemical* aspect, it is the *polemogenic* one that sets the citational activity in motion. In fact, if the possibility of a concrete *pòlemos* is central, it is the friends' acquired awareness that the conflict requires their readiness to kill and to be killed that turns it into a political conflict. The decision is therefore the polemogenic (in the sense of generating a fundamental disposition to fight) recognition of a specific intensity of the conflict, which urges the friends to join together and to acquire a new awareness of who they are and who they have to fend off. This interpretation of Schmitt's conception of the political squares with Vinx's nuanced interpretation of Schmitt's conception of how a people comes about. In his "Introduction" to the Schmitt-Kelsen debate on the guardian of the constitution, Lars Vinx avers that for Schmitt,

> a people's "political existence" is manifested in its willingness to assert itself. . . . [T]he unified will of the people . . . in fact exists for as long as a people is willing to take (or rather to support) genuinely political decisions; decisions on the exception that constitute political community, in an extra-legal space, by drawing the line between friend and enemy.[17]

Based on this, it is our claim that an exceptional reading of Schmitt's work of the 1920s is conducive to an *epistemic understanding* of the law and the political. While in *Political Theology* Schmitt aimed to debunk positivism as an approach to the proper conceptualization of law, in *The Concept of the Political* he intended to illustrate how a group, a population, a people, a community come into life. As far as the legal order is concerned, understanding its generative dynamics entails going beyond the constitution in force and scrutinizing the creational moment when the order is established. As far as the political community is concerned, the analysis of the institutive, creational moment demonstrates that those generative dynamics rest upon the jurisgenerative force of a group of people conceiving of itself as a group of people vis-à-vis an incipient threat. This epistemic understanding of Schmitt's theorizing shines an interesting light on a far less substantive notion of politics than one might attribute to him.

Although this epistemic understanding makes sense of many of Schmitt's concerns in his decisionist phase, we believe the connection between *Political Theology* and *The Concept of the Political* is looser than the exceptionalist reading would have us believe. In particular, while the epistemic interpretation accurately foregrounds the virtual and performative nature of the friend-enemy opposition, it fails to grasp Schmitt's main concerns at the ends of the 1920s. The following section will suggest approaching *The Concept of the Political* from an alternative angle. *Political Theology* marked a transitory phase in Schmitt's thinking, one that was heavily indebted to the notion of exception. A few years later, he extensively revised decisionism in a way that led him to drop exceptionalism and to concentrate on the more salient aspects of normality and the normal case.

TOWARD A CONCRETIST READING

As we mentioned above, recently some scholars have argued that traces of an institutional thinking were already manifest in Schmitt's writings of the 1920s, such as *Political Theology* and *Roman Catholicism and Political Form*.[18] For example, Leila Brännström maintains that an institutional attitude tinges Schmitt's exceptionalism because it is "only when the authorized subject of sovereignty makes an effective decision on the state of exception that 'actual power' and 'the legally highest power' come together. This, however, presupposes that the authorized subject can be identified prior to the decision."[19] However intriguing this interpretation may be, we have already explained why it does not withstand scrutiny. Indeed, we believe it is imperative to cast light on the different background against which Schmitt gradually came to espouse an institutional theory of law. This analysis brings to light a remarkable change in how he conceived normality and its role in yielding the contents of the legal order.

There is no denying that Schmitt was concerned with the concreteness of the political community before the end of the 1920s. For example, it is true that in *Roman Catholicism and Political Form* he extolled the exemplar way in which the Catholic Church had long enacted the principle of representation in "antithesis to the economic-technical thinking" that (he claimed) dominated his time. He clearly dismissed a notion of representation as delegation (*Vertretung*) and insisted on genuine representation being "the concrete foundation for a substantive form."[20] This is evidence that the problem of the concrete, material constitution of the social is a recurring trope in his theorizing, which is hardly reducible to bare existentialism. However, Schmitt returned more intensely to the issue of the concrete foundation of the order in between the end of the 1920s and the early 1930s. More in particular, as we will explain in detail later on, between

1933 and 1934 he put forward his "concrete order and formation thinking" and clarified that decisionism cannot stand on its own feet, because, like positivism, it neglects important societal elements that are foundational to the law. Before examining the outcomes of this crucial transition, we would like to point out early symptoms of his dissatisfaction with exceptionalism towards the end of the 1920s. To do this, we will present *The Concept of the Political* as a first decisive break with the exceptional paradigm that saturates *Political Theology*.

In the 1963 "Preface" to *The Concept of the Political* Schmitt rebuked those who claimed he had disproportionately paid heed to enmity and overlooked friendship. Those critics, he wrote, "neglect that all movements of a legal concept, by dialectic necessity, always proceed from negation. In the life of law as well as in legal theory, entailing negation implies no 'primacy' of that which is negated."[21] Then he went on to say that in criminal law the concept of punishment presupposes wrongdoings, but this does not imply criminal law's eulogizing crime. While also in this case enmity is presented as a conceptual possibility condition for the constitution of the friend (just as the crime is a conceptual presupposition of criminal law), what matters here is that enmity is portrayed as a threat to an existing order. If we take this remark as the pointer to an alternative reading of *The Concept of the Political* Schmitt offered in 1963, it would be helpful to understand what the threat was that he had in mind more than thirty years earlier. We believe a further telling lead can be found in the first of the three corollaries that appear in the 1963 German edition of *Der Begriff des Politischen*. This corollary, originally written in October 1931, discussed alternative meanings of the notion of state neutrality. One of them, the fourth, relates to the state granting equal consideration and equal opportunities to the various substate groups. In this passage Schmitt concerned himself with social, cultural, and religious pluralism and tackled the question of whether the state can really be neutral when it comes to this key issue. His argument was that this type of neutrality "is feasible only with regard to a relatively small number of legitimate groups and only by a relatively uncontested allocation of power and influence among equally legitimized partners."[22] In other words, the state has to recognize some substate groups of different sorts (cultural, religious, or driven by other associative interests), but it behooves it to identify a criterion for selecting some of them and selecting out others.

A few important conclusions can be reached based on these passages, in particular one concerning Schmitt's social ontology and the other concerning his view on how the state should grapple with the question raised by this social ontology. First, Schmitt was sociologically more realist than one might think. As he had already clarified in one of the most revealing, and yet neglected, writings, "State Ethics and the Pluralist State," which appeared in *Kant-Studien* in 1930, Schmitt rejected the Hobbesian ontology of a civil society comprising discrete monads that stand in a direct relationship to the state. Schmitt acknowledged that pluralism is a permanent condition of all complex societies. Drawing from a few key Western thinkers, from Aristotle to Hegel, he acknowledged that social reality is composed of a variety of groups and associations and that no political government, however centralized and powerful it may be, could or should completely homogenize them. This is a key indication of one of Schmitt's main concerns, namely, *pluralism and its thorny relation to the political center.* If this is the case, then the second important conclusion is that, for Schmitt, there is no easy recipe to handle the innate plurality of social life. In fact, if the state gets symbolic and material resources out of the rich plurality of substate groups, it would be both myopic and counterproductive to exert authority in such a way as to damage their microsocial life and to disrupt their intimate normative texture. Needless to say, however, this does not mean that Schmitt had converted to a pluralist theory of the state. Rather, this means that he was trying to solve this theoretical predicament by striking a balance between a tenable conception of social pluralism and the need for political homogeneity. Keeping this, let us make our way into *The Concept of the Political.*

Schmitt begins with a basic warning: "The concept of the state presupposes the concept of the political."[23] The message conveyed by this famous opening is that statehood is conditional upon the concept of the political and not the other way around. As we illustrated in Chapter 1, most German jurisprudence and public law theory between the last decades of the nineteenth century and the first three decades of the twentieth century had revolved around the state as the source of both sociality and legality. It was presented as the fundamental ground for the existence of a political community. Moreover, the common view was that the state is not only the cradle of politics but also its destiny. The political is contingent on there being a state as the supreme law-giving entity, outside of which there can be no politics whatsoever. Schmitt wanted to debunk this view because it postulated a transhistorical link between the state as a political form and the political as a conceptual category and a field of human existence. It neglected the transient nature of the state as the entity that gained the monopoly on the political and consequently on the *jus belli* (that is to say, the right to use force when it comes to ban an internal enemy or to fight off an external one). Schmitt rather believed that the state is nothing other than a transitory configuration of the political, with a beginning and an end, one that could cease at any moment to be the political entity par excellence. It is worth stressing that, for Schmitt, the state monopoly on the *jus belli* was inseparably tied to its capacity to inhibit the formal metamorphosis of nonpolitical conflicts, and thus to prevent intersectional *social* conflicts of different nature (moral, economic, religious, and so on) from escalating into *political* conflicts. When the state loses this key prerogative, it can no longer claim to be the political entity par excellence. By the same token, when the members of a group "decide" on their own that the conflict they are engaged in requires their disposition to kill and be killed, at this very moment this group morphs into a *political* group and (whether intentionally or not) lays a claim to the *jus belli*. This performative act produces a collision between the symbolic and material aspects of the political: a group's performative claim entailed by their decision that the conflict is a political one turns at once into a challenge to the state as the supreme political entity. The mere claim—or better, the mere *possibility* of a particular group's envisaging a concrete *pòlemos*—sets off the collapse of the state as the supreme political entity. This means that control over pluralism entails control over the conceptual grid whereby substate groups conceive of themselves.

If this interpretation holds true, Schmitt's chief concern in *The Concept of the Political* was not with explaining how a political community comes about at the moment it counters an enemy, but with *that which the state has to forestall if it wants to preserve its monopoly on the political.* The exceptionalist reading that glues together *Political Theology* and *The Concept of the Political* presents the friend-enemy antithesis as a condition that the state has to nurture in order for the group of friends to be assembled. Quite the reverse, the concretist reading we champion here presents this antithesis as something that merely plays a theoretical and a pragmatic function. From a theoretical vantage point, the friend-enemy one is a fundamental *conceptual* criterion that allows determining what the entity is that enjoys the monopoly on the political. From a pragmatic, political vantage point, it identifies a virtual possibility that the state has to ward off. Schmitt elaborated on this criterion to draw attention to the fact that, if at a given moment in time the supreme political entity is the state, this does not mean that it will continue to be the state forever. Indeed, one day it might turn out that, by applying the friend/enemy criterion, we will have to conclude that there are more (or different) supreme political entities, that is, all the entities which, at that moment, will be laying claim to the right to engage in political conflicts. If this is the case, pragmatically the friend-enemy antithesis is something that should never materialize for the state to continue to hold the monopoly on the political. It is a state of things that radically changes the configuration of the social because of the rise of new political actors.

In sum, whereas *Political Theology* portrays the state of the exception as the original moment in which normality is created, *The Concept of the Political* portrays the opposition between friend and enemy as a condition that the political community has to obviate strenuously. This idea that Schmitt's core concern was with the friend and a community's internal stability rather than war and the enemy is also advocated by Ernst-Wolfgang Böckenförde in his perceptive article on Schmitt's constitutional theory.[24] He explains that in *The Concept of the Political* Schmitt's objective was to show that the chief end of the state—what makes the state the fundamental political entity—is "to relativize domestic antagonisms, tensions, and conflicts in such a way as to facilitate peaceful debates as well as solutions and ultimately decisions in accordance with procedural standards of argumentation and public discourse."[25] The state has to preclude the possibility that one or more components of the civil society get to nurture the desire for or feel the need to intensify their opposition to the state or to other groups. If the state failed to do so, an effect of political self-constitution would be triggered, and the state political unity would ipso facto be relativized. This is why, Böckenförde rightly points out, "the political in the Schmittian sense is what underlies, facilitates, and shapes the political unity as unity: a degree of intensity of that association which supersedes conflicts and antagonisms in such a way as to provide both form and organization and furnish and maintain a working political order."[26]

Why did Schmitt introduce such a significant amendment to his previous conceptualization of the exception? Our hypothesis is that since the late 1920s Schmitt's interest in pluralism had grown significantly. For one thing, he devoted close attention to pluralist theories of the state. Schmitt was two-minded about them. On one side, he found them enlightening especially as to the conception of the social they propounded. On the other, he sensed that their advocates did not understand the lethal risks that pluralism involves. Schmitt viewed Gierke's idea that the state is an association of associations as a "decisive step" to the pluralist conception of the state. It opened the door to the further demotion of the state to a neutral apparatus governing the relations between associations. While taking issue with Duguit's theory, Schmitt recognized that he rightly debunked "uncritical metaphysics of the state and personifications of the state." Yet Duguit eventually missed "the actual political meaning of the concept of sovereignty."[27] The same applied to Anglo-Saxon theories of the pluralist state. According to Schmitt, in one way or another they all failed to tackle the key political question of "which social entity . . . decides the extreme case and determines the decisive friend-and-enemy grouping." However, in Schmitt's eyes, this was not the neglect of the sovereign decider, as was the case with *Political Theology* when he argued that positivist legal theories failed to theorize the original moment at which a law is established. Rather, his argument was that if the state relinquishes its monopoly on the extreme case, then it is destined to perish as a political form:

> That the state is an entity and in fact the decisive entity rests upon its political character. A pluralist theory is either the theory of state which arrives at the unity of state by a federalism of social associations

> or a theory of the dissolution or rebuttal of the state. If, in fact, it challenges the entity and places the political association on an equal level with the others, for example, religious or economic associations, it must, above all, answer the question as to the specific content of the political. . . . The state simply transforms itself into an association which competes with other associations; it becomes a society among some other societies which exist within or outside the state. That is the pluralism of this theory of state. Its entire ingenuity is directed against earlier exaggerations of the state, against its majesty and its personality, against its claim to possess the monopoly of the highest unity, while it remains unclear what, according to this pluralist theory of state, the political entity should be.[28]

In other words, the concretist reading we are advancing in this section submits that *The Concept of the Political*, and more generally the works Schmitt produced between the last couple of years of the 1920s to the first years of 1930s, hinges on a "constructive" idea of the political. He intended to explain what the state should do to maintain the preeminence it had acquired as the key political form of the modern age. In this light, the enemy as well as war are but conceptual devices that proceed from that which is negated in order to cast light on that which is affirmed. If this is the basic assumption of the concretist reading, our interpretive scheme has to take a further step to show what the friend really consists in. To achieve that, it is imperative to pinpoint what Schmitt regarded as the most serious menace to the state. In fact, if he thought that substate intersectional conflicts might destabilize the existent state order, why did he think the mechanism of the exception was no longer enough to neutralize the internal enemies and ban them? Why could the state government not take matters in hand and declare the state of exception to purge society of its internal vulnerability? The main reason that Schmitt came to believe that this solution would fall through is that he had embraced a more nuanced notion of the friend. Or better, he had come to pay more heed to the societal element that lies beneath any social and legal order. His conception of what a society is had evolved to accommodate elements of an institutional theory of law, one that laid stress on the order being composed of social practices and the normative webs developed within them. In other words, the abstractive nature of an unjustified and unjustifiable decision came to appear in Schmitt's eyes as the main shortcoming of his theory of law and politics.

INSTITUTIONALISM VERSUS DECISIONISM

The revealing 1930 essay, "State Ethics and the Pluralist State," which engages with pluralist theories of the state, offers a telling clue to his renewed preoccupation with state and public law theory from a point of view that bespeaks a noticeable change of mind. As we will discuss in some detail, Schmitt abandoned the view of the social that underlay his work of the early 1920s and embraced a more realist conception particularly alert to the normativity of the social. However, quite unsurprisingly, it is exactly the normativity of the social that became his major cause for concern. It is worth expanding on this theoretical evolution to grasp the decisive paradigm change that led Schmitt to espouse the model that can be called "institutionalist decisionism," as the combination of a radically antipluralist institutionalism and an amended decisionism.[29]

Although Schmitt's initial discussion focuses on the virtues and flaws of the pluralist paradigms that we examined in Chapter 1, what should strike the reader is his brisk rejection of the theoretical monism of state-based conceptions of politics and law, which he straightforwardly presented as abstract and misguided:

> Political unity can never be understood as absolutely monistic and destructive of all other social groups. . . . When constitutional lawyers speak of the "omnipotence" of the sovereign—the king or the parliament—their baroquely exaggerated formulas should be understood as owing to the fact that in the state of the sixteenth to eighteenth centuries the issue was overcoming the pluralist chaos of the churches and estates. One makes one's task too easy if one adheres to such idioms. . . . State unity was always a unity from social pluralities. At various times and in various countries it was very different but

> always complex and, in a certain sense, intrinsically pluralist. A reference to this self-evident complexity can perhaps refute an extravagant monism but does not solve the problem of political unity.[30]

Schmitt's notion that any society includes a variety of groups builds on two implicit premises. First, social subjects acquire their identities within group-based normative contexts, while the social world is but an aggregation of these normative contexts. Second, these practical sites cannot either be reduced to their individual components or dispersed into greater normative entities. In this regard, he bought the social ontology of the champions of pluralist theories of the state. This means that he did not disagree with them on what the social world is composed of. He rather disagreed on the conclusion they reached based on this social ontology: "They aim not only to negate the state as the highest comprehensive unity, but above all to negate its ethical claim to be a different and higher sort of social relation than any of the many other associations in which people live."[31] From the bare fact that individuals are members of a series of distinct groups that most of the time overlap, pluralist theories of the state inferred that the state is also one of those groups. It is at this point that Schmitt relied on his conception of the political to reject this conclusion:

> Among pluralist theorists of the state as nearly everywhere, an error prevails that generally persists in uncritical unconsciousness—that the political signifies a specific substance, next to the substance of other "social associations"; that it represents a specific content besides religion, economy, language, culture, and law; and that, therefore, the political group can be understood as standing coordinately next to the other groups—to church, combine, union, nation, cultural and legal communities of all sorts. Political unity thus becomes a special, new substantial unity, joining other unities. Any debates and discussions on the nature of the state and the political will become confused as long as the widespread idea prevails that a political sphere with its own content exists side by side with other spheres.[32]

Evidently, while Schmitt's objection to monist theories of the state had to do with their conceptualization of the social world, his objection to pluralists concerned the political. Moreover, this also attests to the theoretical frame in which he was elaborating his view of the political, that is, the increasing pluralism of contemporary societies. For it is at this point that Schmitt defined the political decision not as that which creates the friend by identifying the enemy, but as that which prevents "all other opposing groups from dissociating to the point of extreme hostility (i.e., to the point of civil war)."[33] As the concretist reading emphasizes, the political is *primarily oriented towards internal politics*, in the sense that it has to forestall the formal metamorphosis of conflicts. The stable coexistence of groups, Schmitt went on to say, enables the stabilization of the normal condition. From this viewpoint, Schmitt at the end of the 1920s can be theoretically defined a *social* pluralist who thought *social* pluralism should never turn into *political* pluralism. In his own words: "It is not a question of denying this existing pluralism and violating it with universalism and monism, but rather of correctly placing pluralism."[34] Put otherwise, contrary to Romano, Schmitt was convinced that the state should be an entity with no normative rivals, one that establishes what is worth fighting for and thus what conflicts possess a political character.

Before we focus on the details of Schmitt's theory of institution, it is worth briefly insisting on the gradual paradigm change in his conception of law and the political. While it is mistaken to overstress his institutional inclination before the end of the 1920s, it is just as mistaken to speak of a precipitous conversion to institutionalism. In the works he wrote late in the 1920s, and above all in Schmitt's most systematic work, *Constitutional Theory*, published in 1928, there are quite a few traces of a deep revision in progress. In this latter book, Schmitt introduced the concept of a *substantial* constitution as the containing structure of a political entity molded in a determinate conformation. More tellingly, if in this context one concentrates on Schmitt's presenting the *constitutional* guarantees as a set of concrete *institutional* guarantees (such as the various, intertwined regulations of the justice administration, religious associations, the educational system, etc.), one can easily come to the conclusion that this famous book is a first, manifest sign of an institutional thinking.

In the two subsequent years, Schmitt expanded on the doctrine of constitution he had advanced in 1928 and emphasized the foundational role of institutions. It is at this juncture that Schmitt upturned his previous exceptionalist perspective. He dispensed with the idea that the institutional guarantees are party to a more comprehensive set of constitutional guarantees and embraced a view of the latter as elements of a broader set of institutional guarantees. These exceed the written constitution, as they are embedded in the normative practices of daily life. This decisive change came to surface in an (usually overlooked) essay Schmitt wrote in 1931, *Freiheitsrechte und institutionelle Garantien der Reichsverfassung* (The liberty rights and the institutional guarantees of the Reich Constitution). In the formal revision he made some decades later (1958), Schmitt himself explicitly averred that this writing marked a turning point in the doctrine of institutional guarantees, originally elaborated in *Constitutional Theory* and subsequently summarized in an essay published in 1932, *Grundrechte und Grundpflichten* (Basic rights and basic duties). From 1932 on, Schmitt came to think of the constitution not as something that rests on its institutional guarantees, but rather as something that is *composed of* its institutional guarantees.[35] As a consequence, he clearly reoriented his analysis towards the normal situation. What was at stake was the relation between norm and normality.

However, as we will explain in more depth at the end of this chapter, rejecting exceptionalism did not entail rejecting decisionism. For Schmitt held onto a basic element of the latter, that is, the genealogical relation between norm and normality: all legal norms hinge on there being unbroken continuity between law and normality. Importantly, he no longer saw normality as the product of a sovereign who decides on the exceptional case. By making a conspicuous theoretical amendment to his conception, Schmitt got to understand normality as a set of general models of conduct that are produced and accepted in a society's ordinary life. This is a crucial institutionalist feature that found no room in Schmitt's previous position and led him to introduce a third type of legal thinking that he had neglected until the late 1920s. He pointed this out in two texts dated 1993 and 1934—the period when he made the most despicable political choices. In the preface to the second edition of *Political Theology*, written in November 1933, he wrote: "I now distinguish not two but three types of legal thinking; in addition to the normativist and the decisionist types there is the institutional one," which "unfolds in institutions and organizations that transcend the personal sphere."[36] The subsequent year, in *On the Three Types of Juristic Thought* he advanced his concrete-order thinking. On his account, this type of legal thought emphasizes the relation between the legal order and the social context in which it unfolds.

Before we go into the details of Schmitt's conception of the relation between normality and the law, it is worth noting that his adhesion to institutionalism was mainly inspired by Hauriou and Romano, whom he regarded as his predecessors: "Hauriou, like Santi Romano, are my masters. . . . Perhaps, rather than masters, it is more appropriate to say predecessors."[37] However, it is easy to realize that Schmitt's peculiar understanding of Romano reduced the latter's nuanced theory to a minor variation of Hauriou's institutionalism. Whether consciously or not, Schmitt neglected the decisive differences between these scholars and especially failed to grasp Romano's point on the innate plurality of the legal world. As we will see, this will prove crucial to capturing the limits of Schmitt's conception of law vis-à-vis pluralism.

The brief sketch of Hauriou's theorizing that we offered in Chapter 2 helps us understand what it is that Schmitt found intriguing in the groundbreaking paradigm advanced by this French scholar. Hauriou's state-centered institutionalism took the state to be the "institution of institutions" and "the legal order of legal orders." Hauriou held a view of the institution as the demiurgic principle of law—"a project-idea underlying an undertaking"—that is accomplished over time *through* the law in a given social context. In particular, Schmitt seized on Hauriou's fundamental ideas of a "directing idea" and the formation of a structuring power, along with the notion of superlegality. In doing so, he radicalized the *politicization of institutionalism* that can be considered as the upshot of Hauriou's theory of institution, especially between the first (1910) and the second edition (1916) of *Principes de droit public* (Principles of public law). Both Hauriou's and Schmitt's institutional frameworks espoused the view that the state is the highest institution, coupled with the antivoluntarism that necessarily follows from such a monopoly on the legitimate enforcement of the legal order. By capitalizing on the inclusion of these two elements and the corresponding exclusion of the liberal connotations of Hauriou's legal theory, Schmitt coalesced the subjective element of the social (individual beliefs shared by social subjects) and the objective and suprapersonal element of an order created by the state.

On Hauriou's account, the "directing idea," in conjunction with the "organized power," conveys the task that a body has to accomplish and how it can accomplish it through self-organization. The organization is thus instrumental in the realization of the directing idea, while the latter is hegemonic toward the former.[38] This is an insight that led Schmitt to make sense of how an assemblage of people turns into a collective body. This transformative process is the source of legality. This means that in both Hauriou's and Schmitt's institutional conceptions institutions have not a legal but a *protolegal* character. Contrary to Romano, Hauriou thought that the institution is the fountainhead of law, in that it is a social project that is meant to achieve a particular objective in light of the organized structure that the directing idea imposes. In this sense, while institution is not law, law never produces institution: "Institutions make juridical rules; juridical rules do not make institutions."[39] The institution is a demiurgic principle of a group project that the law permits accomplishing. Therefore, the law is nothing other than the visible conformation of a social project that seeks to achieve its structuring goal. In the same vein, Schmitt never claimed institutions are legal entities. Rather, the new key role they took in his amended theoretical framework is that they are the source of social normality. At the same time, this theoretical move assigned normality an unprecedent task. While in the previous exceptionalist framework, normality is the product of an unjustifiable, groundless decision on the part of a sovereign, as we will illustrate shortly, in the institutional thinking, normality becomes the lynchpin of a society's concrete order.

In this new conceptual setting, norms are nothing but standard cases that are given a stable form through legislation. Legal norms are a set of stabilized typical cases, declared as binding, which originate from reiterated patterns of conduct. They characterize the contexts in which they are practiced and acquire normative force. They are *exempla*, exemplar instances offering guidance for conduct to all those who are involved in the kinds of activities that the norms claim to govern. Institutions, as a recognizable ensemble of typical models within practical frameworks, are key components of a concrete form of life, which are reflected in the political form and must be preserved by legal means. In a genuinely Hauriouian fashion, institutional practices can be said to be at one and the same time originally related to, but ultimately independent of, both subjective wills and individual beliefs. They are *constituted of* a mix of subjective wills, individual beliefs, and reiterate activities, but are not *constituted by* them. But before we analyze the main elements of Schmitt's institutionalism, we would like to illustrate in what sense this novel position was intended to overcome the essential flaws that affected the decisionist solution to the problem of legal and political order.

As we noted above, decisionism implies a decision being made regardless of any justifiable criterion. Based on this, the criterion of recognition required to determine the state of exception relies on a self-founding logic that characterizes the sovereign action. The exception brings itself about and provides the unit of measurement for its own application and enforcement. This eventuates in an absolute lack of criteria for determining if a decision is adequate. The conclusion is a sort of irrationalist nihilism: an a priori rejection of any *ratio decidendi*. This proves a serious flaw, as decisionism fails to indicate what fundamental bonds are shared by the members of a given community, how they emerge, and how they put together the members of a given political reality. In the end, Schmitt's decisionism never tells us what a friendship relation is. It sheds light only on the polemical and polemogenic function of the political. However, it never accounts for the factors that induce unrelated individuals to team up and give life to a political association. Decisionism only clarifies that a population's enemy is whoever negates that population's way of life. But who are the friends? Under what conditions can an ensemble of human beings be considered to share one way of life? How can something be determined by comparison with something undetermined?

In sum, the decisionist approach does not indicate the positive content (i.e., the friendship relationship) able to substantiate the concept in question (i.e., who the friend is) independently of any reference to its opposite (e.g., the friend as the nonenemy). It is also to unravel this impasse that Schmitt overhauled his decisionism and set forth his institutionalist theory as a solution to it. In short, institutions, depicted as consistent and widely accepted patterns of conduct, are social devices able to turn scattered individuals into interacting agents who form the "political friend." Institutions achieve this "quasi-ontological" aim by singling out, among the whole set of descriptive features characterizing a given social context, a particular set of basic and essential elements that are believed to constitute the distinctive traits of *such and such* course of action. This shift permitted Schmitt to leave the metaphysical level of a groundless and essentially imagined community and to reach the political level of concrete social agency. In this frame, it is no longer a predetermined identity that permits to identify the distinctive way of life adopted within a given social reality. Quite the contrary, it is the joint nature of interactional practices that shapes a social entity and confers on it a distinctive political relevance and identity. What ultimately characterizes individuals is that which they concretely do in their daily, ordinary life, that is, the adoption of reiterated, recognizable patterns of conduct. All individuals who share the same patterns of conduct and the same interactional practices can be said to be "friends," since they are bound together by common interests and relevant aspects of their everyday life that greatly contribute to making them a social group and (at least potentially) a political actor essentially different from all the others.

LAW AS A SIEVE

The gist of the analysis above is that Schmitt's endorsement of institutionalism was not an opportunistic move, despite what a few interpreters submit.[40] As David Bates pointedly notes in his account of Schmitt's adhesion to institutionalism, his "institutional theorization in 1933 and 1934 was not therefore merely opportunistic, nor was it intrinsically fascist."[41] This does not mean that his relationship with this theory of law was unproblematic. Despite his attempt to show that a few key figures of the German tradition (such as Luther and Hegel) were conscious of the importance of institutions to the good health of the German culture, he knew that legal institutionalism was foreign to the German jurisprudential tradition. His professed skepticism of the word *institution* bespoke Schmitt's reluctance to any facile adoption of a non-German jurisprudential thinking as well as his fear that the Nazi establishment might dislike legal institutionalists' extolling the virtues of a self-organizing society.

Schmitt's misgivings about the lexicon of institutionalism are manifest in his change of mind as to the term that was meant to express his novel view of the legal phenomenon. As we pointed out above, in the preface to the second edition of *Political Theology*, he had declared that he wanted to revise decisionism by integrating institutionalism into his revised jurisprudential paradigm. However, in 1934 Schmitt was clear that none of them fully captured his idea of institution. He noticed that the word "institution" in German has a problematic semantic status, as three discrete words might be used to translate it: *Einrichtung*, *Institution*, *Anstalt*. *Einrichtung* was too general and only referred to the factual existence of a social entity. *Anstalt* by that time, he claimed, had acquired a polemical meaning that made it unusable. *Institution* and its Latin root evoked a fixity and rigidity that was at odds with the flexibility of institutional practices.[42] He eventually concluded that "concrete-order and formation thinking" was unequivocal. It is highly likely that Schmitt reckoned that an institutional conception of law entails a bottom-up view of politics and thus was at variance with the Nazis' concentration and centralization of power. It is no coincidence that in that very preface to *Political Theology* he admitted that "an isolated institutional thinking [i.e., without the support of normativism and decisionism] leads to the pluralism characteristic of a feudal-corporate growth that is devoid of sovereignty."[43] In reality, as again Bates remarks, Schmitt's endorsement of institutionalism coupled with his moving away from decisionism evoked a theory of law that sets a limit on the decider's sovereign power: "Schmitt suggested that an 'institution' marks the legal form of a 'concrete order' that defines both the limit of sovereign decision and the essential foundation of any normative constraint."[44]

In short, on one side, Schmitt got acquainted with the limits of decisionism in the light of institutionalism; on the other, his endorsement of the latter was by no means unreserved, because institutionalism is coupled with the pluralist view of social life that he had excoriated in "State Ethics and the Pluralist State." Thus, he had to tease out what he needed and to throw away what he deemed unacceptable. The text in which Schmitt took issue with this theoretical conundrum is *On the Three Types of Juristic Thought*, published in 1934. Although erratic and slim, this text offers a core conception of law that intends to integrate three notions that, for him, reflect three material features of law that cannot be overlooked: *norms*, *decisions*, and *institutions*. The problem, he reasoned, is that legal theories tend to attach privilege to one aspect to the disadvantage of the others, while a complete picture of the legal phenomenon cannot do away with any of them. Norms, decisions, and institutions are equally key to there being a legal order, because they all contribute to making sure that the concrete order gets reflected and incorporated into the law. Therefore, a legal theory that aspires to be complete should be able to reflect the way these elements integrate each other. While sovereign decisions are required only in specific, particularly tragic moments of a community's life, norms and institutions are devices that draw out and solidify the normativity of social life on a daily basis. In this new theoretical scenario, law is no longer the top-down imposition of a sovereign decision, but a protection for those social institutions that bring a political community into life and make it flourish. At the same time, what emerges as the mainstay of this more complex image of law is the notion of normality. To acquire a sound conception of Schmitt's institutional theory and his take on pluralism it is important to pinpoint three elements: his novel critique of positivism, the notion of institutional standards, and the legal instrument that is known as "general clauses."

Schmitt's Novel Critique to Positivism

In *On the Three Types of Juristic Thought* Schmitt advanced a theory based on a mix of transcendentalism and contextualism. For he makes two claims that point to partly divergent directions. First, normativism, decisionism, and concrete-order thinking are three fundamental aspects of law that make the law what it is everywhere—regardless of if and how different legal traditions privilege this or that aspect. Second, every legal tradition takes a developmental trajectory of its own that is conducive to a particular configuration of the law and the relative legal science. This means that, on one hand, there is no law that does not comprise norms, decisions, and institutions. On the other, law is always contextual. In short, the contextual nuance is determined by the specific mix of the three basic elements of law. This was particularly relevant for Schmitt's purposes as he was at pains to renovate legal science for it to be able to account for the serious modifications that German law was undergoing after the Nazi takeover. Based on this mix of transcendentalism and contextualism, Schmitt unfolded a two-pronged study based on conceptual and historical analysis.

What matters for our purposes is the type of critique he addressed to positivism and its spurious normativism. While in his decisionist phase he charged positivists with ignoring the relevance of a seemingly nonjuristic notion to the emergence of the legal order, in *On the Three Types of Juristic Thought* he mainly concerned himself with the relation between legal norms and social reality. His argument came to be that positivists misread their relation and construct a mistaken hierarchy between them. In a way that distinctly recalls Romano's critique of rule-based theories in *The Legal Order*, Schmitt argued that the legal order is neither norm nor a combination of norms and metanorms.[45] Normativism is a theoretical attitude that screens off the decision and the concrete order and seeks to found the whole legal order on the alleged self-sufficiency of norms and norms over norms. However, more than decision, Schmitt insisted on the concrete order and how it shapes norms. It is important to stress that "concrete" here gestures to the actual organization of the juridical machinery: "For a law cannot apply, administer, or enforce itself. It can neither interpret, nor define, nor sanction itself; it cannot—without ceasing to be a norm—even designate or appoint the concrete men who are supposed to interpret or administer it."

Therefore, it is no surprise that Schmitt made a rather liberal use of Romano's theory, which he defined as "very significant." At the end of the first chapter, he quoted his Italian colleague as the latter wrote that "the legal order, taken as a whole, is an entity that partly moves according to the norms, but most of all moves the norms like pawns on a chessboard—norms that therefore represent the object as well as the means of its activity, more than an element of its structure."[46] It should not go unnoticed that Schmitt translated Romano's expression "comprensivamente inteso" (taken as a whole) into "ist ein einheitliches Wesen" (is a unitary entity). As we argued in Chapter 2, this betrays a questionable interpretation of Romano's notion of order and at the same time lays bare Schmitt's idiosyncratic misuse of his institutionalism. For he wanted to integrate Romano's theory of institution into his concrete-order thinking and, at the same time, to expunge what in his eyes was its most detestable consequence, that is, the intrinsic link between institutionalism and pluralism.[47] This differentiates Romano's and Schmitt's approach to normality, as we will discuss later on with regard to this latter notion. Despite this, however, there is no doubt that the two scholars agreed on blaming normativism's unjustified elision of the machine-like character of law to the exclusive advantage of one aspect.

Normativists—and above all the school of legal positivism, which pushed normativism to its extremes—defended two basic tenets. First, there is no ontogenetic relation between norms and social reality, as they dwell in discrete realms. Legal norms lie in the realm of the ought and are impermeable to all that happens in the realm of the is. Norms are nothing but a *technique of description* that is valid regardless of whether individuals follow or break them. Second, legal norms can be used to describe social reality in an entirely different way than the way the ordinary language of everyday life would do. For they give life to a metalanguage by which experts can speak about reality in a special manner, that is, according to the set of fact-types that are yielded by the legislator. As we discussed in Chapter 2, that the language of law is a special language is something that Romano fundamentally concurred on with positivists, while Schmitt did not. He identified a major sticking point between institutionalism and positivism on how these paradigms regard law's specialty. For Schmitt, the error of normativism is that it portrayed law as something norm-abiders use for interpreting and predicting the conduct of the other norm-abiders. Law is reduced to a coordination mechanism, just like a "the framework of a scheduled railroad traffic."[48] Interestingly, Schmitt rebuked this view because it obliterates the relation between norms and the behaviors that norms are intended to repress or promote. If the law is a special technique, this is not because it is a regulatory framework for the rational agents of the bourgeoisie, but because it is a potent means for consolidating the conducts that make a community that community. Accordingly, norms are not indications for rational agents to plan their actions, but pieces of a concrete order for the promotion of conducts that are beneficial to the political community and the eradication of those that are detrimental to it.

Therefore, it makes sense to say that it is the connection between law and conventional morality that Schmitt was concerned with. If the law is reduced to a coordination mechanism, a norm prohibiting a crime such as murder is turned into an undesired consequence intended to discourage one from killing another. In other words, the norm prohibiting murder threatens a disadvantage, i.e., a punishment that occurs if somebody kills somebody else. Murder then is not an act that defies and jeopardizes the concrete order, but an instrument for one to plan one's action whereby one is put in the position to consider the advantages and disadvantages of doing something. Instead, Schmitt thought legal norms encapsulate behavioral standards that are produced by social institutions within ordinary life. Like Romano, Schmitt denied a norm being the sanction that accompanies a behavioral standard, as the sanction is a piece of the machinery as a whole. As Romano put it: "The sanction can be neither contained nor threatened by any specific norm: it can be immanent and latent in the mechanisms, in the organic apparatus of the legal order taken as a whole, it can be a force operating indirectly, a practical guarantee that does not give rise to any subjective right, and thus to any norm from which this law emerges, a constraint that is inborn in, and necessary to, social power."[49] While, as we illustrated in Chapter 2, Romano did not think that norms are related in any way to morality and looked at the machinic nature of sanction within law, Schmitt gave this view an ethical twist: the concrete order is an all-encompassing ethical system.

On this account, conventional morality is the condensation of moral standards produced by those institutions that are compatible with the concrete order. We will shortly see that at the basis of this interplay between social institutions and the concrete order there is still a decider playing a pivotal role—although the decision's role is strikingly different than the one

Schmitt had in mind in the 1920s. What matters here is the relation between legal norms and moral standards—which is indeed more correct to define *institutional standards.* For the adjective "institutional" is more appropriate than "moral," or, as Schmitt himself wrote, normality, as the latter term conjures the idea of a spontaneity of social habits, while on the contrary institutional standards are the outcome of a selection process. While this will become clearer as we go along, it now leads us to the notion of normality.

Institutional Standards

In Schmitt's view, institutional standards are prototypical types of behavior, stabilized and established as binding within the normative contexts in which they arise. These are frequently recurring patterns of conduct that characterize the contexts in which they are generated and applied. As they get incorporated into legal norms, the law renders them into exemplar cases offering guidelines for conduct to all those who are involved in the kinds of activities that legal norms claim to govern. They are concrete models "growing out of the order of the concrete 'conditions.'"[50] It is *widespread normality* that generates typical models of conduct embodied by norms, not the other way around:

> A legal regulation presupposes concepts of what is normal, which develop so little from the legal regulation that the norming itself becomes so incomprehensible without them that one can no longer speak of a "norm." A general rule should certainly be independent from the concrete individual case and elevate itself about the individual case, because it must regulate many cases and not only one individual case; but it elevates itself over the complete situation only to a very limited extent, only in a completely defined sphere, and only to a certain modest level. If it exceeds this limit, it no longer affects or concerns the case which it is supposed to regulate. It becomes senseless and unconnected. The rule follows the changing situation for which it is determined.[51]

While in the 1920s Schmitt thought that normality explained nothing and the exception everything, he completely revoked his distrust in normality, so much so that it became the keystone of legal regulation. In this new institutional frame, the legal order is a filter that is set to select in institutional standards that are instrumental in the homogeneity of the political community and to select out those that threaten to jeopardize it. The "good head of family," the "brave soldier," the "duty-conscious bureaucrat"[52] are examples of models that the law, on Schmitt's account, has to incorporate and foster. Certainly, these standards cannot be displayed in any easy manner. No propositional statements comprising the text of a norm is ever able to specify all of their characteristics: "The cohabitation of spouses in a marriage, family members in a family, kin in a clan, peers in a *Stand*, officials in a state, clergy in a church, comrades in a work camp, and soldiers in an army can be reduced neither to the functionalism of predetermined laws nor to contractual regulations."[53] Although they are not designed to detail institutional standards, legal norms are instruments in the hands of officials to support and stabilize these models. Officials are required to make sure that the norm may always follow the changing situation and that the latter is adequately reflected in legal regulation.

To put it otherwise, legal norms are tasked with determining those that in specific institutional settings establish themselves as normal cases. The law makes them binding and confers on them the force of legitimate authority. Social reality and the law are entangled in a special relation of sieving and stabilization whereby a normative content is drawn out from social institutions and transformed into a stable evaluation standard for all members of the political community. Norms are supposed to follow reality, while reality is molded in accordance with selected legal standards. If this is the case, normality cannot be identified with normativity. Though the former is the cradle of the latter, these two spheres remain distinguished and distinguishable. Interplay does not entail coalescence. Based on this, we can now discuss how this interplay occurs.

General Clauses

In *On the Three Types of Juristic Thought* Schmitt wrote that "the extent to which the age of juristic positivism has ended is most clearly recognizable today in Germany" because the positivistic idea of certainty had been superseded by the "so-called general clauses" (*Generalklausen*).[54] Those are "indeterminate concepts of all kinds, reference to extralegal criteria, and notions such as common decency, good faith, reasonable and unreasonable demands, important reason, and so on." The notion itself of general clauses entails giving up certainty and calculability. They allow officials to perform the job Schmitt thought pertains to the law as a filter and a stabilizer. The main advantage of general clauses is that they do not predefine any given contents, but leave it to the judges to determine them case by case.

In German law, general clauses had become subject of controversy since they were first introduced by the 1900 German civil code, the Bürgerliches Gesetzbuch. General clauses were generic principles or maxims addressed to officials for them to be able to deal with circumstances not specifically regulated by the code. Thomas Krebs comments that in fact these clauses were a double-edged sword. On one side, the legislator meant to use them to make sure that legal officials might cope with unregulated cases. On the other, general clauses inevitably imply various degrees of discretion, and thus empower judges significantly. As Schmitt himself underlined, these concepts were characterized by a high degree of fuzziness and thus granted much flexibility to judicial activism.[55] Yet it was not fuzziness itself that Schmitt appreciated, but the way-out of positivism general clauses suggested. As he explained in *State, Movement, People*, German law was bound to navigate through the Scylla of total uncertainty and the Charybdis of an impracticable return to positivism.[56]

It is here that Schmitt gave away the decisionist flavor of his institutionalism. As the relation between social reality and the law is based on a controlled filtering, general clauses are the main instrument in the hands of officials to see to this process. However, officials cannot be granted complete freedom, as they are the instrument in the hands of an ultimate decider who is able to identify those institutional standards that fit the political community. This means that judges are to be formed in such a way that they are naturally sensitive to the inputs of a leader as the ultimate decider. Schmitt put it as follows:

> There is only one road. The National-Socialist State has been treading it with great firmness, and the Secretary of State Freisler has given it

> the clearest formulation in the call: "no reform of justice but reform of jurists." If an independent administration of justice must continue to exist, even though a mechanical and automatic commitment of the judge to predetermined regularization is not possible, then it all depends precisely on the *breed* and *type* of our judges and civil servants. Never has the question "*quis iudicabit*" had any such crucial importance as today.[57]

What Schmitt had in mind was a pyramidal edifice where the various nodes of a well-structured network are connected to the various subleaders up to the ultimate leader. As a spontaneous convergence on the meaning of the law is impossible, "we demand their commitment without which all the guarantees and freedom, all the independence of the judges, and above all, that 'creativity' would be but anarchy and an especially noxious source of political dangers."[58] This kind of leadership feeds off an intrinsic relationship between the leader and his following, one that has to do with *ethnic identity*. The followers' loyalty does not hinge on any sense of administrative responsibility but on a substantive identity that ensures social homogeneity. Obviously, this is at odds with an institutional view that is sensitive to the spontaneous emergence of social patterns of conduct and models of life. Spontaneity endangers the relation between the leader and the people.

As a final aside, it is worth stressing that this bespeaks a major change in Schmitt's key notion of homogeneity. The law is the product of a selection of institutional standards from practice-based normative sources that devoted officials handle with recourse to general clauses and in compliance with the leader's view of the community. The leader is the interpreter of the common ethnic identity, which, as a concept, owns a "*systematic* force . . . that pervades all the judicial deliberations."[59] This makes Schmitt's institutionalism an "institutionalist decisionism," as the conjunction of an antipluralist state monism with an amended decisionism. In such a revised decisionist framework, deprived of its previous exceptionalist allure, the homogeneity of the social cannot be obtained through recourse to forceful, abrupt decisions on the part of the leader. Rather, it is a result to be achieved over time, with patience and accuracy in the selection of institutional standards through norms and general clauses—and importantly, in keeping with the view of a leader. As the social naturally tends to produce differences, the legal order is called upon to protect the uniformity of concrete order, based on the identity between the leader and the people.

CONCLUDING REMARKS

In this chapter we concerned ourselves with Schmitt's telling revision of his own legal theory, and the comparison with Romano's proved enlightening in a few junctures. While either was always reluctant about the notion of law as system, Schmitt was the one who pushed the notion of law as order to the extreme. Romano was obviously on the side of the order versus the system, but his view made no room for the idea that law incorporates a form of life and promotes social homogeneity. While for Romano the task of law is that of making orders compatible with each other through technical forms of negotiation, Schmitt tasked law with preventing the rise of an order vis-à-vis another within state borders. The law, Schmitt believed, is an instrument for the leader and his loyal officials to tease out the institutional standards that feed into the ethnic homogeneity of the people and shore it up. The order, then, graphs onto a form of life that has an ethical and an ethnic nature. Therefore, it is hardly surprising that two theories of law as order, despite many key aspects in common, came to irreconcilable visions of pluralism.

Still, the juxtaposition of Romano and Schmitt is useful for another reason. It shines a light on their blind spots. Romano's trust in the autonomy of legal science obliterated the issue of political power. An order always requires someone selecting among a variety of normative sources that coexist even in a context of plurality of pluralities. Romano thought the law can rely on its special nature to handle the potentially uncountable conflicts between institutions. The order is implicitly associated to a spontaneity of a functional mechanism of self-production and self-regulation. Schmitt overturned this view. His conception casts light on the relationship between the production of legal norms and the reverberating effects of selection and social normalization that these norms bring about on the social world. Even within liberal democracies, the core of legislation scarcely lies in the production of shared standards that are neutral vis-à-vis private lifestyles and alternative conceptions of the good. On the contrary, legal norms are instrumental in fostering some lifestyles and conceptions of the good to the detriment of others. In doing so, Schmitt's theory serves as a warning to those who neglect the mechanisms that turn certain institutional standards, produced in the here and the now of particular contexts, into universally valid norms.

Based on Schmitt's analysis, the legal field appears as a platform where social identities are given social legibility and political "speakability" insofar as they abide by the "rule of the game," that is to say, the acceptance of law's normative preeminence over any other type of normative repertoire. The utmost duty of political institutions is to "tame" the innate force of social practices and to impose on them a common understanding of what is normal. The "normal" is given by the individual conducts and interactional models that are formed within the most widespread and age-old institutions of a given country (such as the church, the army, or the bureau). Schmitt was particularly adroit at showing that the "normal" stems from an arbitrary process of selection that defies the passage from "is" to "ought" by transmuting social patterns of behavior into binding legal standards. While he obviously thought this is indispensable for a healthy community to survive and thrive, this is a lesson that those who appreciate pluralism should take to heart to lessen detestable effects of exclusion.

CHAPTER FOUR

Costantino Mortati and the Material Constitution

THE EDUCATION OF A REALIST THINKER: CONTEXT AND CONCERNS

An analysis of the legal theory of Costantino Mortati (1891–1985) is the most appropriate follow-up to the previous chapters. This is the case for three reasons: Mortati's reflections on the nature of the legal order constitute a third wholly distinct type of legal institutionalism that will find wide recognition after World War II in many legal orders; at the same time, and this is the second reason, his major intellectual points of reference were precisely (although not exclusively) Romano and Schmitt. His work can be read as an attempt to take these institutionalist authors seriously by going *with them, beyond them*. As we will see, Mortati combines the organizational aspects of Romano's institutionalism with Schmitt's constitutional realism with a view to produce a new institutionalist synthesis. The third reason is that Mortati has directly addressed the role of pluralism within the remit of this synthesis. It follows that Mortati's work does not only point to another institutionalist route for addressing the question of pluralism; it will also allow us to put both Romano's and Schmitt's types of institutionalism in the right perspective.

Slightly younger than Romano and Schmitt, Mortati became a scholar after the consolidation of Fascist Italy, that is, after the full transformation of the Italian legal order into an authoritarian "regime" with the key laws approved between 1925 and 1928.[1] After having graduated first in law and in philosophy, then in political science,[2] Mortati started his academic career in an advantageous position for addressing a series of questions that were relevant to the constitutional functioning of the Fascist regime.[3] As we will see, the historical context dictated his main academic concerns. Mortati indeed wrote some of his major works during the 1930s[4] and he did take seriously how fascism tried to address the constitutional anxieties of the age.

The advent of the Fascist regime has been read as an authoritarian reordering of the Italian state after the crisis of the liberal political system and the so-called red biennium that followed the end of World War I.[5] The destabilizing effects of the advent of the masses on the political system was tackled by the Fascist Party with the penetration of the party itself into the organization of both society and the state and, constitutionally, with the subordination of parliamentary politics to the centripetal forces of executive power, concentrated in the hands of Mussolini. Mortati's intellectual profile was formed in those crucial years of constitutional transformation. For him the opening up of the state legal order to the masses, and accordingly to a growing number of intermediate groups, represented a crucial issue and threat to constitutional unity. Moreover, the debate on the nature of the Fascist regime and its relationship with the previous liberal constitutional order influenced and shaped his legal and political thought. In fact, the flexible constitution originally enacted in 1848 by the king, and still in use during the liberal period, was never formally repudiated by the Fascist regime, giving rise to a genuine legal quandary about its status in the new political context. Hence, understanding which type of state and constitutional order were instantiated by the Fascist regime represented a genuinely decisive question for Mortati. In the debate between those who saw the Fascist regime as disruptive of the previous constitutional order and those who thought that it was just a development of it, Mortati sided with the former. A key component of this interpretation was provided by the way fascism dealt with the new type of social pluralism that emerged after World War I. The influence of the context on his intellectual formation is reflected in some of the key themes taken up from the inception of his academic career.

One of these key themes was the role of political and social homogeneity.[6] Mortati, like others of his contemporaries, was seriously convinced that without some kind of political homogeneity the legal order could not be stabilized and would be constantly exposed to centrifugal pressures. His reaction to the fragmentation of social and political claims was driven by the constitutional ethos of building and stabilizing the legal order. The new subjects who were entering the political sphere unsettled previous dominant conceptions of homogeneity. The political body had been shaken and fragmented by the appearance of these new subjects. Liberal public lawyers had ignored this novelty because they had addressed it with a formalist and positivist approach based on the dualism of social and legal relations. In Germany the question had already been addressed, in the context of Weimar, at times with different and innovative views on the question of homogeneity such as those put forward by Rudolf Smend and Hermann Heller. Both authors exercised a profound influence (especially Smend, as we will see later in the chapter) over Mortati's intellectual development, and it is fair to note that his position on homogeneity and pluralism has been certainly shaped in dialogue not only with Schmitt and Romano but with these two authors as well.

In the 1920s, Smend's reflection started from a specific interrogation: how to avoid that the loss of organic links within society, due to the rise of the multiclass state,[7] would bring about destructive effects upon the unity of the state. The way to cope with this crisis of political unity was to conceive constitutional development as a form of social integration through law. This worry is based on material grounds because the loss of organic links produces distortive dynamics (of psychological and sociological nature) between the individual and the community, and the consequences for the stability of the social order are extremely negative. Reflecting on his own intellectual development, Smend would later remember that the originating factor of his "integration theory" was "the sight of the political chaos of the sickly constitutional state of the 1920s, out of which emerged a desire to offer in contrast the original healthy sense of the constitution."[8] Only a dynamic conception of the constitutional order could ensure that this "sickly constitutional state" (i.e., the state of affairs of the

Weimar epoch) would eventually recover. However, Smend gave a peculiar twist to that dynamic and pitched his enquiry at the psychological level of the individual conscience. The stability of the legal order was made to depend largely on the psychological convictions of the individual in relation to the wider community. The way to avoid the side effects of radical social and legal pluralism was to integrate constantly (this is the dynamic aspect) psychic and cultural elements into the life of the legal order. The aim of integration was simply to produce and then stabilize the political unity of the state. There is no other content nor aim for integration. In brief, the process of integration would be functional to the constant amalgamation of the social order and its own reproduction.

Heller's starting point is not much different, as he assumes that political unity is an essential feature of any legal order and therefore pluralism is a condition that ought to be governed: "The politically decisive acts establish and maintain a legal order, whose existence, positivity, or validity remain permanently dependent on the existence of that unity of acts, which must therefore asserts itself when necessary even against positive law itself."[9] The requirement of political unity is so constraining that it is possible to sum it up with a remarkable synthesis: "All politics consists in the formation and maintenance of this unity."[10] A political community holds together only if society is artificially molded in a way that realizes a certain degree of homogeneity. Unlike Smend, Heller believed that the only real option was to build social homogeneity in virtue of governing activities whose direction can be either bottom-up (and in this case, the government is democratic) or top-down (in which case, the government is authoritarian). Heller describes explicitly the internal relation between social homogeneity and political unity. In his view, the social and political spheres are not neatly separable: "It is thus the case that the degree to which it is possible to form a political unity depends on the extent of social homogeneity."[11] Once again, homogeneity is a process and not a static outcome, and it requires the mobilization of a number of cultural, social, and political aspects. The legal order plays a key function because it provides a number of juridical principles that are not external to the community but derive from its social practices.[12] The production of social homogeneity can unfold around these principles. In fact, these principles operate at the same time as a fixed reference with a relatively open content around which social relations can be mediated and reorganized.

Mortati shared with Smend and Heller the concern for the artificial creation of a certain level of homogeneity as the best way to cope with pluralism; however, instead of thinking of homogeneity in cultural or social terms, he provided a more political version. He did think that the new pluralism ought to be addressed with a different conception of the legal and constitutional order and be made productive, rather than disruptive, of political unity. Given the latter's persistent centrality, the quest for the *suprema potestas* remained, in his account, a relevant juristic practice that could not be discarded because of the rise of pluralism. Identifying the *suprema potestas* and its manifestations is part and parcel of the same process of understanding the formation of political unity. Anticipating the conclusions of this chapter, we can state that Mortati's legal institutionalism (like those of Smend and Heller) advocated a form of integration as a path for addressing the question of pluralism.

The complexity of society would require the overcoming of the checks and balances model, where each of the three functions of the modern state counteracts the others and protects individual freedom. Instead, Mortati postulated the existence of a fourth function ensuring the formation of political homogeneity and the pursue of the state's fundamental aims. Overall, his main contribution to the political understanding of the legal order is to be found in having attributed this constitutional function (the function of governing society) to political forces and, late in his trajectory, to a constellation of different intermediate powers.[13]

This perspective is compatible with the description of the functioning of the Fascist regime. What remains an open question is whether this is just a theory for the Fascist regime or it aspires to be a general theory. The nature and quality of Mortati's support for the Fascist regime persists as a controversial topic for historians,[14] as it is, more generally, the contribution given by the Italian mainstream legal culture to the development of the regime.[15] His political biography seems to suggest that his work would be connected to the development of the Fascist regime only in an incidental way. In fact, after the fall of the Fascist regime, Mortati applied to become a member of the Christian Democratic Party and soon after was elected as member of the Constituent Assembly in 1946. In this role, he contributed to the formulation of decisive parts of the final text of the Italian republican constitution.[16] Later, after a truncated political career, he went on to become a judge in the constitutional court.[17] Furthermore, in the works published after the end of World War II, Mortati would adapt his previous reflections to the new republican reality in a series of works ranging from the history and theory of constituent power to analyses of the Italian constitution and its core components.

While recognizing changes in some dimensions of Mortati's writings, this chapter will assume that there has been continuity in his legal thought.[18] This working hypothesis inspires the structure of the argument of this chapter. We will first reconstruct Mortati's legal theory and then the notion of the material constitution[19] will be unpacked. Finally, the relation between Mortati's institutionalism and the challenge of pluralism will be broached.

A REALIST VERSION OF LEGAL INSTITUTIONALISM

Mortati's legal theory rests firmly within the tradition of legal institutionalism, even though he grafted a peculiar blend of political (but not legal) realism onto that type of legal theory. While Romano put forward a juristic conception of institutionalism and Schmitt a political one, Mortati twisted the insights offered by both authors (and, as mentioned before, others as well) to obtain a realist version.[20] The intellectual debt owed to Romano is the most evident as it is testified by the fact that *The Constitution in the Material Sense* (possibly Mortati's major work) is dedicated to the great Italian jurist. Mortati takes from Romano the idea that the main unit of legal analysis is the legal order. More specifically, the legal order is an institution, or a set of institutions, to be understood as a pattern of organizations animated by a *telos*, an aim or a principle. Therefore, an institution is essentially an organized unity (with different degrees of cohesion) that contains fundamental normative elements. However, the aims or principles that animate the legal order should not be conceived only in deontological terms. Rather, they are conceived by Mortati as teleological elements.

The adoption of this starting point comes with two advantages. Legal institutionalism is indeed concerned with the institutional dimension because it highlights the structural coupling between societal formation and legal ordering. The legal order and its institutions take shape internally to social development, and not outside of it. The synthesis of these two aspects (social organization and normative framework) is what makes an institution, or a set of institutions, a legal order.

Methodologically, such a move requires viewing the autonomy of law in a nonpositivist manner. Of course, according to Mortati law can take up any content. The specificity of a legal norm (against social or moral ones) cannot be found in its content, but in its normativity, which is (as we will see) closely associated to its enforceability. Under this aspect, Mortati's institutionalism is not categorically different from classic legal positivism. And as it is for most versions of legal positivism, the normativity of legal norms is based on a specific function: consolidating or stabilizing the social order by helping it to achieve fundamental aims.[21] At the cost of simplifying what has become a sophisticated and rich constellation of different positivisms,[22] the main differences between Mortati's legal institutionalism and his contemporary versions of positivism lie in the epistemic consequences of the link between social facts and the legal order. Most forms of legal positivism of the first half of the twentieth century remained loyal to Hume's law and respected the separation between is and ought. They tend, therefore, to portray the relation between social facts and the normative order as an external one, so that the legal system is conceived as a scheme of intelligibility applied to an already existing social reality. Mortati insists that the opposite is the case. Of course, it is possible to separate for analytical purposes societal formations and legal orders, and even to treat them as distinct, but the jurist always ought to bear in mind that this is an *internal relation*, that is, the legal order does not grow or emerge from the outside of society. Rather, the creation of the legal order is already embedded in societal formation and development, and vice versa. The intention of the author is not to extract a sociological approach to law out of legal institutionalism.

And this is not because Mortati despises sociological approaches to the law. It is possible, in his view, to observe the societal factors undergirding the development of the legal order. However, such an observation concerns only sociological knowledge and not, strictly speaking, legal knowledge. But if Mortati had stopped his reflection at this point, he would have adhered to the classic legal-positivist distinction between sociology of law and legal philosophy. His project is different because the jurist ought to focus on the internal relation between social formation and the legal order as the latter's proper juridical foundation:

> The jurist does not do sociology, because she does not look out for the factors that determined the rise of forces and ideologies on which the state is based; nor does she express any opinion about them. By tracing the features that are necessary for conducts and social relations to acquire legal significance, she delineates the facts that emerge out of these very relations as they unfold within a given order.[23]

In brief: it is one thing to study the relation between society and the legal order from a sociological perspective with a view to becoming aware of the natural, material, and cultural factors that have brought together a social group and to assess the congruence between formal legal structures and social reality; quite another thing to look for those social elements that already contain the seeds of legal normativity. The jurist's task is to penetrate the organizational dimension of social reality in order to find those elements which integrate the formal legal orders and breathe life into them.

From this way of conceiving the relation between society and the legal order derives the second important difference. As we discussed at the outset of Chapter 3, Mortati also refers to the notion of order rather than system because he conceives law as more than a system of norms.[24] From this premise, Mortati extrapolates two key tenets of his legal institutionalism. First, institutions do precede, at least logically, the system of norms because, second, they intrinsically contain their own order organized around a telos or finality. The first tenet establishes that norms become legal precisely because they are embedded in an institution. The latter comes as a consequence of the former: an institution is an already organized unity whose identity is given not by its ever-changing norms, but by the aim or telos animating it. Norms can change, but the identity of the legal order remains (under certain aspects) the same. The requirement of an organized unity entails that roles and functions within that unity have been already distributed.

Differentiation within a social group requires ordering processes (that is, *normative facts*) and ordered structures (that is, a *constituted authority*). Hence, the legal order rests on five organizational and normative building blocks: First, the ensemble of the subjects linked by common interests that require cooperation for their realization (in a nutshell: one or more social groups). Second, the presence of an authority that can objectify a legal will applicable to all the members of the group. Third, one or more fundamental aims. Fourth, a system of social relations juridically qualified. Fifth, an array of means (normative and not) through which legal certainty is established (mostly in virtue of its enforcement).[25]

It is worth giving more consideration to these building blocks by bearing in mind that all of them must be present at one and the same time for a legal order to come about. The first one refers to the subjects whose interests and needs provide the reason for associating in the first place. The second postulates that the group is internally structured and bestows a special position upon some members. The third establishes the teleological nature of legal orders by assuming that each and every institution is created or brought about for an instrumental reason, that is, to realize certain goods or values. The fourth and the fifth, concerning respectively the interaction among subjects and the means to govern it, require a system of legal norms. The latter point needs a supplement of explanation.

Legal norms are distinguished from the other types of norms (norms of etiquette, moral norms, and social norms) because they are fundamentally imperative. According to Mortati, the imperative character of norms contains two tenets. First, positive law is in the end reducible to a command that affects human conduct and, second, this feature of law threatens, in case of disobedience, a sanction or the loss of an advantage or privilege. The command is not autonomous and categorical (as it is in Kantian moral law) but heteronomous and parasitical on the interests of the subjects for compliance. Given that a legal order has to be not only valid but also (even though not necessarily always) effective, the disobedience of the command will trigger, at a certain point, an obligation on one of the organs of the legal order to enforce the violated norm.[26] The imperative and enforceable aspects of legal norms are intrinsic components because the legal order is also an instrument of societal formation and not a mere recognition of a state of affairs.[27] Law is not a tool for imagining alternative social relations, as it is an instrument to select or impose some of them over others.

At this point, a further clarification on the nature of legal orders is necessary. Being built on institutions, Mortati's legal theory is in principle open to the recognition of the plurality of legal orders. As there are an infinite series of interests (of the general, common, and individual kind) and needs, there must also be a multiplicity of legal associations. Yet, Mortati's real concern is not with the proliferation of this type of pluralism. Even the relation among institutions (and legal orders) can be organized, and often is, by the differentiation among their functions and aims. Such a differentiation introduces also a hierarchy, which is part and parcel of a wider legal order. In fact, legal orders (and therefore institutions) can be of different kinds of which Mortati sketches a tentative classification. A crucial distinction is between legal orders with a single and specific aim, and legal orders with general aims.[28] Orders with only one specific aim can be socially, culturally, or morally oriented (charity or forms of sports associations, for example). Here Mortati is not fully explicit, and it remains uncertain whether every order with only one finality can really qualify as juridical. Possibly, the lack of clarity comes because of the lack of interest in the issue.

Nonetheless, the author of *The Constitution in the Material Sense* is adamant when he addresses those legal orders with general fundamental aims, which are qualified as *political* orders. These are defined as political because general aims (for example, maintenance of peace among different social groups) can in principle address almost any interest or need as long as this is instrumental to the pursuit of the fundamental aim. These political legal orders can be *original* (*sui juris*), when they derive their nature internally, or *dependent* on another superior order (derivative orders such as, in the modern state, regions, or provinces). The former are sovereign legal orders as well.[29] Here, sovereignty means that the authority intrinsic to the legal order can find its origin in an internal principle of order that is not imposed from the external world. Accordingly, within its jurisdiction, this type of legal order remains hierarchically superior to the others.[30]

Central to this reconstruction is the ordering principle internal to each original legal order. Such a principle (or series of principles) operates necessarily under certain conditions, otherwise it would not be able to perform its proper function. The operational activities of the principle are required at least during these phases: as already mentioned, the principle cannot be derived from the external world, but has to be immanent to societal organization; at the moment of forming the legal order, the principle molds some of its defining traits into it; at the moment of integrating the system of norms with new norms because of gaps in the legal order, the principle fills the gaps; at the moment of guaranteeing legal certainty and legal stability, which is actually a self-limiting moment, as the ordering principle limits itself according to the aims the legal order is supposed to pursue.[31]

Another basic aspect of Mortati's institutionalism should be pointed out. According to him, a legal institutionalist approach paves the way for a *concrete* study of the legal order, that is, a study centered on its organizational aspect and the differences and articulations that the organization bestows upon it. It should be noted that on this point Mortati found Romano's theory rather abstract and vague. While Romano was clear on the priority of the organization over the norm, he did underestimate the internal ordering properties of each organization. Each institution, according to Romano, is moved by a vital principle; but, the objection goes, this principle "cannot perform its function . . . if it did not have the character of uniformity and constancy, that is, if it were not a norm; this norm would be without any doubt different . . . from those disciplining directly behaviors, but still similar in its function."[32]

In several instances, Mortati recognized explicitly his debt, not only toward Romano, but also to some of the contemporary institutionalist authors. It is helpful, for the purposes of illustrating and assessing his legal theory, to go through his analysis of the differences between legal institutionalisms.[33] At this stage, it is possible to anticipate that his engagement with the authors of the canon of legal institutionalism is animated by a Janus-faced frustration: either these theories are juridical but not realist, or they are realist but not juridical.[34] For this reason, we qualify his version of institutionalism as *realist institutionalism*: when he addresses original and autonomous legal orders, his theory pivots on the synthesis between the legal order and the political system. In a nutshell: his methodology is fully in line with a political conception of law. This means that the mediation between social formation and legal ordering is realized by political subjects through political agency.

Before exploring his engagement with other institutionalist authors, one comparison with a scholar belonging to a different tradition of studies is helpful. Despite being highly critical of his legal theory, the confrontation with Kelsen is central for Mortati's legal thought and for understanding his main difference with Romano's. According to Mortati, Kelsen has put forward the wrong solutions, but he has asked several relevant questions. The biggest issue is Kelsen's methodology because it unduly restricts the epistemic boundaries of the legal theorist's research. Mortati cannot accept the pureness of the pure theory. This is the case despite the fact that the pure theory contains precious insights. For example, according to Mortati the idea of the basic norm should not be discarded entirely. The problem lies in the way it is presented by Kelsen, and this is because it is based on wrong assumptions. While, according to Mortati, it is laudable to anchor the legal order upon a unitary, objective point of reference, it is not acceptable to understand the basic norm in terms of an hypothetical norm. Conceived in this way, the basic norm cannot perform its epistemic role. This is because its epistemic value is limited to legislative outputs but cannot extend to the sphere of discretion or the sphere of interpretation. In fact, only those norms that descend logically from another norm belong to the legal system. Moreover, a basic norm that is conceived as hypothetical cannot contribute to the identification of the main distinctive characters of the legal order. Therefore, even when there is a substantial change of the fundamental tenets of a legal order, the basic norm as hypothesis does not register it as relevant in terms of legal knowledge. As also noted by Alf Ross, the mere command "obey to the supreme organ" is too vague because it is possible that the same organ would change dramatically without any formal legal registration of the change.[35] Therefore, Mortati was firmly convinced that to make sense of the basic norm the legal theorist ought to begin by taking into account *facts*.[36] In this way, the basic norm would not operate as a precondition of conceivability of the legal order, but as its validity-condition. Mortati believes that to be operative as a condition of validity, the basic norm[37] must be effective.

Based on these considerations, two precious lessons can be learned thanks to the engagement with Kelsen. First, observing facts cannot be deemed to be outside of the field of legal knowledge. Second, the existence of the legal order, as "it emerges from the observation of the facts is a necessary element for attaching the property of legality to the norms,"[38] but it should be excluded that it assumes a distinctive value from that of validity and becomes relevant, so to say, only a posteriori. In the end, Mortati believed that Kelsen's account should be turned upside down. The normative system can be estimated to be valid if it is efficacious in its entirety. It follows that the ground of the normative system should be looked for in social reality. More specifically, under a normative order one can always find a real or social relation that operates as a source of juridification. But if the social fact bearing the normative order is organized and already contains normative elements, why should it be left outside of the realm of legal knowledge? Such a move allows Mortati to put at the center of his legal theory the relation between the constitution of society (the real constitution) and the legal constitution (the juridical one) by reframing the way social facts and norms interact. Unlike empirical and critical positivists, Mortati's institutionalism is conducive to the postulate that both levels are normative and juridical as well. The juxtaposition between what is and what ought to be is tamed and transcended because the identification of what is the case, unless described as an empirical phenomenon, presupposes an evaluation of it as a legal phenomenon. The legal theorist cannot simply describe the effects of human behavior, but ought to interpret them in light of a particular concept of law and, more accurately, "on the basis of a concept of valid and efficient legal order."[39] This type of institutionalism avoids the ontological difference between societal formation and legal ordering. It is therefore a type of institutionalism that intertwines what is and what ought to be the case.

Within the institutionalist family, Mortati is indebted most heavily to the German tradition[40] (whose main works he had read extensively during the 1920s) and less to the French version. Among institutionalist authors, Carl Schmitt was one of the most important for Mortati,[41] despite some remarkable differences.[42] What Mortati finds compelling in Schmitt's work is the constant reminder that to explain the legal order, it is necessary to include the concrete social order and the emphasis put on the creation of political unity through a decision. To put it briefly, Mortati holds Schmitt's approach to the legal order in great esteem. He also praises Schmitt's apparent commitment to the concrete order. However, he reproaches Schmitt's institutionalism for its two major limits. The first is that it still maintains norm and order as strictly separate entities; the second is a dramatic deficit of concreteness affecting Schmitt's analysis, despite his methodological claims.[43] This type of deficit undermines two key points of the concrete conception of the legal order. First, who should be the author of the decision on the form of the political unity remains utterly underdetermined. Second, the two elements that make up the legal order, the existential and the normative, are kept distinct and, crucially, understood to be an expression of different realities.[44]

As already mentioned at the beginning of the chapter, another important point of reference for the Italian constitutional lawyer is Rudolf Smend.[45] From him, Mortati takes the idea that, despite its political nature, the legal order is potentially integrative. The formula employed by Smend, "constitution as integration," is intuitively appealing to the Italian lawyer because it thematizes the indissoluble link between society and the legal order. The problem, again, is similar to the one that affected Schmitt's theory.[46] One can spot two deficits of concreteness in the way Smend developed the idea of the integrative process. At one level, there is nothing legally distinctive about the three types of integration (personal, functional, and real) discussed by Smend. At another level, there is no real bearer (*Träger*) behind the legal order and therefore the integrative process is diffuse throughout an underdetermined social consciousness. The link between social forces and state institutions is not openly addressed and "it seems that according to Smend they remain juxtaposed, moments of distinct realities, expression of two worlds, that of the is and that of the ought, which do not communicate."[47]

Similar charges are directed against French institutionalists. Carré de Malberg and his notion of national sovereignty is a predictable target for two reasons.[48] First, he separates neatly between facts and law, politics and the legal order. Heir to a solid French tradition, Carré de Malberg posited the nation as the bearer of the legal order. Although the nation is an already organized group (an institution), in a rigorous positivist fashion he kept separated the seat of political authority and the sources of the legal order. As is the case with other institutionalists, Malberg still falls prey of a methodological dualism that betrays the premises of the theory. The second reason of criticism is to be found in the lack of specification and concreteness. The nation is an ideal construction loosely based on the abstract idea of the common interest. Its homogeneity is postulated rather than reconstructed in political terms. Because of this, Malberg's national sovereignty cannot explain away the formation of the legal order (because the nation is considered already formed before it) or qualify the nature and character of its concrete identity.[49]

Mortati's assessment of the work of Maurice Hauriou is rather different. He is credited by Mortati for having understood which element could work as an aggregative factor of the social community and for having found it in the directive idea (*ideé directrice*). The directive idea has been conceived as internal to the institution, and it is not surprising that Mortati saw it favorably. However, Mortati detects an oscillation in Hauriou's theory of the institution.[50] On one hand, the institution is described as the almost spontaneous formation of a collective will (even if unorganized) or the outcome of a natural balance among social interests and forces through which facts become law. If this were the case, the institution would be perfected before the appearance of the juridical world. On the other hand, the institution is sometimes represented as proper to the most sophisticated juridical organism, up to the point where "it requires the will of a founder . . . and a correlative authoritative organization."[51] In this case, conjuring up such a notion of the institution limits the concept of the legal order instead of widening it.

To sum up the analysis so far, one can conclude that all these doctrines represent sources of argumentation for Mortati, but he believes they are ultimately disappointing because they end up contradicting their own institutionalist premises. In fact, he believes they all actually suffer from a deficit of concrete analysis: they collapse the complex and real organization of the state into the legal order as something separated from the realm of facts.[52] To the other extreme, some of these institutionalist thinkers do not care to provide the criteria for the identification of the power to found, stabilize, and direct the development of the constitutional order. In this way, this latter trend is exposed to the plausible accusation of sociologism because it confines its analysis to the territorial and personal elements of the legal order.

Two final observations are necessary for a proper understanding of Mortati's conception of law. First, Mortati's understanding of law is mostly inspired by an imperativist model, that is, by the idea that law can be described as a command.[53] This might represent an element of internal tension as legal institutionalists do not need to adopt an imperativist conception of law,[54] which is often (but not necessarily) associated with a positivist approach. Romano, for example, does not hold that an imperativist conception of law is a conceptually necessary tenet of the notion of institution. Contrary to that, Mortati's description of state law is permeated by imperativist themes: for example, the state legal order is defined as "stable, authoritative, coercive, and total."[55] Basically, a legal order is formed around the choice of certain fundamental aims and, consequently, the rejection of others. Crucially, this entails the establishment of a *differentiation* between rulers and ruled.[56] Law as a command describes most of the legal phenomena that regulate the relation between rulers and ruled. Moreover, among the main characters of the legal order, Mortati always lists the authoritative and the coercive. As for the former, the process of distinction among subjects within the same legal order requires the formation of authoritative structures. As for the coercive aspect, Mortati states openly that legal norms are necessarily connected to sanctions. The legal order belongs to the world of the "ought," and this entails the need to ensure that on average the members of the social group conform to the legal norms. Accordingly, this requires recognizing that there are officials with the normative power of commanding over legal subjects. Command comes always with the possibility of sanctions:

> The opinions that exclude the element of sanction from legal norms are perhaps the outcome of an inappropriate mode of understanding it and they cannot avoid being tied to inextricable contradictions. . . . Experience shows that as soon as it [the threat of sanction] disappears or weakens, the selfish instincts of individuals explode and the social order is shaken.[57]

Therefore, legal norms have to transcend the will of those to whom they are addressed, and they have to operate "not only as the current judgment of past behaviors (applied by the authority which embodies the objectified common will), but as commands doomed to be realized even coercively in case of transgression."[58] As we will see, this is part and parcel of the political understanding of the legal order promoted by Mortati.

Second, Mortati's legal theory does not accommodate radical pluralist tones. Unlike some of his fellow institutionalist colleagues, and despite his favor for intermediary powers and groups, he rejects expressly social law as genuine law. In fact, as we will see in the fourth section, the primacy of the constitutional order implies that social normativity does not qualify immediately and automatically as legal. Like Romano and other pluralists, Mortati does not have any problem in recognizing that there is a wide variety of extralegal norms. Yet, on the same wavelength with Schmitt, he thinks that if these norms are not selected and supported by dominant political forces, then they cannot be considered to be part of the legal order. In other words, the mediation between unity and pluralism is delegated to the political sphere and registered at the juristic level only at a later stage.

This attitude toward social normativity applies also to the classic distinction between public and private law. It is quite interesting to note how

Mortati deals with the liberal recognition of a space of private autonomy that can be productive of bodies of law mainly through contracts between private subjects. In fact, by observing how he tackles the issues of private autonomy and social claims, it is possible to grasp why he stayed loyal to a *political* conception of the legal order throughout his career. Mortati considers discretion an essential component of political power and a building block of every state-based legal order.[59] As already mentioned, every legal order contains a finality made of fundamental aims. The political moment in the formation of the legal order is represented by the discretion exercised by political forces in selecting those aims. The liberal understanding of private autonomy as a source of law is incompatible with this view. In particular, Mortati cannot accept the idea (already introduced by Article 5 of the Declaration of the Rights of Man and of the Citizen of 1789) that everything that is not forbidden by law cannot be hindered, from which it is often assumed that in the sphere of what is not explicitly prohibited, every social or private action can be interpreted as allowed by law. The statement that any action taking place in a relation among human beings can be potentially relevant to the law is true only in the sense that those actions are promoting, or at least compatible with, the fundamental aims of the legal order. Consequently, Mortati rejects "those theories that posit determined extralegal norms as necessarily linked to any type of order and therefore endowed of their own validity, independently from any reference to positive law."[60]

It is time to take stock. There is no doubt that Mortati's legal theory is a version of legal institutionalism. The latter granted the Italian constitutional lawyer access to the understanding of the relation between society and the legal order. But Mortati did not propose a sociological theory of the legal order, let alone, normatively speaking, a pluralist one. His intention is to valorize the role of politics in the formation and development of society and law. For this reason, he gives a realist twist to his legal institutionalism. Only by looking at how political forces operate (that is, by choosing fundamental aims and pursuing them) is it possible to obtain a proper knowledge of the valid and effective legal order. Mortati does not conceive of the legal order without norms; yet, the political element of his theoretical construction introduces a teleological aspect to the most fundamental norms of the legal order. The teleology that animates these norms is not necessarily implicit in the form of the norm itself, but it is rather an imprinting of political power. A consequence of this conception is that no legal order can exist and flourish without organized political groups and without the effective exercise of political discretion. This is the realist component of his legal institutionalism, and, as we will see, it represents both an original insight and the source of some theoretical tensions that will be addressed in the next couple of sections.

THE CONSTITUTION IN THE MATERIAL SENSE

In order to account properly for the realist conception of institutionalism, it is necessary to introduce Mortati's most innovative contribution to legal studies: the *juristic* idea of the constitution in the material sense.[61] Possibly, the idea came about because Mortati needed to account for the ordering principle of each legal order, understood as the synthesis between social formation and legal order. Mortati was facing the problem of an activity, such as governing, whose normativity forced him to recognize the juridical nature of the substance lying under the formal legal order. In this sense, the material constitution was found to be that part of the legal order which would produce (and guarantee the solidity of) an ordering principle. Mortati formalizes this idea in 1940, that is, when the Fascist constitutional order is firmly established and formally already well developed.[62] Undeniably, sections of the monograph devoted to the material constitution are influenced by that context. However, the gist of the idea has proved to be heuristically so fertile that it transcends its context and still represents an essential analytical tool for understanding legal and constitutional reality. Mortati himself kept referring to the notion of the constitution in the material sense in the period following the end of the war (although sporadically) and gave it a twist that made it the basis for understanding the new type of constitutionalism spread across the Continent. In a nutshell: pluralism was to be mediated and managed through the material constitution. In the following subsections, the main tenets of the notion will be dissected:

the object, the subjects, and relation between the formal and the material constitution will be broached in the subsections below.

The Governing Function: Political Unity

The crisis that invested different European legal orders in between the two world wars had changed how the relation between society and the state legal order was being thematized. The crisis of the liberal state (as a legitimist state opposed to the absolutist state), and the diversification of European states (with, for example, the revolutionary change in Russia and the rise of fascism in Italy) had made it evident that the form and functions of the state would not necessarily overlap. In the liberal state the form of the constitutional order, drawn around the organization of powers, coincided with its function of preserving individual freedom for those who qualified as active citizens. The simple observation of the diversity of constitutional projects across the Continent pushed European public lawyers to address a new challenge: understanding the changes concerning the identity of the state legal order.

Due to path dependency and material circumstances, such a quest took up its own jargon within each constitutional tradition, but many of these faced the same issues of governing a deeply divided and disordered societal organization. One example is represented by the tensions created by the appearance of corporatist claims, which were pushing for a different involvement of the state (and a different methodology) in managing class-based social conflicts.[63] As known, this was usually coupled with the growing weakness of parliamentary politics, at least for its capacity of steering institutional politics toward a stabilizing and firm direction.[64] A common concern for public lawyers during the Italian Fascist regime was to locate the essence of the state and of its unity as well in the executive function. This was a legacy of Vittorio Emanuele Orlando's school of public law that was dominant before the advent of fascism. According to this approach, political acts were still deemed to be administrative acts with special political relevance. From the constitutional perspective, the mainstream school of public law would qualify political action as a branch of one of the state functions. Orlando, the doyen of public law scholarship in Italy, had come to the conclusion that governmental acts do not form a separate and distinct category.[65] As such, they were still qualified as administrative acts.[66] Government and administration would comprise the executive function within the classic tripartite separation of functions. In this way, in the absence of potentially disruptive social forces admitted to the political sphere, the question of the destabilizing effects of a strict separation of powers could be sidelined.[67]

As a general phenomenon, the executive function might have had its competences increased in the aftermath of World War I to cope with the new social challenges. Hence, a quantitative increase of executive power might have given the impression that the liberal state was undergoing a change of the balance among powers. Such a transformation would be assessed from the liberal perspective of the principle of the rule of law and the protection of civil rights. Yet, we should be careful in carving out the reasons standing behind the debate around an autonomous governing function. At this stage, a nonformalist (even if at times still positivist) stream of scholarship gained momentum on the background of a different explanation of the rise of governmental powers. In fact, it seems that the question of a new and distinct function emerged precisely out of the pressure for holding the political unity of legal orders together despite the emergence of new social and political actors. Once the form and functions of the state legal order were visibly disjointed, it became clear to public lawyers that political unity could not be obtained in virtue of the balance among powers or through an invisible hand. The political unity of the legal order was, and always had been, an effect of politics. At this stage, and still conceded that unity was an epistemic preliminary condition for sovereignty, it became impossible to ignore the nomic force of politics in the life of constitutional orders.

Mortati's background and aim were compatible with this new Weltanschauung. As for the background, Mortati's academic environment and intellectual points of reference were intensely engaged with the issue of the nature of governing. Both the Italian and the German debates were divided, but definitely animated by this question. Historically, his initial interest in the question of the nature of the governing activity might have been motivated by the sweeping reforms approved by the Fascist government from

1925 onward, which forced Italian lawyers to face two key constitutional questions: whether governing had become the supreme and autonomous function of the state and whether the advent of the Fascist regime amounted to a constitutional transformation.

The problem that the theorization of an autonomous governing function was supposed to tackle was the constitutional issue of political unity. The urgency of the latter was dictated by the question of managing social pluralism. Mortati's core intention was indeed to separate the function of governing from the executive power with a view to make the former into the *Ur-Funktion* of the modern state. In fact, this is the core concern behind his first book (*L'ordinamento del governo*), where he sketches out the peculiar and autonomous nature of the governing function.[68] The definition of governing action presents clear political traits:

> absolute discretion, direct derivation from constitutional statute [*legge costituzionale*], the aim of realizing in an immediate way the unity of state action; its explicating mode through impulses and control over the other constitutional organs; an expansive tendency that brings it to reach state action when the latter seems to be relevant for the political direction.[69]

It is possible here to see why Mortati eventually found legal institutionalism fitting for his intellectual enterprise. Conceiving governing as an autonomous function entails thinking that the legal order and society shape each other in terms that cannot ignore political action. And the required extent of this political action varies according to the fundamental political aims that governing is called to realize. For this reason, the constitutional crisis of the modern state engendered by the pluralization of social actors and claims should be addressed politically, which basically means that unity can be secured (though not exclusively) by political action. But Mortati takes the question beyond historical circumstances. While the bulk of his first monograph focuses mostly on the legal order of the Fascist regime,[70] he still takes time to unpack the peculiar nature of the governing function in historical and theoretical terms. Unlike some of his institutionalist predecessors (and in particular, unlike Romano), he examines the governing function on a juridical terrain (meaning: governing is also legally fruitful because productive of unity in a substantial sense) and makes it an autonomous function of the state.

Mortati is not the first author to formalize the notion of an autonomous governing function. A similar idea can already be found in other works, albeit in a rather underdeveloped form. A clear point of reference can be identified in an early work by Smend[71] (which Mortati knew very well) and, later, by his mentor Sergio Panunzio (an extremely influential Fascist public lawyer).[72] In fact, as early as 1923, Smend clearly referred to an autonomous and distinct governing function.[73] Government and public administration were complementary but distinguishable functions that are not "occupied" by the legislative and the jurisdictional functions: more specifically, the governing function would be related to the constitutional role of political activity, that is, the moment where the state qualifies its identity. Five years later, Smend made the idea of an autonomous and distinct governing function even more explicit when in his *Constitution and Constitutional Law* noted that what is missing in the classic theory of separation of powers is the "conclusive moment," which can be defined government (*Regierung*) or directive power (*furstliche Gewalt*). Smend defined governing as the internal and external activity of the state, functional to the determination of the state's identity.[74] Smend's contribution was seminal because it linked the governing function to the integrative property of the constitutional order. The unity enhanced by governing is not only political, but it operates across society with ordering force.

In the Italian context, Panunzio formulated the idea of a fourth function of the state directly connected with the organization of society. This is quite interesting because Panunzio drew a clear connection between the fourth function of the state and the governing of society itself (and not just of the formal powers of the state). In particular, Panunzio stated that the state ought to address social relations between capital and labor by building up an autonomous function to be called the "corporatist function."[75] Even Antonio Gramsci, in his *Prison Notebooks*, credited Panunzio for the "invention" of this new function by interpreting his theory of the corporatist state as the first theorization of an autonomous fourth function and noted that the question had emerged because of the weakening of parliamentary politics under the Fascist regime.[76]

While Smend and Panunzio made important exploratory contributions to the theory of the governing function, Mortati was the author who produced the systematic and original doctrine, describing it as an *essential*, *autonomous*, *supreme*, and *distinct* juridical function of every type of state legal order. It is through the exercise of this function that political power is embedded into the constitutional structure. Mortati tried to build the legal order of the state on this function, and this is why he defined it as essential. In his view, the governing function is a nonfungible component of political unity. Left to the simple separation of the classic functions, a legal order might just be torn apart, and this for a predictable reason: a certain degree of social homogeneity is necessary as a basis for a working state legal order, but it is not available in nature. Primordial or elemental forms of homogeneity can be generated by social normativity, but in order to expand and drive societal change, homogeneity has to be produced artificially (for Mortati this means *politically*). In this sense, the governing function necessitates an underlying *nomic force*, which can be provided (at least in Mortati's view) only by organized political actors.

The other three characters of the governing function are no less important. Obviously, the autonomy of the governing function has to be understood not in relation with societal development because, as already stated, the governing function is a political activity whose aim is to shape important social relations. The autonomy operates vis-à-vis the other functions: government can influence the other classic functions, but the opposite cannot be the case. In a nutshell: the autonomy of the governing function postulates the heteronomy of the other traditional state functions. Given this type of autonomy, it is necessary to assume the primacy of governing over the other functions as well. Mortati thought that if the governing function were just another function among many, then it would not be capable of performing its peculiar task.[77] Finally, the governing function ought to be distinct from the other in its form and manifestations; otherwise, given the directing impulse inherent to its essence, it would not be cognizable and outside of juristic knowledge. As we will see, this means that, despite its deeply political nature, the governing function can be located in one organ and assume a juridical form, so that its primacy is not expressed in an arbitrary way, but in typified and constant forms. Juridical science is indeed invited by Mortati to identify and systematize these forms.[78]

For the reasons just stated, in the first part of his career, Mortati linked his research on the governing function to the quest for the *suprema potestas* within a legal order. He found that the governing function (and in particular the imprint given on society by organized and institutionalized politics) had to find an institutional expression—a seat—in one organ (or in a unitary complex of organs). Here, Mortati introduced a challenging but controversial relation between function and organ. It is as if the governing function had to irradiate from an identifiable central organ to the other functions and, with a cascade effect, throughout society. In fact, the association of the governing function to an institutional organ enables two things: a clearest communication to the rest of society of the main aims of government and the certainty of translating the principles behind the governing impulses into juridical norms. During the Fascist regime, for example, Mortati was convinced that "in Italy, the Head of Government, dux of fascism, and the Great Council, an organ at the same time of the party and the state . . . have acquired the character of being supreme."[79] As known, whether Mortati's analysis was correct is debatable because other constitutional lawyers supported the idea that only the head of government was the supreme organ. But, for the purposes of our analysis, it is important to highlight two aspects of Mortati's interpretation. First, institutional form still matters, as his quest for the supreme organ shows. It is only by attributing the function to a specific organ (or set of organs) that governing as a function can become effective and registered by juristic knowledge. The second key insight is to be seen in the intimate relation established between the organs deemed to be supreme in the Fascist regime and the political party. The fact that the Great Council of Fascism is an organ, at the same time, of the party and the state proves the necessity of a permanent bridge between society and government to make the governing function effective.

The party makes sure that an internal relation is established between these two poles as it inhabits both spheres.[80]

The Object of the Governing Function: Fundamental Political Aims

The definition of the four main characteristics of the governing function is necessary but not sufficient for a full understanding of the process behind the creation of political unity. Considering its teleological nature, an analysis of the governing function without mentioning its object (its telos) would be largely incomplete.

The object of the governing function is political finality. The governing function served the purpose of introducing and, in a loose sense, juridifying political action within the state legal order. Basically, the centrifugal forces of society can be governed only by a coherent and juridified political action. As already noted, this is the distinctive blend of Mortati's institutionalism: only the introjection of politics into the legal order as its main source enables the project of governing society or, at least, fundamental parts of it. On the most important level, the governing function is instantiated by the choice and implementation of one or more fundamental aims. Governing is a function with teleological pretension: there is always a telos (whose content can vary from order to order) that constitutes the finality of governing and that serves, in the long term, as the glue for holding the political unity of the legal order together. This finality sets up the field for political action of constitutional relevance by objectifying values and providing also the boundaries of the possible language games playable within it.[81] In order to work as a condensing factor for the dominant social forces, the fundamental aim has to be

> so comprehensive as to allow the evaluation of different interests gathered around the state in a unitary way and so rigid to be able to act as point of reference even through the possible oscillations of power relations that occur over time, but at the same time, so elastic to allow certain required adaptations necessary for the development of collective life.[82]

Another important aspect of the fundamental aim to consider is its normative character. The material constitution has a juridical nature, and this character is reflected in the status associated to the fundamental political aim. While the choice of the fundamental aim is the most intensely political action within a legal order, its apprehension is always already juridical. In fact, Mortati's material understanding of the constitution should not be confused with a purely political approach.[83] The selection of fundamental political aims is a political act, but it has to be endowed, as a necessary condition for its success, with nomic force.

By describing the governing function as a crucial moment of societal formation, Mortati made another essential contribution to the understanding of modern states' legal orders. Governing qua a state function does not entail only the unity of the political and the legal systems. Governing requires the capacity of forming and pursuing certain finalities. Of course, the aims pursued by a polity cannot have been fully obtained at the moment of adopting them, hence they remain in an important sense external to the action of governing. The governing function is key in defining the relation between society and legal order because, through governing, political subjects exercise a shaping pressure over social groups and steer their development in the future.

Finally, the choice and pursuit of fundamental aims is also critical for the definition of the constitutional identity of the legal order. What is distinctive of a particular legal order is prominently, but not exclusively, its fundamental aims and the undergirding social organization whose purpose is to realize them. The fundamental political aims may recall Smend's "supreme political values" and the role they play in his theory of the constitution as integration.[84] While it is likely that Smend partially inspired Mortati, a key difference sheds light on the hiatus between the constitution as integration and the material constitution. Smend's supreme political values are inscribed in social consciousness. Accordingly, they can mutate as long as society does. In this way, the constitution as integration is closer to the idea of a living organism whose positive law is reinterpreted according to the changes in the undergirding social perception. Unlike Smend's supreme values, the fundamental aims are of political origins and, actually, their selection is probably the most important political action in the sense of being the least constrained by the legal order. In fact, Mortati introduces, unfortunately without further developing it, a double layer of political action:

> From what we have said one can infer that it is necessary to distinguish politics as a critical activity, pushing for a change in the ideology of the regime and the instauration of a new one, from the politics that consists in the search for the necessary means for realizing the aims typical of the valid constitution.[85]

Hence, Mortati envisages two kinds of politics: one is an instrumental activity, while the other is an activity setting the agenda for the constitutional project. This distinction resonates with Italian constitutional doctrine, whereby political choices of the government have been traditionally indicated with the expression "political direction" (*indirizzo politico*).[86] In fact, it is more appropriate to draw a distinction between the political direction imprinted upon a constitutional project (at times referred to as "constitutional political direction" [*indirizzo politico costituzionale*]) by selecting the fundamental aims and the ordinary policy-making power (or general policy, at times defined as "ordinary political direction" [*indirizzo politico ordinario*]), mostly concerned with the achievement of the main aims of the government of the day.[87]

This distinction, which is not fully developed in Mortati's work, also hints at specific relations between law and politics according to the kind of political action involved in them. In the latter case (ordinary politics), Mortati notes that "politics does not identify with law, but it appears in the position of means as well, both dedicated to the realization of the same aim."[88] Law and politics in the ordinary sense do not run through separate channels, as they are imbricated in the same order because the selection of the appropriate means and sub-aims still requires what Mortati defines as "law in movement." Accordingly, the judgment on the adequacy of norms and directives to be adopted for attaining the fundamental aims always admit of a certain margin of maneuver and adaptation to the state of affairs.

It is, however, necessary to add a clarification here. The political trajectory is a substantial function of the material constitution because it can be defined only by making reference to its content and, therefore, unlike the other standard functions of the modern state, it does not have a typical and unique form that makes possible to identify it. In other words, the legislative function can be exercised by different organs (or a set of organs), but its form is not subject to many variations; the same applies, for example, to the jurisdictional function. It can be exercised by nonjudicial bodies (at times, for specific crimes, parliamentary bodies are attributed this task), but it is usually communicated in the form of decisions upon concrete applications of general norms. Being conceptualized by Mortati as a function, governing can be exercised by different organs, but it should take up a specific form. Could it be that its defining trait is exhausted by the choice of fundamental aims? According to Mortati, what defines the type of state and its identity is not the supreme organ, or the organs in charge of the governing function, but the nature of the fundamental aims that the governing function is called upon to realize:

> Each individual state arises on the basis of assumptions that are the purpose and raison d'être of its founding and interpenetrate with its structure, arranged in a way to implement that foundation. It derives this purpose from sociological factors . . . but once it has emerged it makes it its own in the way we have seen, so that it then ceases to be a de facto prerequisite, to become the true validity condition for acting.[89]

This goes to the core of the notion of the material constitution because it invites scholars to look at the substance of the fundamental aims for grasping the constitutional identity of the state. But it is not immediately clear why, according to Mortati, governing should be conceived as an autonomous function given that it consists in choosing and realizing political aims. One might suspect that the reason is to be found in the alleged introjection of the fundamental aims into the normative system. At times, it seems that without the autonomy of governing (and its separateness from the other functions) there would not be proper authority and, accordingly, it would not be possible to make the fundamental political aims easily cognizable by legal knowledge. It is as if there were an imperativist remainder in the description of the notion of governing: Fundamental political aims can become an object of knowledge only if they are communicated as commands by a distinct organ.

It should be noted that it is not always clear what the constitutional effects of the fundamental political aims in Mortati's thought are. Such ambiguity is probably immanent to the idea itself. How concrete can the specification of these aims be? Can the determination of the content of these fundamental aims be separated from the ordinary policy-making function? Part of the answer can be found in *The Constitution in the Material Sense*, where the determination of the political trajectory is codified in purposive or teleological norms (*norme di scopo*). In this sense, these norms operate as *the basic norm of the material constitution*; this is not in the formalist sense of distribution of competences, but as a norm or principle with certain contents and not others, capable of leaving an imprinting upon the rest of the legal order. "Political law" (*diritto politico*) is what Mortati calls the introjection of the general political aim of the state into the legal order.[90]

This peculiar construction of the fundamental norm of the state legal order has enormous consequences for the jurist and for juridical sciences. First of all, the direct translation of the choice of fundamental aims into a normative form makes it impossible to reduce the study of the constitutional order to a sociological enterprise. While analytically distinct, the governing function and the choice of fundamental political aims are incorporated into the normative order because they take the form of teleological norms: "We can conclude that the political aim, when incorporated in a state institution, not only does not belong to a prejuridical condition, but by shaping the essence of the constitution itself become the primary source of state law."[91] Mortati's position on the relation between the fundamental aim and the legal order is resolutely nonpositivist. He takes time to prove that if a legal order is endowed with nomic force, then the aims animating it are juridical from the very beginning and carry this character throughout the life of the legal order itself. Sometimes, these aims are translated into formal norms, but sometimes they are not. The jurist can always infer them by observing the whole legal order and, as we will see in the following section, the intentions of the bearers of the material constitution.

The Subjects of the Material Constitution: The Role of the Political Party

In the previous two sections we illustrated how the production of homogeneity is driven by the convergence of certain political forces around common fundamental objectives. However, Mortati's realist methodology imposes an addition of concrete analysis. Mentioning generic social or political forces is not enough. For this reason, at the core of the formation of the material constitution one can find two analytically distinct processes. Both hark back to the internal relation between societal formation and constitutional ordering. A constitutional order is not given or applied to an already formed political community. Moreover, in terms of legal analysis, it is too vague to refer to the undergirding society as an undifferentiated whole.

It is worth noting that without a process of differentiation, a group or a society cannot have nomic force, partly because it would not be capable of acting. The recognition of this conceptual and factual necessity is part and parcel of Mortati's effort to overcome (as we saw in the previous section) the two dominant traditions within Italian and German scholarship. Neither the subsumption of the constitution under the sovereignty of the state as person nor the reference to the abstract ideas of nation or people are an appropriate starting point for legal analysis. It is possible to organize society in a way that enables collective action on its behalf or name only through processes of political representation. Recognizing this aspect of the formation of public powers is a precondition for an accurate constitutional analysis.

Critically, according to Mortati, the driving differentiation for every constitutional order is the one between command and obedience. Each constitutional order is animated by the formation and reformation of differentiating processes and especially of the individuation of the ruling class.[92]

The governing function is premised upon the division between those who are in the position to command and those who are supposed to comply. As recently remarked by Martin Loughlin, "the business of governing invariably requires the drawing of a distinction that has become fundamental to the activity: the division between rulers and ruled, between a governing authority and its subjects."[93] This is such a foundational distinction for the material constitution that at the end of his career, confronting once again with Schmitt's work, Mortati will make clear that the relationship of obedience is more basic and foundational than the dyad friend/enemy. More specifically, the antagonism between friend and enemy is but a specification of the more general principle of obedience, and it is instantiated in those cases where obedience is firmly contested.[94] The political party plays an obvious role during the process of differentiation because it acts as the vector through which differentiation in society takes up an institutional form and imbues the formation of the constitutional order.[95] With an effective formula, it has been noted that "the political party . . . is nothing but *an instrument of construction of the state through the differentiation of society*."[96]

The principle of specification implies the identification of the social and political forces whose dominance constitutes a condition for the exercise of the governing function. It goes without saying that this idea is heavily indebted to the Italian tradition of political philosophy and science, and in particular to the works of the Italian elitists and, indirectly, even to the work of Gramsci.[97] Mortati does not address the further question of the interaction between differentiation in the political and in the social spheres. However, it seems safe to assume that this principle is proper, not only to the political system, but to the organization of society as well, as it is mostly visible in the modern phenomenon of division of labor.[98]

In modern constitutions, differentiation and specification are usually brought about by specific agents (not necessarily with legal personality), but the mediating role is exclusively attributed to political parties. What Mortati has in mind is a specific conception of the political party:

> It [the party] is here understood in a more specific conception as that association—endowed with a general view encompassing the life of

> the state in all its aspects—that tries to translate the general view into concrete state action, with the exclusion of the conflicting conceptions. . . . Political parties are pushed to shape into an organization that, despite the personal autonomy of their chiefs, put as the predominant element a general political idea . . . capable not only to hold together the group that assumes it, but also to represent a center of attraction for new adherents and the conquest of state power.[99]

This is the distinctive trait of the modern political party. Unlike premodern parties, the modern political party is characterized by an ideology and works as a factor of unification for the whole political system.[100]

It cannot be denied that the reconstruction of the role of political parties in *The Constitution in the Material Sense* is compatible with the political regime of the Fascist Party. Actually, at times, his author seems to postulate that the material constitution requires a monoparty system: "The party, in the specific sense, is the active element of the original institution, a necessary one for it to assume a political form, and for this reason it can't be but unique, as unique is the principle of any political form."[101] Moreover, the basis for understanding the relation among the state, the party, and the constitutional order is originally conceived during the 1930s, at the zenith of the Fascist regime, and it will provide the theoretical background for the works of the more mature period.

Despite all this, it is fair to note that his constitutional doctrine cannot be reduced to an endorsement of the Fascist regime for two reasons. In the context of the debate between the traditionalist public lawyers and the constitutionalists of the new regime, Mortati recognized the novelty of the regime but did not fully accept the latter's thesis. The public lawyers of the regimes pleaded that the governing function of the state had been basically "conquered" by an external element, that is, the Fascist Party. For the apologists of the Fascist regime, the party had taken over the state and the latter had been reduced to a simple tool in the hands of the revolutionary party. Mortati conceived the party as a state organ, which for him meant subsuming the party under the state. On one hand, he recognized that in order to understand the modern state and its material constitution, the public lawyer ought to take into account the governing function and the role of the party. On the other hand, he believed it necessary to address these new issues still in terms of functions and organs to be ultimately referred to the exclusive domain of the sovereign state.[102]

The second reason is to be found in the way Mortati overhauled the doctrine of the material constitution for the new constitutionalism of post–World War II. He replaced the monoparty system for a political system comprising several and different parties. Already in the essay on the constituent assembly (1945),[103] he had swapped the single party for a multiparty system. The difference with the previous regime is that in the age of fascism all interests and finalities were processed by the same or within the same party. In the incipient republican regime, the process of differentiation and the selection of fundamental aims was going to be left to an array of different (and at times remarkably diverse) political parties. But the components of this group could still coalesce around some fundamental political aims through a *political compromise*.

Such a solution might prove to be more vulnerable to internal contradictions and conflicts,[104] but it still entails the exclusion of a series of aims pursued by other collective subjects and the rise of the specific political difference between those who rule and those who are ruled. In other words, Mortati's main focus is on the political system and its capacity to realize and stabilize the form of political unity by selecting fundamental aims. Of course, the constitutional lawyer still needs to pay due attention to the details of the political system, in particular because the qualification of an issue as constitutional is basically in the hands of the dominant forces.[105] But it is important to note that the possibility condition of the material constitution is the presence of a collective subject (a bearer) capable of realizing (or at least to try to accomplish) some fundamental political aims. In light of these remarks it is opportune to clarify that the red thread that spans across Mortati's works is the idea that political differentiation has to be coupled with some form of unity among those who rule. Monoparty and multiparty systems are both compatible with the formation of the material constitution as long as they can ensure they are capable of pursuing common aims. As Mortati would make clear in the last years of his academic career, even in presence of a multiparty system, the potential antagonistic groups have to be excluded or marginalized because forms of political antagonism are disruptive of the material constitution:

> The word *party* has not been used to indicate the specific groups in conflict among them, but the ensemble of the political forces that are homogeneous and around which the state is organized. Bearing in mind this meaning, the necessity of the unicity of the party, in which the ruling class is included, has been confirmed.[106]

From an external perspective (that is, from the outside of the political system), what counts for the material constitution is the convergence of the ruling class[107] around a political system. Whether internally (i.e., from inside the political system) further differentiation is a reality or not, this does not affect the unity of the political system.

A further point deserves to be discussed in relation to the nature of the agreement among the political forces bearing the material constitution. Given that this agreement bestows normative force upon the material constitution, its understanding is fundamental for the definition of the correlated legal theory. It is possible, in principle, to interpret what Mortati writes during the period of the constituent assembly (1945–1947) in a less imperativist fashion. As a way to illustrate the new role that the parties of the anti-Fascist resistance had taken up, Mortati placed emphasis on the idea of an equilibrium (or a truce) among different and often hostile political forces. Of course, the necessity of political homogeneity is still present, but in post–World War II this homogeneity is no longer a given. Mortati is committed to the idea that the definition of the form of the state is always dependent on a series of agreements on concrete aspects (interests, principles, etc.). Therefore, the material constitution is still intimately related to the political and social reality, but in the context of a plurality of sometimes dramatically different parties.

It is possible to read into this dynamic the formation of a new ground for the constituent phase (and its relative strength), which is not to be found in sheer force any longer, but in a convention.[108] In fact, it is possible to find some textual basis in support of this interpretation. While reflecting on the role of the constituent assembly, Mortati draws a clear line between the social contract approach to constituent assemblies and the idea that the constituent agreement among a plurality of different political forces is not an expression of the logic of the social contract.[109]

The conventionalist interpretation might explain the logic behind the agreement in the constituent assembly, that is, in a context where the main parties were radically opposed one to each other. Philosophically, conventionalism has always proved an appealing approach for those who wish to understand why agents decide to converge on certain stated interests and principles, even though their internal motives might be quite different. Conventionalism represents an alternative to the standard social contract story on the origin of the political community and the state.[110] As an approach to the creation of the legal order, conventionalism is less demanding than contractualism because it does not require explicit agreement on all aspects of the original setting. Following the contemporary leading legal conventionalist theorist, Andrei Marmor, a legal convention can be defined by two tenets: (1) it could have taken another form, that is, it could have been constituted by a different rule,[111] and (2) it underdetermines the relation between reasons and law, securing a space for the autonomy of law.[112]

A conventionalist reading of the material constitution might make for an interesting amendment to Mortati's realist approach. The key point of this interpretation is that the convention among parties (or, more generally, among the involved actors), and *not* the content of the convention, would provide the source of the constitutional obligation. This entails that the ground of the constitutional obligation would be found in the way conventions address basic human needs.[113] In this way, other reinterpretations of important aspects of Mortati's doctrine of the material constitution would become available. For example, a conventionalist reinterpretation would give a different meaning to political compromises and it would justify the ambiguity of the language of certain constitutional clauses. The function of the normative/formal constitution would also change because it would acquire an autonomous status before the political subjects. In classic conventionalist fashion, the disagreements among political forces would find not a solution, but a point of convergence that remains (partially) independent from their interests. Such an approach would also provide a justification for the so-called "clausole dilatorie" ("postponing clauses"), that is, those clauses which postpone the resolution of a concrete conflict among political forces:

> Historical experience shows, at times, that the possibility of the creation and the guarantees of longevity for many constitutions depend precisely on those decisions that leave unaddressed the regulation of issues around which is not possible to reach an agreement, or, to adopt an inaccurate formula, which can be interpreted differently. This is done with the intention to leave to the subsequent changes of the political forces and the evolution of political ideas the task of defining what remained vague in the first place, or to affirm one of the possible meanings that can be given to the same norm.[114]

If a conventionalist interpretation were to be accepted, then the material constitution might be thought cunningly as a conventional rule of recognition around which the main political forces can converge. In this way, the imperativist tenet of Mortati's legal theory would be dropped or, at least, limited, and the material constitution would be made more attuned to a liberal interpretation of the political pluralism emerging out of World War II.

However, if one had to look at the coherence of Mortati's trajectory, it would appear that there is more continuity than discontinuity with *The Constitution in the Material Sense* and the previous works. Crucially, the type of belief postulated as necessary for the activation of constituent power is not a conviction entirely based on the intrinsic goodness of the convention itself. As happens in many of its instantiations, the conventionalist approach underestimates the case when participation in a convention is coerced (not necessarily by force, but sometimes by circumstances or by the environment).[115] It is worth further reflecting on the role played by conviction in Mortati's scheme. He discriminates between voluntary and necessary associations and attaches different types of conviction to them. For voluntary associations, conviction is generated by the link between adhesion to an aim or finality and the acts undertaken to achieve it. One performs certain acts because they are instrumental to the pursuit of specific goals. In necessary associations (such as the state, that is, associations whose membership is not voluntary), conviction is not necessarily related to the link between means and ends, because the ends might be imposed through the processes of differentiation and specification within the association. Rather, conviction can be one's awareness of the consequences deriving from one's complying or not with the command of the authority.[116] Here we see again at work a prudential and realist assessment of the formation of necessary associations. Mortati assumes that, in accordance with processes of differentiation and specification, a number of associates (usually quite conspicuous, if the association has to be stable and lasting) should purposefully contribute to the achievement of the same social aims. Yet many others will perceive the same aims as an external imposition, while their obedience to the legal norms of the association will be dictated by a series of considerations that are more utilitarian or strategic in nature.

Other reflections, written around the same time, are available in support of a nonconventionalist interpretation of the material constitution. In the essay written on the constituent assembly, Mortati notes that "each constitution is nothing else than the formal expression of a determined relation of force, of an equilibrium achieved by active political groups, and it represents only an instrument for the stabilization of the equilibrium itself through a constellation of legal institutions."[117] In another important writing introducing the Italian translation of the constitution of the Weimar Republic, Mortati stated unambiguously the link between societal differentiation and the material constitution. His diagnosis of the failure of the Weimar constitution (and of the Spanish constitution of 1931) is adamant and adopts tones that are not compatible with a conventionalist reading. Mortati thought that the Weimar constitution contained an essential contradiction between its constitutional forms and the underlying reality of social life. When social and political homogeneity was threatened by the universal suffrage, the institutional center of political life, i.e., parliament, became unable to perform its function of a forum for solid compromise. In other words, parliament fell prey of a plurality of corporative interests that made the constitution unstable. Mortati suggests that on a concrete level, the failure of Weimar was due to two factors. First, the nonelimination (tolerance) of those interests which are in radical antithesis with others. Second, the absence of new constitutional forms that would have made sure that the new social reality could be taken properly into account and would have concurred in finding a new balance among forces (which is, in short, a failure in integration).[118] The contradiction is the following one:

> If, on one hand, planning of the economy is attributed to the state and new social rights are conferred to individuals as a way to obtain substantial equality . . . and, on the other hand, the substance of the traditional liberal state framework is maintained by sticking to an interpretation of the individual sphere of freedom as a negative *status*, a contradiction then emerges, one that cannot but have an impact on the solidity and longevity of the constitution.[119]

Finally, in the essay on the concept of the constitution, Mortati reminds us that "political forces, in giving birth to a formal constitution, tend to bestow on it the specific function of consolidating and guaranteeing more firmly their dominium."[120] From these remarks, we can deduce that a conventionalist reading of Mortati's constitutional thought does not hold. This is the case for two reasons. First, it does overemphasize the autonomy of the formal legal and constitutional rules vis-à-vis the undergirding societal organization. After all, according to Mortati, it is only by looking at the aims of the constitutional order that we can grasp its specific nature. Second, the conventionalist reading might be made compatible with the political character of the distinction rulers/ruled only at a very high price. If the adherence to or compliance with the legal order is seen only as an arbitrary convention, then the peculiar political dimension of the material constitution is lost.

Popular Sovereignty and Constituent Power

The role of the political system is so central to Mortati's construction that he is compelled to come up with a rather original conception of two classic doctrines of modern law: the principle of popular sovereignty (which is also recognized by Art. 1 of the Italian constitution) and the notion of constituent power. Both notions are central for understanding how Mortati deals with the question of social and political pluralism.

As already noted, Mortati refused to reify all the abstractions that are common in legal and constitutional theory, such as the people, the community, or the nation. Even when writing about the principle of popular sovereignty in the Italian constitution, he made it clear that the reference to the people could only be understood in symbolic or political terms, but had no juridical status. Only in virtue of the action undertaken by certain collective subjects (like political parties or trade unions) it is possible to vindicate the ideal of the principle of popular sovereignty. For example, in the case of the Italian republic, he thought that it could have been only a "republic of political parties."[121] Differentiation is always already operative within the principle of sovereignty, which is therefore conceived as the opposite of a decision taken in the middle of a chaotic context.

Constituent power is conceived in juristic terms as well. Mortati engages with the concept both during the Fascist regime and the republican phase. In both cases, it is possible to detect a red thread that spans across these periods. Parties (and organized groups) still play a major role. The dominant positivist view of constituent power portrays it as a set of facts taking place in a prejuridical condition.[122] In the classic version of the positivist approach, the constituent moment belongs to the realm of facts and conveys its impulses to the normative order of constituted powers.[123] Once these impulses have passed from one realm to the other, the constituent retreats into a state of latency or even disappears completely. Such a reconstruction of constituent power either requires the reification of the collective subject (nation, people), in which case there is a lack of differentiation and specification, or, in alternative, constituent power is seen as the equivalent of living law, that is, as a jurisgenetic adaptation of the legal order to social change, in which case the constituent element and its realist properties slip outside the picture once again.

Coherently with his own legal theory, Mortati's view cannot adhere to this portrayal of constituent power. His realist institutionalism pushes him to recognize nomic power intrinsic to the constituent force. In other words, the materiality of social organization is already producing ordering effects as constituent force. From an institutionalist perspective, this is not really surprising. Antonio Negri has interpreted Mortati's conception of constituent power as another expression of an "integrative" form of legal institutionalism, more or less along the same lines of Smend's integration theory.[124] Negri is onto something here, in particular when he blames lawyers like Mortati for identifying constituent power with sovereign power. In fact, in Mortati's words, "constituent power is the term that designates the active side of the process of differentiation, which derives from the political idea posited as the center of unification of behaviors and of the authoritative apparatus in charge of its protection." Even more clearly, we are told that "constituent power, . . . when it obtains the diffuse conviction that it is capable of realizing the order for which it is the bearer, can then be identified with the state, because it becomes the state itself, that is, a sovereign juridical organization."[125] As these quotes show, the passage from constituent into constituted power comes about without any real discontinuity. The key point is that a constituent force is necessarily already an organized force, hence it contains important elements of constituted (or ordered) power.

There is a heavy Hegelian moment in the way Mortati imagines constituent power. The constituent realizes itself only through its negation, that is, only the moment it becomes constituted.[126] Mortati defines this coupling of constituent and constituted as the paradigmatic "normative fact."[127] Constituent power is a normative fact because its factual existence contains in itself a norm (or a principle, understood as a normative principle) that unfolds while the organized constituent force shapes a new order. A normative fact is "a fact which has in itself its own law and the guarantees of its persistence in the future."[128] Strictly speaking, in Mortati's thought constituent power is that force which can pose new fundamental aims for the state constitutional order. In this strict version, constituent power manifests itself as ordering the initial formation of a state constitutional order, setting up the main aims of that particular form of the state.

According to this perspective, the formation of the state is always a juridical phenomenon. Constituent power coincides with the transformation or utter re-creation of a state if it comes with a process of differentiation that introduces a structure of authority. According to Mortati, the mere intention of a group or an association does not suffice to instantiate constituent power.[129] The moment of negativity is essential for the recognition of constituent power. When a force is constituent it will have to give up to part of its constituent quality in order to exercise its ordering activity.[130] Here, the levels of the ordering and the ordered cannot be fully separated. In this way, a potential objection is avoided. One might note that it is not possible to have a subject who seriously has the will to commit to rules or norms that it has posited. The intuition behind this objection is the following one: in order to follow a command or a rule, a will ought to be different from the one that posited the norm or the rule. But this is precisely Mortati's point on constituent power. By being a normative fact, the constituent is always intertwined, at a certain level, with elements of constituted power. As a consequence, it is not acceptable, for Mortati, to conceive constituent power as an irrational force or a moment of pure rupture precisely because it carries with it ordering qualities emanating from its ordered nature.

Finally, a key question that is necessary to address at this point is the role of the party. Is it essential or is it possible to have a material constitution without political parties? The question is heavily loaded because according to the answer it is possible to assess the relevance of Mortati's theory for the contemporary intellectual landscape. Mortati has always deemed the political system, either a one-party system or a multiparty system, as an essential feature of the material constitution of the modern state. Nonetheless, in his more mature writings, he conceded that other actors from society were becoming as important as political parties. In the essay on the concept of the constitution, the political party is substituted by the wider notion of the "ruling class." This interpretation seems to be confirmed in his last publication, where the principle of differentiation (with which comes a form of domination like the distinction between rulers and ruled) is still deemed to be the essential condition for the formation of the material constitution.[131] To sum up: the elements that are truly indispensable for the constitution in the material sense are the principles of differentiation and specification, a series of fundamental political aims and collective subjects whose ordering capacities are robust enough to fulfil these principles. In modern times, the political party is the organization that has mostly (and often exclusively) monopolized the process of differentiation and effectively ensured the governing function.

CONCLUDING REMARKS

Mortati's realist institutionalism provides the background for understanding and addressing the issue of social and legal pluralism in a distinctive, but not authentically pluralist, way. As we argued so far, despite its formation and development during the age of Fascist Italy, such a conception of the legal order became one of the most powerful and accurate formulations of constitutionalism post–World War II. Mortati was able to bring together normative and factual elements through the combination of political realism and legal institutionalism. This is how he tried to tackle the issue of the potential dissolution of the legal order caused by the proliferation of groups and claims that was putting contemporary societies under pressure. By committing to the idea of political unity and using the expansive potential of the normative principles enshrined in the material constitution, he tried to set up a theoretical framework that could, at the same time, save the main tenets of classic constitutional law and cope with the challenges posed by the incipient social forces animated (in casual order) by labor, gender, sex, culture, and religion. As we have seen, what emerged out of the coupling between political realism and legal institutionalism was a peculiar blend that established the supremacy of the constitutional order, and whose core, the material constitution, would produce fundamental political aims whose normative strength would serve as an internal limit for its political bearers.

Yet, despite the reference to the values of the legal order, a residue of relativism surfaces in Mortati's constitutional thought. In particular, his political realism seems to suffer from a form of "occasionalism" and an underestimation of the social normativity of groups. In his account, indeed, the dominant political forces are often portrayed as becoming hegemonic in virtue of their sheer force and strength (that is, as if they would become hegemonic in virtue of their will to power). It is surprising that despite the emphasis on the processes of representation, differentiation, and specification, Mortati did not develop a proper account of the link between societal formation and political hegemony. In other words, the formation of the material constitution is at times represented as an outcome of the political autonomy of the political party or, in cases of political pluralism, the political system as a whole. This reconstruction ignores the social factors that still have a horizontal impact on societal formation and that are also part and parcel of the construction of political forms of representation. At times, Mortati's description of constitutional change is more indebted to the idea of the autonomy of the political rather than to a material understanding of the legal order.[132] Even though it should be stressed that this is not always the case, the materiality of the legal order is at times presented simply as the molding of political forces around political aims, in a process that seems bootstrapped out of nothing.[133]

In the end, because of what has been just highlighted, pluralism itself is tamed and twisted in support of the state constitutional order. In fact, Mortati did recognize the striated structure of society but did conceive it as functional to the construction of political unity. Hence, he admitted of three levels of societal organization: the person, the intermediate social groups, and the state.[134] Mortati undertook the issue of social pluralism by focusing the idea of the person (as opposed to the individual) and its undergirding social philosophy:

> In order to understand the issues raised by the organization of society in each of the forms it assumes and the phases it is divided into, it is necessary to move from the consideration of the nature of man, susceptible to directing her freedom of determination or in the sense of ordering her own behavior according to a standard of rationality and an ideal of morality; or, instead, remaining exposed to the anarchy of instincts that lead to disobeying an order even if it is seen to be necessary for the achievement of ends indicated by reason.[135]

This version of the person owes much to a simplistic anthropology: the person is a moral agent, but it is also exposed to the possibility of acting for the wrong reasons. What is most relevant for the purposes of this chapter is Mortati's rejection of the anonymous person belonging to the mass, to the point that he is convinced that

> the main problem of modern democracy is to arrange in an ever more perfect way the amorphous masses into differentiated organisms according to the various types of social interests and to make emerge in them the great possible number of individuals making them always more consciously active for the state.[136]

A person, under this conception, has to be part of intermediate concrete bodies that support her flourishing. Crucially, these intermediate associations are not always the offspring of spontaneous social normativity or, even, of the satisfaction of natural needs and impulses. In the end, intermediate bodies are conceived as utterly functional to the creation and development of the constitutional order's political unity. In this way, intermediate associations integrate masses into society. Their task is to gather and unify experiences that would otherwise remain scattered, but at the same time, they are called to divide bodies into a series of groups. As has been astutely observed: viewed from below, intermediate bodies aggregate, but when observed from above, they divide.[137] These bodies are called upon to differentiate society without harming its unity. Within this logic, one can identify the potential and the limits of social differentiation. On one hand, forms of cultural pluralism and institutional pluralism as well are encouraged because these open up spaces for formation and participation of the person.[138] Mortati's support for a regionalist type of constitutional order (that is, an order where public power is partially delegated to regions) is symptomatic of his recognition of the importance of certain forms of pluralism (in this case, institutional).[139] But, on the other hand, the limit of possible forms of aggregation and separation is dictated by the level of homogeneity that is necessary for a well-functioning constitutional order. The disruptive and at times innovative force of social pluralism has to be constrained and properly ordered. The role played by the selection operated by institutional figures for achieving homogeneity in Schmitt's thought is performed by differentiation and specification in Mortati's constitutional scheme. Intermediate bodies can offer spaces for enhancing persons' freedom and culture.[140] But they have to ensure that they will work toward the strengthening of the constitutional project and not its disruption. The division of society in a number of groups should not affect social homogeneity, which is difficult to realize, and given its artificiality, quite a demanding good. In this way, one can also explain Mortati's favor for the introduction of an institutional space where representatives from capital and labor would be able to meet and bargain.[141]

How is relative homogeneity preserved despite the possibility of pluralism intrinsic in societal alternative normativities? Mortati's response is based on two pillars. The first one is constituted by the processes of differentiation and ranking of both subjects and interests. Differentiation, by itself, is a necessary condition but not a sufficient one. Drawing differences and distributing roles within the legal order is not sufficient to obtain and secure political unity. Only the ranking of interests and positions (the process of specification) makes possible to establish substantial unity. For this reason, legal pluralism (in particular in its radical versions) cannot be admitted by Mortati. Given that radical legal pluralism postulates de-hierarchization of interests and needs, then it threatens the core of the process of unity building; hence, it is not functional to the integration of the person into the state and to the consolidation of political unity.

The supremacy of the constitution and of its principles represents the second shield against the centrifugal forces of pluralism. Mortati emphasizes the normalizing effects of the application of constitutional principles across society (which includes their horizontal effect) and even of the managing of states of exception and emergency. In particular, the material constitution allows understanding the emergency not as a constitutional rupture, but as a discrepancy between the formal constitution and the political integrity of legal reality, which needs, as a matter of necessity, to be normalized. Mortati developed a keen interest in all the liminal figures of constitutional law, including the state of siege and the declaration of war.[142] Even if it is conceded that formal parts of the constitution can be temporarily suspended,[143] constitutional principles still retain juridical force. They can function either as a limit to the suspension of the constitution (meaning that the suspension cannot impact upon the core of the material constitution) or, in cases of internal emergency, they maintain an integrative and inclusive potential. Mortati is adamant on the possibility of managing the emergency or the state of siege *contra legem* but *secundum constitutionem*.[144] Accordingly, even in the silence of the formal constitution, it is possible to retrieve criteria, provided by the material constitution, to select the organ in charge of managing the emergency. The rationale behind the criteria is to avoid any confusion between constitutional emergency and transformation because the point of addressing the situation of crisis is not to modify surreptitiously the constitutional order, but to preserve its integrity. This allows Mortati to come to the conclusion that the competent organ for managing constitutional emergencies should be the same responsible for the governing function. Indeed, in both modalities (emergency and governing) the finality is the same: protecting and consolidating the fundamental political aims. In conclusion, in cases of escalating conflict, Mortati does not opt for the crude Schmittian excision of any destabilizing factor, but for its constitutionalization,[145] so that the emergency can be reinterpreted as an opportunity for further inclusion into the material constitution.[146] Yet, while this solution might accommodate a certain degree of social and institutional pluralism, it cannot welcome radical or strict legal pluralism. Indeed, the political dimension of the material constitution requires that interests qualify as political only as long as they are general enough to apply to the whole of society (even against those who are reluctant) and therefore still be ranked as superior to the others.

Finally, another moment of constraint of legal pluralism is represented by Mortati's realist approach. As already mentioned, Mortati's belief in the central role of political parties was shaken during the last phase of his career. In his last few essays, he had to concede that glimpses of a remarkable incipient transformation could already be observed, with new social and political forces emerging and replacing decaying ones. Quite interestingly, he widened the notion of the bearers of the material constitution to the "governing class," which includes more than those ruling through the formal political system. Indeed, by 1962 this class had come to include

> all the individuals and the groups holding various positions which, de facto, can ensure their predominance, such as control of the army, or land ownership, capital accumulation, or the spiritual patrimony, as constituted by cultural and religious values.[147]

By noting the limitations of the political system in addressing the new circumstances, he began to explore new institutional avenues to cope with these challenges. However, most of these institutional channels were forms of constitutional engineering and include things such as electoral laws and referendums, which come across as institutional devices for consolidating the governing function in a context of progressive weakening of the political actors[148] and not much as opportunities for bottom-up political action.

This is not surprising. In fact, Mortati had been and remained throughout his intellectual path the champion of an institutionalist conception of the constitutional order. From his point of observation, the pluralist challenges of the second half of the twentieth century, whatever their sources and their nature, could only be tackled by consolidating the supremacy of the constitution. Accordingly, the measure and the extent of integration had to be dictated by the stability of the constitutional order. In such scheme, pluralism is admitted and legitimate, but it is not an end in itself. It rather serves, within a certain context, the instrumental role of strengthening the legal order. Beyond that point, pluralism has no legitimate space to expand further.

CHAPTER FIVE

Pluralism and Order

Two Interpretive Axes

THE ANALYSIS ADVANCED in the preceding chapters foregrounds a common thread in Santi Romano, Carl Schmitt, and Costantino Mortati. This thread lies much deeper than the level of assonances and resonances, convergences and divergences. These towering figures of twentieth-century legal and political theory tackled the same fundamental issue from the same starting point (the idea that law is first of all organization) but came up with three prototypical solutions to it. The issue is how to reconcile social normativity's irreducible tendency to self-differentiation with the antithetical need for order and stability. All of them delved into the crucial question of how social practices organize themselves and how this organizational activity rubs off on the legal regulation of society. Despite the fact that all three authors might have shared certain tenets of the dominant form of legal positivism (which is hardly surprising, as it provided the hegemonic legal view of the time), the way they framed the question is what made their theories into a genuinely original theoretical inquiry. The relation between social facts and the legal system (as legal positivists would frame it)[1] is conceived, by these authors, (1) as a qualitatively different relation because it does not just apply the legal onto the social, and (2) is qualified not as a relation made exclusively of norms, but also of institutions and concrete orders. This is one of the reasons why we claim this stream of legal thought is better equipped to address the challenges of pluralism,[2] although its scarce visibility in the Anglophone world has severely impaired its contribution.

In the three chapters devoted to these authors, we made this point by taking up Romano's, Schmitt's, and Mortati's irreconcilable perspectives on the *nomic force of matter*. In doing so, we explained why the lesson we have to learn from this juxtaposition is more valuable than an account of each of them in isolation. Although they all contributed to the development of what is called classic legal institutionalism, it is in the different function they assigned to institutions and the legal practice that a major theoretical conflict in the history of Western law comes to surface—one that still haunts contemporary accounts of the relation between law and politics.

As was the case in the foregoing chapters, to grasp the richness of this subject matter we can refer to a double relation whose intertwinement is concretely impossible to disentangle: *juristic* versus *political* conceptions of law and the interplay of *matter* and *nomic force*.

The first dichotomy concerns the understanding of the role of legal science. Romano advanced a juristic conception that emphasizes the role played by legal science in the composition of the social world. Mortati regarded legal science as instrumental in the discovery and consolidation of institutional facts, that is, those institutional phenomena that possess the capacity to persist over time. Schmitt is of particular interest because of his progressive movement from an idea of legal science as the investigation into the origin of law (which he identified with the sovereign's decision) to an idea of legal science as the interplay of three essential elements of all legal orders, namely, norm, decision, and the concrete order. The relation between the juristic and the political affects how they deal with the relation between matter and nomic force. Romano thought that matter—that is, bare social interactional practices—is not nomic in itself, in that its normative value requires a type of knowledge being developed about it, one that goes hand in hand with practice. Mortati believed that the aggregation of political forces around certain aims was the institutional phenomenon out of which jurists should draw nomic force. Contrary to Romano's view, Mortati thought this political aggregation does not require the production of legal knowledge in the first place. For it is that which produces the institutional facts that function as a grid for identifying the nomic force of an institution. Legal knowledge plays the function of consolidating and enriching nomic force. Schmitt is interesting once again because his adhesion to an institutional view of law remarkably affected his understanding of the interplay between nomic force and matter. His earlier decisionism assigned the sovereign's decision a demiurgic potential, so much so that he deemed the normal case—the materiality of everyday practices—to be conditional on an effective decision being made. On the contrary, his institutional revision assigned genuine and original nomic force to social practices, whose normative power must be tamed by the activity of the political ruler and her loyal officials, lest the political community be eroded by an uncontrolled fractalization.

Accordingly, the main claim we will make in this chapter is twofold and it offers an important insight into the current debate on legal pluralism and global law. The first is that it is not so much the different understanding of law that marks the theoretical distance between Romano, Schmitt, and Mortati as it is the different understanding of legal science and the contribution it is supposed to give to the life of institutions. Their views on the function of legal science proves crucial to their notion of how law should interact with politics. This is conducive to the second main claim. These authors viewed the question of how legal orderings mold societal formations in terms of nomic forces giving shape to the materiality of social relations. Their theories represent three paradigmatic instantiations of how legal institutionalism deal with such a complicated relation.

JURISTIC VERSUS POLITICAL

Chapter 1 traced the rise of legal science as a discipline. We wanted to give the sense that, from its very inception, the legal orders of the rising states provided the battlefield for the conflict between the juristic and the political. The struggle on codification that took place in many European countries, and was particularly fierce in Germany, started a confrontation between jurists and legislators on who the authoritative interpreters of the people's customs and will should be. The notions of *Juristenrecht* and *Professorenrecht* reclaimed a role for legal science that exceeded mere description and called for juristic analysis of legal sources and legal consciousness to issue law. Although this understanding of the legal phenomenon was mainly based on private-law concepts and principles, it nonetheless reflected a centralizing push intended to assist the fragile structure of the newly minted state. In a sense, therefore, the advocates of the juristic in the first half of the nineteenth century did not intend to question the state as the supreme political entity. Rather, the opposition of its advocates to purely legislative law bespoke skepticism of the idea of the state as a mighty god autonomously issuing laws. The later contest between Paul Laband and Otto von Gierke was the acme of this irresoluble contradiction. Correspondingly, two notions of legal theory came to a head: legal theory as the interpretation of positive law based on purely jurisprudential method versus legal theory as the philosophical, political, and juristic analysis of an all-encompassing living body comprising a multiplicity of other bodies.

Doubtless, the legal order as a top-down production of the state legislative apparatus was destined to efface all rivals. But Gierke's theoretical effort was a rich seam to mine. His teachings infiltrated the interstices of legal theorizing and inspired a remarkable swathe of pluralist theories in a variety of countries that were more averse to the state as a monolithic entity. The modern conception of the state from Hobbes to nineteenth-century legal positivism had nurtured a fictional figure and had unwittingly endowed it with unlimited power. Gierke's epigones argued that state-based theories had robbed associations of their nomic force. Their critique of legislative law entailed that associational ties are the cradle of normativity and thus associations possess nomic force well before the state recognizes (or does not recognize) them. It is in this context that the notion of "juristic" exhibits its theoretical strength. On this account, the term *juristic* comes to emphasize a type of normativity that cannot be easily reduced either to conventional morality or to state legality. Group-based practices create normative orderings that are not immediately legal (and this is what Romano will deny) but are certainly organizational. Gierke's pioneering eulogy of "juristic orders" extolled the capacity of social agents to engender normative power and to build interactional contexts around it. This theoretical move effected a radical break with the modern theory of statehood as it entailed that the state is by no means the only producer of normativity. Indeed, the normative hinges upon the nomic resources triggered by nonstate entities.

"Juristic," then, signified a staunch opposition to the idea that the political is the possibility condition for a legal order to come about and work. It exalted the autonomy of legal agents (although most of pluralist theorists thought of collective agents) in the creation of normative contexts. While Romano departed from Gierke's organicism, as we illustrated in Chapter 2, he was certainly sensitive to this line of thought. As he pointed out in the 1909 essay on the crisis of the modern state, the French Revolution had turned out to be a missed opportunity. It had initially voiced the grievance of several unrepresented entities that the Old Regime refused to recognize and yet it soon suppressed their aspiration to a more varied form of representation. The processes of constitution building and codification that the Revolution ignited all over Europe were largely founded on the image of a vertex radiating ordering force on an otherwise unordered society. This is how political conceptions of the law took over.[3] What was at stake was not so much the artificial nature of law. Most juristic conceptions, too, regarded the law as an artifact requiring a creative as well as interpretive activity on the part of experts. Law is always the outcome of craftspeople exercising their skills and competences as the representatives of a complex legal tradition. However, the advocates of political conceptions exaggerated the relation between political and legislative power: law is nothing other than the product of one or more authoritative craftspeople entrusted with unlimited *power* to legislate.

The passage from juristic to political conceptions of law had a major impact on the understanding of the sources of law that simultaneously brought about a decisive change in the understanding of legal science. Unlike in the Middle Ages and early modernity, legal science was not conducive to the determination of the contents of the law. It became ancillary, as it was instrumental in making sense of the contents of something that it did not contribute to producing. While Savigny's main goal was to emphasize the intrinsic relation between legal science and the production of law, his main worry was the infelicitous event that legal science be reduced to a mere activity of description—one that had nothing to do with the definition of the contents of the law. As a matter of history, Savigny was one of the leaders of a school of thought that was going down to defeat. A team of resolute legal scientists across Europe was paving the way for a conception of municipal law as innately tied to the creative activity of the legislator; for an understanding of courts as organic agencies of the state apparatus; for a view of legal science as propaedeutic to the cognition of valid law and to the formation of legal officials. The parliament was the only legislator, the judges were loyal appliers, professors of law were educators.

The political understanding of law prevailed, especially within the positivist tradition that ties the work of John Austin to the work of Hans Kelsen. What Kelsen praised in the work of Austin was precisely his clear intention to draw the boundaries and systematize the science of law and to differentiate it from other sciences. Austin was convinced that this process of specialization and systematization presupposed a clear differentiation from other sciences, as he suggested when he wrote that the main purpose of his book was "to describe the boundary which severs the province of jurisprudence from the regions lying on its confines."[4] Such an intent to reorganize the field of legal theory was the main rationale of Kelsen's vindication of the "pureness" of legal science. He insisted that legal theorists have to carry out a strictly *cognitive* task:

> The interpretation of law by the science of law (jurisprudence) must be sharply distinguished as non-authentic from the interpretation by legal organs. Jurisprudential interpretation is purely cognitive ascertainment of the meaning of legal norms.[5]

The main goal of this basic division of labor between legal scientists and legal officials (whether law makers or law appliers) was to give legal scientists the task of determining whether something is a valid law (that is, whether something belongs to a given legal system) by applying accurate theoretical schemes. This is the reason why, according to Kelsen, it was necessary "to free the science of law of all foreign elements,"[6] namely, from psychology, sociology, ethics, and political theory. Only this *purified* theory of law can provide a description of law as it really is, freed from any deceptive contamination.

The notion of the juristic as well as the conceptual battles that took place around it during the nineteenth century are particularly relevant to the argument of this book. For classic legal institutionalism shares with pluralist theories the aversion to state-centrism, in the sense that institutionalists refused to locate exclusively the source of law either in the legislative activity of the state or in the collective practice of state officials. From this viewpoint, Romano, Schmitt, and Mortati are thoroughly institutionalist thinkers. Although, as we have demonstrated, they disagreed on where the origin of law is to be found, the issue of the juristic versus the political vibrantly resonates in their elaborations. The interesting form it takes in their analysis of the relation between the nomic and the material is worth some further scrutiny.

THREE VARIATIONS OF THE NOMIC FORCE VERSUS THE MATERIAL

As we explored in Chapter 2, Romano's is a peculiar institutionalism. He wanted to preserve the *productive* (namely, *not merely descriptive*) function of legal science even though he was fundamentally a legal positivist. Firmly rooted in his conception of a pure legal science, his positivist theory of the institution was well placed to reject the (alleged) essential connection between state and law and opened the door to legal pluralism. In brief, his understanding of legal theory was instrumental in the amendment of positivism in such a way that the latter might be turned into a juristic conception. In a book that is the epitome of Romano's constitutional theory, *Principii di diritto costituzionale* (Principles of constitutional law), he insisted that legal science should be determined and delimited. The juristic method can only rely on the juristic point of view. He emphasized the scientific limits of the metalanguages of other disciplines and contended that legal science was at a stage where it could give up the support of other sciences. The synergy between disciplines had too many disadvantages, "inherent in their union," which most often "amount to confusion."[7] Like many positivists, and Kelsen in particular, he concluded that scientific syncretism was not only ineffective, but detrimental. The job of legal science is to determine the forms and the contents of the legal lexicon *from within* to account for the reality that surrounds the law. However, unlike Kelsen and other positivists, he thought that the pureness of the legal lexicon has to perform not only the task of *description*, but also that of *translation*. Let us briefly touch upon these two crucial activities of the law in Romano's view.

In the end, the way Romano thought of description is less close to Kelsen's than to Niklas Luhmann's. For both Romano and Luhmann, speaking of a certain scientific field *as a field* contributes to drawing its boundaries and consolidating its systemic nature. A self-description taking place from within works as an operator with which a system generates, affirms, and reiterates its own identity.[8] It is a description that selects some elements and isolates them as distinctive features within a wider environment comprising other systems that in their turn produce their own self-descriptions. Though Romano obviously never used the language of systems theory, he had in mind this type of self-description of the legal field: an autological discourse that only speaks of itself. Again, like systems theory, law is not the product of the will understood individually as a psychological faculty. It is also (and emphatically) not the act of a sovereign will.[9] Accordingly, it is not surprising that Romano postulates that institutionalism should be not essentially linked to the centrality of the person and legal personality:

> My claim is that an institution is a social entity or body, in the sense that it is a manifestation of the social, not purely individual, nature of human beings. This does not mean that the base of an institution cannot be but human beings connected to each other. . . . There are institutions with a different base that are composed of an array of means, whether material or immaterial, personal or real, patrimonial or with an ideal nature.[10]

But given that reason as well cannot ground the legal order, and in the absence of any external foundation, law can only be self-referential.[11] While engaging in the self-description, according to Romano, the legal order reproduces itself by functioning almost like a communicative system composed of relations among institutions or legal orders.[12]

This explains why, as illustrated in Chapter 1, "The Modern State and its Crisis" begins with a reference to the study of political institutions. It is an approach to the law that is not reliable because it comes *from the outside*. Jurists are required to stay within the boundaries of legal science and to describe the law from *within*. Such a direct relation between the description of a scientific field and its contents, as well as its capacity to exert effects on what surrounds it, provides a precious key to the beginning of the 1909 essay through to the late book on constitutional theory: Romano's lifelong effort was to reclaim the operative force of law, which requires an utter independence from other disciplines.

Attached to the notion of self-description is the notion of translation. If it is the case that the legal is a scientific field discursively producing itself, then the only way to get access to it is a process of linguistic conversion. Here we hear again traces of a motif that will be later developed by systems theory and then societal constitutionalism. Luhmann speaks of structural couplings between institutions of law and other systems that work as evolutionary achievements.[13] Romano indeed admitted that the legal field is a special venue where the social gets reformulated as it is described with exclusive reference to juristic categories within the juristic field. In this way, he postulated a communicative exchange at the heart of the translating process. Yet, we should be cautious about extending this parallel between structural couplings and translation as almost identical processes. An important difference remains. In Romano, the institution is intrinsically a legal order and generates law, while, according to systems theory, structural couplings are mostly a learning opportunity for the system, that is, a chance to select information from the environment as a process of adaptation to irritations, surprises, and unpredictability.

Be this as it may, Romano was convinced that social frictions and conflicts can be overcome as they get reframed through the legal lexicon. Even more importantly, he regarded the law as a compositional technique insofar as it not only settles conflicts but yields new compositions of the social. For all legal orders—that is, all organized entities—that enter forms of legal negotiation produce new conformations of the social. Law is a space with linguistic borders that makes room for those legal entities that assemble themselves and get reassembled as they interact with other legal entities. Romano's legal translation is therefore a process of juristic production through juristic law: semiotic transposition of signs into other signs, description of social conflicts through the legal language with an eye to repairing and composing.

Thus, it is interesting to note that Romano's juristic notion of law is the reverse side of his obsession with the pureness of legal science and his amendment to positivism. On his account, description is far from purely cognitive, as *legal description always involves translation*: as the law describes through its technical language from the juristic point of view, that which is described gets formed and transformed. The law is a productive technique that exerts effects by way of its performative language. This means that for the material to acquire nomic force, a discursive practice is indispensable. As we explained in some detail in Chapter 2, this does not presuppose the material being antecedent to the nomic. While nomic force is thrust upon practice, it cannot exist independently of it. These two elements of legal reality are on a par. Despite this, materiality itself has no nomic force until a knowledge production process gives formal structure to its contents. The law always emerges as the interplay of discourse and practice.

Schmitt's notion of this interplay is somewhat more rudimentary because it misses the subtlety of Romano's portrayal. Chapter 3 of this book focused on his progressive movement from decisionism to concrete-order thinking. In this conceptual revision, what changes is the role of nomic force vis-à-vis materiality. In his decisionism of the early 1920s, materiality is confined to a state of anomic normality that awaits a sovereign decision to obtain an ordered form. The sovereign is the one who manages to make a decision that effectively molds normality in such a way that normal life can function properly. The nomic rules over the material. It can always revoke its ordered structure when a state of exception is brought about to suspend normal life. We argued that at the end of the 1920s Schmitt gradually came to terms with the severe limitations of this view as he took stock of Hauriou's and Romano's institutional theorizing. Within Schmitt's concrete-order thinking, nomic force becomes an innate property of the practices that people produce in ordinary life. The decider no longer orders them through a miraculous conferral of nomic force, but makes sure that practices are compatible with each other with a view to preserving political homogeneity. The law becomes a sieve that promotes some practices and rules out others. The means to this end is the set of general clauses that officials faithful to the leader's view of the community use to determine if and to what extent particular practices jeopardize the homogeneity of the political community.

The relation of nomic force to materiality changes remarkably. The law is a selective machinery playing a political function. It does not produce normativity but fosters state ethic. Its function is jurisdictional not, as is the case with Romano's theory, in the sense that the law makes normative entities compatible within a pluralist framework, but in the sense that it curbs their tendency to self-differentiation within a monist framework. It is this difference that marks the theoretical distance between Romano and Schmitt. In keeping with Romano's idea of the interplay between nomic force and matter, pluralism can always become the vehicle for new compositions of the social. In Schmitt's understanding of law's selective function, pluralism is a danger to be guarded against. Such a difference between Romano and Schmitt should come as no surprise in light of their understanding of the juristic versus the political and how it affects materiality. For if the material is reduced to a state of normative inertia, then it inescapably presupposes the creative performance of a discursive inception. On the contrary, if the nomic is deemed to coincide with the materiality of institutional practices, then the law does not add any nomic force but the seal of state legitimacy. In this latter case, the law is reduced to a mechanism of political selection. Schmitt's case is particularly interesting because his understanding of the relation of materiality and nomic force changed visibly, as he moved from one extreme to the other. In his decisionist phase, nomic force is totally extrinsic to normality; in his institutional phase, totally intrinsic. Romano's unswerving conviction was that the relation between nomic force and materiality is not a matter of substance but a matter of process. The law is neither a conferral of normativity on inert matter nor a jurisdictional machinery selecting normative social practices. Rather, it is an ongoing process in which normativity is continuously produced and transformed. If this is so, then the encounter of law and practices is a channel for social transformation.

Because of his reduction of the juristic to a selective machinery, Schmitt's political notion of law seems to be not just reactionary but also oversimplistic. Law's political task is limited to the restraining activity of curbing pluralism and ensuring homogeneity. Mortati offered a more robust alternative to Romano's juristic account of law. His political notion of law has the virtue of grasping the fundamental interplay of materiality and nomic force. The materiality of normative facts always precedes any discourse about law, although the juristic account of normative facts proves crucial to the formation of a legal order. Mortati's seminal insight is that the material constitution always contains nomic qualities. These qualities, however, are neither self-standing nor self-sufficient. The homogeneity they require to work properly is not meant to preserve the homogeneity of the political community, as Schmitt maintained. Rather, it provides the necessary basis for a functioning legal order. As we insisted in the previous chapter, according to Mortati, homogeneity is attained through the selection of fundamental political aims. Contrary to Schmitt's, this is a political notion of law that does not incline to reductionism because the selection does not hinge on an extrinsic view of how the political community should look like—as is the case with Schmitt's idea that general clauses respond to the leader's view of the community. In other words, Mortati viewed homogeneity as mobile because it is a juristic construction and can thus be adjusted—though within certain limits and according to the changing circumstances. The selection is itself a juristic act that requires juristic wisdom. The political and the juristic coincide when it comes to the inception of the material constitution: normative facts furnish the material content that political forces are meant to turn into the set of fundamental aims that enliven the legal order. *The political is juristic.* The governing function already-and-always requires a nomic force triggered by the selective activity of those political actors that set the community's fundamental aims.

Therefore, for Mortati, the constituent power resides in those nomic forces that call for a political act of elicitation. While Schmitt's view paradoxically leans towards randomness, as what really counts is not the practices that are to be selected, but that they prove instrumental in the attainment of political homogeneity, on Mortati's account it is all about the capacity of political forces to give life to the material constitution, how they establish the fundamental aims, and what these aims are. If and when these forces cease to be active and hegemonic, then the material constitution ceases to be alive.

This demonstrates that Mortati's political notion of law is in the starkest contrast to Romano's juristic mainly because of, as it were, their underlying legal ontology. Romano envisaged a plurality of entities in a nonhierarchical relation of relevance or irrelevance to each other. No superstructure or overriding legal entity is to be posited, to such an extent that only from its own point of view is the state legal order superior to the other orders whose existence does not depend on the state. It is the ontology itself of the legal that is inherently pluralist. In this scenario, the interaction of the nomic and the material develops into a continuous process of order making and negotiation between orders. Mortati thought of the emergence of *a* legal order that incarnates *the* material constitution and oversees the pursuit of its fundamental aims.

Here, we can identify two key differences with Romano. Only certain subjects can bootstrap the legal order into existence. In short, while for Romano all organizations and groups are potentially endowed with nomic forces, for Mortati only certain organizations (in his case, mostly political parties) qualify for this task because they need to imprint upon the whole of society their fundamental aims. The second key difference is that, on Mortati's view, institutions and legal orders are still nurtured by a voluntaristic idea of political action—one that is completely exogenous to Romano's theory. This approach to the formation of the legal order underplays the compositional qualities of law and emphasizes its exclusionary pull. While in Romano the logic of the law operates within the boundaries of its own rationality, in the case of Mortati the law is not fully autonomous, but functional to the governing activity. Crucially, all these differences remind us that Mortati regarded the law as intrinsically imperative. Its organizational nature is instantiated by a series of commands that are directed by the rulers to the ruled. Unlike Romano's theorizing, Mortati's is hallmarked by an acute awareness of the power dimension of legal relations as well as their exclusionary nature. Such a view, however, greatly underestimates the jurisgenerative capacity of societal actors and remains blind to any form of societal constitutionalism.

In the end, Mortati is closer to Schmitt's realism when the former postulates that the material constitution can only be brought into life around general political aims (namely, aims that are applicable to the whole of society), whose quality is therefore "imperial" and not simply associative.[14] In fact, the activities of the social organizations constituting the legal order entail, at first, the exclusion of other social forces or groups as long as the latter are not prepared to accept that the legal order pursues certain political aims and not others. Constituent power, then, always contains seeds of constituted power—one that admits no peers and resents rivals. This implies a hierarchical ontology where the legal order of the constituted power hovers over other forms of normativity. But unlike Schmitt, who theorized that the way to manage social self-differentiation is simply to curb it, Mortati introduced a peculiar logic of integration of other social forces according to a move that would become predominant in many legal orders after World War II.[15] Pluralism would be allowed, but only within the perimeter drawn by the teleological dimension of the legal order under the assumption that the fundamental political aims are socially expansive. The tension between social differentiation and legal ordering would be managed by strengthening the integrative force of the fundamental aims. Still, in order to achieve a stable development of the process, juristic knowledge will have to be mobilized.

In the end, the way Mortati conceived of integration can easily be interpreted as an inspiration for the development of European constitutional orders in the second half of the twentieth century. This is where Mortati conspicuously departs from Schmitt. The fundamental aims set by the material constitution recognizes the impossibility of state neutrality, and hence the possibility of a militant order.[16] However, in Mortati's constitutional theory the instruments of integration operate for the inclusion of social relations under the state. Inclusion should not be conceived, at least during this phase, in purely sociological terms, à la T. H. Marshall, or rather, as the enlargement of the scope of the status attached to citizenship. Rather, inclusionary processes are deployed to constitutionalize sectors of society previously excluded or exempted from the reach of the political and constitutional system. More precisely, in a value- or rights-based constitutional order, fundamental rights and principles perform a double function. On one side, they are means for managing increasingly complex claims and demands coming from society. On the other, they carry out an inclusionary practice by extending the reach of the political system into society, in particular with their horizontal application.[17] As previously highlighted, pluralism is protected by the constitutional umbrella, but also shaped by the political substance of the constitutional order.

In conclusion, this chapter has drawn two interpretative axes for reading the works of Romano, Schmitt, and Mortati on the basis of a couple of key distinctions: juristic versus political knowledge and matter versus nomic force. The two axes intersect at the crossing point where the question of how we get to know the law in a pluralist context becomes salient. We should like to note that we did not mean to impose those axes on the authors. Rather, we extracted them from a systematic reading of these authors' theorizing. As we will briefly explain in the concluding pages, it is our firm conviction that reading Romano, Schmitt, and Mortati against this background strengthens our capacity to understand the dynamics of contemporary legal orders and their relation to politics.

Conclusion

THIS BOOK WANTED TO REFRESH knowledge of three leading figures of twentieth-century legal thinking. Their contributions exceed the realm of legal philosophy, as they penetrated the heart of a persisting issue in social and political theory, that is, how order and pluralism can coexist. So, while one of our objectives was to bring back to the fore the work of three outstanding representatives of a Continental tradition that is usually labeled "legal institutionalism,"[1] there is a further objective that should not go unnoticed. We concerned ourselves with the comparison between Romano's, Schmitt's, and Mortati's theorizing because it allowed us to cover the full spectrum of the continuum we illustrated in the Introduction.

Romano's juristic notion of law exalts the compositional force of law that always produces new conformations of the social. The order is something that can be always reinvented as new problems emerge and the existing composition of legal entities need adjustments. Schmitt re-elaborated his influential idea of the sovereign decider because he had underrated the eruptive force of social practices. The order is not created ex nihilo, as he himself had erroneously postulated. It rather calls for constant scrutiny on the part of loyal officials who are called upon to secure social homogeneity by selecting practices in accordance with the instructions of a leader. Order is the outcome of a process of social selection under the supervision of a political leader. Mortati's political understanding presents pluralism as tenable and desirable only within the normative framework of a material constitution entrenching fundamental aims. Order is obtained by harnessing pluralism with a view to using its energy to consolidate political unity.

Importantly, these authors offer theories that best capture a concrete historical change in the forms and practices of managing the multiplication of social groups. In other words, each of them portrays the specific form taken by the legal order as a coping mechanism before the challenge of social pluralism. Romano's prophetic contributions in the first two decades of the century are not only moved by concerns about a disordered society. They should also be viewed as a penetrating reconstruction of the impact of the first globalizing wave on state legal orders. Schmitt's reflections in the third decade of the century have also cast a discerning gaze on the transformations of the state into authoritarian or even totalitarian forms of government.[2] The selectivity of legal ordering does not entail anymore bootstrapping the order out of nothing, but it is an activity of suppression of the potential legal alternatives to the creation and preservation of homogeneity. Mortati's material understanding of the legal order as put forward during the fourth decade of the century provides a third option for dealing with the inherent tension between pluralism and ordering. In particular, in his constitutional theory he came up with the idea of an integration of pluralism into the legal order. Such a state of affairs would be the outcome of the constitutionalization of the legal order. Pluralism can certainly be tolerated, but only to the point where it remains instrumental in achieving the main goals, principles, or values that are at the core of the legal order. Mortati's solution to the riddle of the societal tendency to differentiation was the one that came closer to what in the second half of the twentieth century would become the European constitutional state.[3] Integration of social pluralism into the constitutional order would occur by introjecting and adapting to legal and constitutional principles various social fragments.

The value of these options does not lie in the fact that one of them is correct vis-à-vis the others. Obviously, one can hardly appreciate Schmitt's reactionary conservatism for what it implies about pluralism. His theoretical amendments to his earlier decisionism made his theory even more detestable. And yet, they cast light on something that he himself had undervalued; which is to say, the force of matter, which no sovereign decider can bring about or erase. The concrete-order thinking of this phase of his work illuminates the logic behind the reaction against the restructuring of society during the first half of the twentieth century. As we have shown, Schmitt suggests a less miraculous task for the sovereign—one that nonetheless requires an impressive mobilization in order to exercise what is, at its core, a jurispathic activity. On the contrary, Romano and Mortati are enlightening alternatives for the contemporary debate on pluralism and its compatibility with ordering activities. Romano's belief that the law is a special semiotic field that should be preserved from politics is in stark contrast to Mortati's belief that law is already and always political. Still, both authors have posed the question of how to articulate law and politics for ordering purposes in the most effective way, and reading their works together can be highly instructive for addressing contemporary issues and debates.

In light of the current developments, it is intuitive, and arguably correct, to prophesize the resurgence of law in a sense akin to that which Romano had in mind. What we have been witnessing in Western legal orders is a transformative move from political unities instantiated by the form of the constitutional state to the growth of transnational public and private regimes, international and global legal orders, regional and sectoral legal systems.[4] These are in state of frequent exchange and mutual irritation.[5] At present, law is more and more a field where people interact to produce acentric bodies of normativity, with fewer and fewer clear hierarchies defining who should do what. This is a common trend for the relation between different layers of legal ordering. Supranational, international, and global law are in a relation of negotiation and conflict with the national, regional, or other specialized legal regimes.[6] New or transformed fields of legal knowledge have now been established: WTO law, international economic law, international human rights, international criminal law, Internet law, just to name a few. As a consequence, legal studies have seen the rise of new approaches for managing this type of pluralism. Global administrative law, for example, has developed an impressive interpretive framework for global law inspired by administrative institutions and practices.[7] In the last decade, global legal pluralism has also flourished, providing an intriguing account and typology of the relations between different legal orders.[8]

Constitutional pluralism is one of the other streams of thought that have addressed questions of ordering under conditions of pluralization of legal sources. According to this approach, the tension between order and pluralism would be managed by constitutionalizing the relation between legal orders. These streams of thought have clearly enriched the debate but, with a few notable exceptions,[9] they have fallen prey of two important epistemic limits. They have adopted—quite controversially—the point of view of the global order and have not addressed the issue of how legal orderings, in conditions of rising pluralism, shape societal formations.[10]

This book has argued that the recovery of the Continental jurisprudence of Romano, Schmitt, and Mortati would not only be valuable in itself. Much more than that, it contributes to confronting the topical problem of how the proliferation of legal orders is changing the configuration of law vis-à-vis politics. So, whether the state in the next few years is likely to decline once and for all or to come back to the fore, it is not the mere destiny of state-form that is at stake. It is the technique that gives shape to the material that is being reconfigured, along with the general perception of the tasks it has to perform. Romano, Schmitt, and Mortati took issue with this wide-ranging process with this awareness and demonstrated that this is key to governing its enormous effects on social life.

Notes

INTRODUCTION

1. S. Romano, "Lo Stato moderno e la sua crisi," in *Lo Stato moderno e la sua crisi. Saggi di diritto costituzionale* (Milan: Giuffrè, 1969), 5–26, at 12.

2. Interestingly, some of these authors (with other institutionalists) were at the core of the early edited collection, W. Jennings, ed., *Modern Theories of Law* (Oxford: Oxford University Press, 1930).

3. It is worth clarifying at the very outset of this book that classic legal institutionalism should be set apart from more recent trends of legal institutionalism. The most influential version of the latter emerged as a set of theoretical proposals to reconcile legal positivism with the theory of institutional facts (originally developed by G. E. M. Anscombe and John R. Searle). In one of the leading works in the field of new institutionalism—N. MacCormick and O. Weinberger, *An Institutional Theory of Law* (Dordrecht: Springer, 1986)—the authors argue that when people reach an agreement, when they take part in a ceremony, when they watch a football match, these all are experiencing institutional facts. Those are particular facts, which are true not because of any inner qualities but by dint of the practices and norms that every participant shares and (at least implicitly) knows. Such facts are "not true simply because of the condition of the material world and the causal relationships obtaining among its parts"; on the contrary, they are "true in virtue of an interpretation of what happens in the world, an interpretation of events in the light of human practices and normative rules" (MacCormick and Weinberger, *An Institutional Theory of Law*, 10). The crux of this type of legal institutionalism is that those institutional facts' *being true* can be only tested hermeneutically: these facts exist as long as the participants believe them to exist. As the members of a community assume an internal point of view, they become inclined to look at the legal rules, not as compulsory menaces, but as practices that are shared and are followed *just* (even if *not only*) because they are shared. These practices organize

the social life of the population by providing standards for assessing and (when necessary) criticizing the conduct of each other. In this hermeneutic light, institutional facts are considered as *occurrences mediated by concepts* that social actors use and apply when they act in the various ambits of social life. Accordingly, institutions are systems of norms that create spheres of meaning. Such norms have the form of constitutive norms (à la Searle) establishing "what counts as an *x*," where the variable stands for a contract, a marriage, a testament, a championship, a parliamentary procedure, and so on. While the context of this footnote is certainly not adequate to explore the differences with classic legal institutionalism, it will soon become evident that none of the classic institutionalists ever reduced law to norms of whatever type. As we will discuss in depth, it is the notion itself of institution that the two institutional families work with that is altogether different. The distance between these two versions of legal institutionalism is made visible by the absence of any discussion of the first wave of legal institutionalism in MacCormick's late reformulations. See N. MacCormick, *Institutions of Law* (Oxford: Oxford University Press, 2007). An in-depth discussion of MacCormick's peculiar approach to institutionalism is available in M. Del Mar and Z. Bankowski, eds., *Law as Institutional Normative Order* (Farnham, UK: Ashgate, 2009). Another recent stream of legal institutionalism is emerging in the US-based debate on the relation between law and the economy, and it is a reaction against the methodology of Law & Economics. It has to be noted that this is, again, a different model of legal institutionalism, one that (against Law & Economics, indeed) aims at retrieving the constitutive function of formal law and social rules for the development of contemporary economies. A concise statement of this theoretical position is given in S. Deakin, D. Gindis, G. Hodgson, K. Huang, and K. Pistor, "Legal Institutionalism: Capitalism and the Constitutive Role of Law," *Journal of Comparative Economics* 45 (2017): 188–200.

4. Unlike the authors at the center of this book, Hauriou and the other French institutionalists have received some attention in the Anglophone debate. See A. Broderick, *The French Institutionalists* (Cambridge, MA: Harvard University Press, 1974).

5. Among legal theorists, see the use of Schmitt in a decisionist fashion by E. Posner and A. Vermeule, *The Executive Unbound* (Oxford: Oxford University Press, 2010); other authors have provided systematic analyses of Schmitt as theorist of sovereignty and the state, focused mostly on his exceptionalist phase. See e.g., D. Dyzenhaus, *Legality and Legitimacy: Carl Schmitt, Hans Kelsen and Hermann Heller in Weimar* (Oxford: Oxford University Press, 1997); P. Kahn, *Political Theology* (New York: Columbia University Press, 2011); J. P. McCormick, *Carl Schmitt's Critique of Liberalism: Against Politics as Technology* (Cambridge: Cambridge University Press, 1997); and B. Schupmann, *Carl Schmitt's Constitutional and State Theory* (Oxford: Oxford University Press, 2017).

6. Although this work is the outcome of a joint effort and ongoing collaboration, Mariano Croce is the author of the Introduction and Chapters 1, 2, and 3, while Marco Goldoni is the author of Chapters 4 and 5 and the Conclusion.

CHAPTER ONE

1. J. Rawls, *Political Liberalism* (New York: Columbia University Press, 2005, expanded edition), 441.

2. R. Rorty, *Philosophy as Cultural Politics: Philosophical Papers*, vol. 4 (Cambridge: Cambridge University Press, 2007).

3. I Berlin, *The Crooked Timber of Humanity* (London: Random House, 1991).

4. On value pluralism see the thought-provoking exchange between Robert Talisse and Michael Spicer: R. B. Talisse, "Value Pluralism: A Philosophical Clarification," *Administration & Society* 47, no. 9 (2015): 1064–76; M. W. Spicer, "On Value Pluralism, Its Implications, and the Nature of Philosophy," *Administration & Society* 47, no. 9 (2015): 1077–86.

5. Berlin, *The Crooked Timber of Humanity*, 65.

6. For an analysis of communitarianism and pluralism as parts of a broader critique of the monistic view of the state see M. Croce and A. Salvatore, *Undoing Ties: Political Philosophy at the Waning of the State* (New York: Bloomsbury, 2015).

7. S. Romano, *The Legal Order* (Abingdon, UK: Routledge, 2017), 15.

8. M. Reimann, "Nineteenth Century German Legal Science," *Boston College Law Review* 4, no. 4 (1990): 838.

9. F. C. Von Savigny, *Of the Vocation of our Age for Legislation and Jurisprudence* (London: Littlewood & Co., 1831).

10. On the *Kodifikationsstreit* (struggle on codification) see R. C. van Caenegem, *An Historical Introduction to Private Law* (Cambridge: Cambridge University Press, 1992), 1–15.

11. See R. Siltala, *Law, Truth and Reason. A Treatise on Legal Argumentation* (Dordrecht: Springer, 2011), 182–83.

12. See G. Mousourakis, *Roman Law and the Origins of the Civil Law Tradition* (Dordrecht: Springer, 2015), 292–93.

13. S. Mezzadra, "Dalla necessità all'occasionalità del positivo. Figure della giuspubblicistica tedesca da Savigny a Jellinek," *Materiali per una storia della cultura giuridica* 1 (1997): 62.

14. See G. Beseler, *Volksrecht und Juristenrecht* (Frankfurt am Main: Weidmannsche Buchhandlung, 1843). See C. Thornhill, *German Political Philosophy. The Metaphysics of Law* (London: Routledge, 2007), 205.

15. A remarkable contribution to the study of the personality of the state is D. Runciman, *Pluralism and the Personality of the State* (Cambridge: Cambridge University Press, 1997). On the introduction on the notion of legal person into English law, see P. Stein, "Nineteenth Century English Company Law and Theories

of Legal Personality," *Quaderni fiorentini per la storia del pensiero giuridico moderno* 11–12 (1982/83): 503–19.

16. See G. Berti, "La parabola della persona Stato (e dei suoi organi)," *Quaderni fiorentini per la storia del pensiero giuridico moderno* 11–12 (1982): 1001–33.

17. Thornhill, *German Political Philosophy*, 196.

18. C. F. Von Gerber, *Über öffentliche Rechte* (Darmstadt: Wissenschaftliche Buchgesellschaft, 1968).

19. It should be noted that Gerber's thought developed through two phases. In a first phase, as he produced *Über öffentliche Rechte* (1852), he implanted public law on the conceptual apparatus of private law, so that public relations were reflections of private ones. In this phase the organicist metaphor was far more pronounced. Later on, when he wrote *Grundzüge des deutschen Staatsrechts* (1865), he had ceded to the fascination for the strong Bismarckian state, which was claimed to be the owner of legal personality and supreme sovereign will, and thus as the only producer of the relations among all public entities. In this latter phase the people is no longer a natural condition arisen on the basis of private law relations, but the byproduct of the state's will and personality.

20. C. F. Von Gerber, *Grundzüge des deutschen Staatsrechts* [1865] (Leipzig: Bernhard Tauchnitz Verlag, 1880), 3.

21. See K. Rennert, *Die "geisteswissenschaftliche Richtung" in der Staatsrechtslehre der Weimarer Republik* (Berlin: Duncker & Humblot, 1987), 22–34.

22. In that respect, it is worth pointing out a key difference between Laband's obsession with methodological pureness and the one pursued by Hans Kelsen, who drew from, and perfected, the former's positivism. While Kelsen's theoretical conceptual effort was not (meant to be) in sync with the actual constitutional setting within which he operated, Laband's systematization was instrumental in harmonizing "the national conservative main currents of the time of the citizenry and the state apparatus" (M. Stolleis, *Public Law in Germany: 1800–1914* (New York: Berghahn, 2001), 236). In other words, unlike Kelsen's pure theory, Laband's theory did reflect and embody a specific geohistorical context.

23. Stolleis, *Public Law in Germany: 1800–1914*, 327.

24. See O. Hintze, *Soziologie und Geschichte: Gesammelte Abhandlungen zur Soziologie, Politik und Theorie der Geschichte* (Göttingen: Vandenhoeck & Ruprecht, 1964).

25. On the meaning and history of these concepts, see M. Richter, *The History of Political and Social Concepts: A Critical Introduction* (Oxford: Oxford University Press, 1995), 58–78.

26. See S. Mezzadra, "Il corpo dello Stato. Aspetti giuspubblicistici della 'Genossenschaftslehre' di Otto von Gierke," *Filosofia politica* 7, no. 3 (1993): 445–76.

27. On the translation of *Genossenschaft*, in his celebrated Introduction to Gierke's *Political Theories of the Middle Age*, Frederic William Maitland wrote: "The English translator must carefully avoid Partnership; perhaps in our modern

usage Company has become too specific and technical; Society also is dangerous; Fellowship with its slight flavour of an old England may be our least inadequate word" (F. W. Maitland, "Translator's Introduction," in O. von Gierke, *Political Theories of the Middle Age* [Cambridge: Cambridge University Press, 1913], xxv).

28. See Runciman, *Pluralism and the Personality of the State*, 36–37.

29. O. von Gierke, *Natural Law and the Theory of Society: 1500 to 1800* (Cambridge: Cambridge University Press, 1934), 41.

30. Gierke, *Natural Law and the Theory of Society*, 43.

31. Gierke, *Natural Law and the Theory of Society*, 61.

32. "Corporation" here should be taken as a term of art qualifying collectives that are endowed with a specific, self-assigned group identity. In an interesting analysis Arthur Machen defines a corporation as "an entity separate and distinct from the constituent members" (A. W. Machen, "Corporate Personality," *Harvard Law Review* 24, no. 4 (1911): 259). Importantly, the identity and nature of the corporation does not change as its members change, while the corporation confers on its constituent members an identity as members. This is the dialectic between the members' identity as individuals and the members' identity as members that the term *corporation* intends to encapsulate. Interestingly, Machen notes that law is not the creator of corporations. It is worth quoting him at some length: "All that the law can do is to recognize, or refuse to recognize, the existence of this entity. The law can no more create such an entity than it can create a house out of a collection of loose bricks. If the bricks are put together so as to form a house, the law can refuse to recognize the existence of that house—can act as if it did not exist; but the law has nothing whatever to do with putting the bricks together in such a way that, if the law is not to shut its eyes to facts, it must recognize that a house exists and not merely a number of bricks. This personality is neither fictitious, nor artificial, nor created by the state, but both real and natural, recognized but not created by the law. When a company is formed by the union of natural persons, a new real person, a real corporate 'organism,' is brought into being."

33. Gierke, *Natural Law and the Theory of Society*, 191.

34. Gierke, *Natural Law and the Theory of Society*, 181.

35. Gierke, *Natural Law and the Theory of Society*, 184–86.

36. E. Barker, "Translator's Introduction," in Gierke, *Natural Law and the Theory of Society*, lxxvi.

37. Maitland, "Translator's Introduction," xxvi. On Maitland's and Barker's different attitudes toward the Germanic root of pluralism vis-à-vis the Romanist legacy, see J. Stapleton, *Englishness and the Study of Politics: The Social and Political Thought of Ernest Barker* (Cambridge: Cambridge University Press, 1994), 71–77.

38. Runciman, *Pluralism and the Personality of the State*, 45.

39. Gierke, *Natural Law and the Theory of Society*, 50.

40. Gierke, *Natural Law and the Theory of Society*, 70.

41. Gierke, *Natural Law and the Theory of Society*, 71.

42. Runciman, *Pluralism and the Personality of the State*, 47.

43. Other authors, however, contest this view of medieval pluralism and claim that the Middle Ages made room for diverse forms of pluralism and dissent. See e.g., P. Grossi, *A History of European Law* (Malden, MA: Wiley-Blackwell, 2010), 1–38.

44. In this regard, a highly revealing text is O. von Gierke, "Naturrecht und deutsches Recht," *Rede zum Antritt des Rektorats der Universität Breslau am 15. Oktober 1882 gehalten* (Frankfurt am Main: Rütten & Loening, 1883).

45. Mezzadra, "Il corpo dello Stato," 474.

46. M. Fioravanti, *La scienza del diritto pubblico. Dottrine dello Stato e della Costituzione tra Otto e Novecento* (Milan: Giuffrè, 2001).

47. See D. Quaglioni, "Il 'peccato politico' di Vittorio Emanuele Orlando," in *I giuristi e il fascino del regime*, ed. I. Birocchi and L. Loschiavo (Rome: Roma TrE-Press, 2015), 373–88.

48. See in particular V. E. Orlando, *Studi giuridici sul governo parlamentare* [1886], in *Diritto pubblico generale* (Milan: Giuffrè, 1940), 345–415.

49. V. E. Orlando, "I criteri tecnici per la ricostruzione giuridica del diritto pubblico," in *Diritto pubblico generale. Scritti vari (1881–1940) coordinati in sistema* (Milan: Giuffrè, 1954), 7.

50. See in particular V. E. Orlando, *Principi di diritto amministrativo* (Florence: Barbera, 1891).

51. Fioravanti, *La scienza del diritto pubblico*, 152–53.

52. Although Mosca himself never used the term "political elite," as he preferred "political class," "ruling class," and "governing class," he was the originator of the concept within political theorizing. See in particular G. Mosca, *The Ruling Class* (New York: McGraw-Hill, 1939). For an analysis of Mosca's work see J. Meisel, *The Myth of the Ruling Class: Gaetano Mosca and the Elite* (Ann Arbor: University of Michigan Press, 1962); E. A. Albertoni (ed.), *Studies on the Political Thought of Gaetano Mosca: The Theory of the Ruling Class and Its Development Abroad* (Milan: Giuffrè, 1982). See also A. Zuckerman, "The Concept 'Political Elite': Lessons from Mosca and Pareto," *Journal of Politics* 39, no. 2 (1977): 324–44; J. Scott, "Modes of Power and the Re-conceptualization of Elites," *Sociological Review* 56, no. 1 (2008): 25–43; M. Christensen, "The Social Facts of Democracy: Science Meets Politics with Mosca, Pareto, Michels, and Schumpeter," *Journal of Classical Sociology* 13, no. 4 (2013): 460–86. It is worth noting that, for present purposes, Mosca's elite theory is less relevant and will be paid scarce attention, as we will refer to his understanding of constitutional studies.

53. Mosca, *The Ruling Class*, 70.

54. R. C. Van Caenegem, *Judges, Legislators, and Professors. Chapters in European Legal History* (Cambridge: Cambridge University Press, 1987), 67–68.

55. Runciman, *Pluralism and the Personality of the State*, 258.

56. P. Schmitter, "Still the Century of Corporatism?" *Review of Politics* 36, no. 1 (1974): 96. It goes without saying that pluralism and corporatism in between the eighteenth and the nineteenth century can hardly be likened to the renewed scholarly interest in corporatism within capitalist states of the late twentieth century. In the latter scenario, pluralism and corporatism were meant to usher in new modes for organizing modern interest-group democracies.

57. C. Levy, "'Sovversivismo': The Radical Political Culture of Otherness in Liberal Italy," *Journal of Political Ideologies* 12, no. 2 (2007): 150.

58. Compare with C. Levy, "Currents of Italian Syndicalism before 1926," *International Review of Social History* 45, no. 2 (2000): 209–50.

59. See J. Davis, *Conflict and Control. Law and Order in Nineteenth Century Italy* (London: Macmillan, 1988), 342–50.

60. Although in this book we cannot delve into Sorel's thought, he was certainly a major figure of the time, to such an extent that some scholars take him to be one of the inspirers of later fascist movements also outside France—see Z. Sternhell, M. Sznajder, and M. Asheri, *The Birth of Fascist Ideology: From Cultural Rebellion to Political Revolution* (Princeton, NJ: Princeton University Press, 1994), 36–91; Z. Sternhell, *Neither Right nor Left: Fascist Ideology in France* (Princeton, NJ: Princeton University Press, 1996). On Sorel's limited influence on Italian fascism, see D. D. Roberts, *Historicism and Fascism in Modern Italy* (Toronto: University of Toronto Press, 2007).

61. See K. H. Tucker, *French Revolutionary Syndicalism and the Public Sphere* (Cambridge: Cambridge University Press, 1996), 131–58.

62. See D. Beetham, "Sorel and the Left," *Government and Opposition* 4, no. 3. (1969): 308–23.

63. See G. Sorel, *Reflections on Violence* (Cambridge: Cambridge University Press, 2004).

64. Sorel, *Reflections on Violence*, 67–71.

65. Sorel, *Reflections on Violence*, 77. On Sorel and violence, see J. J. Roth, *The Cult of Violence: Sorel and the Sorelians* (Berkeley: University of California Press, 1980); K. Steven Vincent, "Interpreting Georges Sorel. Defender of Virtue or Apostle of Violence," *History of European Ideas* 12, no. 2 (1990): 239–57.

66. Along with John N. Figgis (1866–1919) and Harold J. Laski (1893–1950), Cole was the founder of English pluralist theory. Inspired by Maitland and his influential reception of Gierke's theory of associations, these pluralists put forward a compelling critique of state sovereignty and made the case for a decentralized form of authority whereby society would be administered by self-governing and semiautonomous associations. See C. Laborde, *Pluralist Thought and the State in Britain and France, 1900–25* (Houndmills, UK: Palgrave Macmillan, 2000); D. Nicholls, *The Pluralist State: The Political Ideas of J. N. Figgis and His Contemporaries* (London: Macmillan, 1975); P. Hirst (ed.), *The Pluralist Theory of the*

State: Selected Writings of G. D. H. Cole, J. N. Figgis, and H. J. Laski (London: Routledge, 1989); Runciman, *Pluralism and the Personality of the State.* On British pluralism as entailing a novel political science methodology, see M. Bevir (ed.), *Modern Pluralism: Anglo-American Debates since 1880* (Cambridge: Cambridge University Press, 2012).

67. See E. D. Ellis, "The Pluralistic State," *American Political Science Review* 14, no. 3 (1920): 399–402.

68. S. Cassese, "The Rise and Decline of the Notion of State," *International Political Science Review/Revue internationale de science politique* 7, no. 2 (1986): 124.

69. In light of the topic of this book, we mainly concentrate on Germany and Italy. In the present section, we will devote some attention to France as it was the cradle of a jurisprudential view that had a significant impact on the authors this book speaks of.

70. Insightful criticisms of these authors are provided in L. Duguit, "The Law and the State," *Harvard Law Review* 31, no. 1 (1917): 1–185.

71. See L. Duguit, "Objective Law. II," *Columbia Law Review* 21, no. 1 (1921): 17–34.

72. L. Duguit, "Objective Law," *Columbia Law Review* 20, no. 8 (1920): 818.

73. Duguit, "Objective Law," 827.

74. This aspect is emphasized in M. Loughlin, "The Functionalist Style in Public Law," *University of Toronto Law Journal* 55, no. 3 (2005): 370.

75. Duguit, "Objective Law. II," 21.

76. Duguit, "Objective Law. II," 24.

77. Duguit, "Objective Law. II," 24.

78. Duguit, "Objective Law. II," 28–34.

79. See L. Duguit, "Objective Law. III," *Columbia Law Review* 21, no. 2 (1921): 130.

80. G. Gurvitch, *Sociology of Law* (London: Kegan Paul, Trench, Trubner & Co., 1947), 101–2.

81. C. Laborde, "Pluralism, Syndicalism and Corporatism: Léon Duguit and the Crisis of the State (1900–1925)," *History of European Ideas* 22, no. 3 (1996): 234.

82. For a discussion of functional representation within British theories of the pluralist state, see Laborde, *Pluralist Thought and the State in Britain and France.*

83. See Laborde, *Pluralist Thought and the State in Britain and France*, 119.

84. Along with Ehrlich, among the most relevant exponents of the Free Law Movement are Hermann Kantorowicz (1877–1940), Ernst Fuchs (1859–1929), and Hermann Isay (1873–1938). On its influence on American legal realism see J. E. Herget and S. Wallace, "The German Free Law Movement as the Source of American Legal Realism," *Virginia Law Review* 73, no. 2 (1987): 399–455; V. G. Curran, "Rethinking Hermann Kantorowicz: Free Law, American Legal Realism and the

Legacy of Anti-Formalism," in *Rethinking the Masters of Comparative Law*, ed. A. Riles (Oxford and Portland, OR: Hart, 2001), 66–84.

85. Gény's seminal insight was that the judge should undertake free scientific research on law and society (*libre recherche scientifique*) for them to make legal decisions based on this research. On the influence of Gény on US jurisprudence through Charles Sander Peirce, see R. Kevelson, "Peirce as Catalyst in Modern Legal Science," in *Semiotics 1980*, ed. M. Herzfeld and M. D. Lenhart (Dordrecht: Springer, 1980), 241–54. See also R. Kevelson, *The Law as a System of Signs* (New York: Plenum, 1988).

86. E. Ehrlich, "Judicial Freedom of Decision: Its Principles and Objects," in *Science of Legal Method; Select Essays by Various Authors*, ed. E. Bruncken et al. (Brookline, MA: Riverdale, 1917), 74.

87. One of the most precious sources for the study of Ehrlich's theorizing is M. Hertogh (ed.), *Living Law: Reconsidering Eugen Ehrlich* (Oxford and Portland, OR: Hart, 2009). See also K. Papendorf, S. Machura, and A. Hellum (eds.), *Eugen Ehrlich's Sociology of Law* (Berlin: Lit Verlag, 2014).

88. On the differences and similarities between this distinction and Roscoe Pound's one between "law in the books" and "law in action," see D. Nelken, "Law in Action or Living Law? Back to the Beginning in Sociology of Law," *Legal Studies* 4, no. 2 (1984): 157–74 and S. Nimaga, "Pounding on Ehrlich, Again?" in *Living Law*, ed. Hertogh, 162–63. On Ehrlich's centrality to American jurisprudence and Pound engagement with his theory, see N. E. H. Hull, *Roscoe Pound and Karl Llewellyn: Searching for an American Jurisprudence* (Chicago: University of Chicago Press, 1997), 109–12.

89. E. Ehrlich, *Fundamental Principles of the Sociology of Law* (New Brunswick, NJ: Transaction, 2009), 10.

90. Ehrlich, *Fundamental Principles of the Sociology of Law*, 39.

91. Ehrlich, *Fundamental Principles of the Sociology of Law*, 85.

92. Ehrlich, *Fundamental Principles of the Sociology of Law*, 85.

93. Ehrlich, *Fundamental Principles of the Sociology of Law*, 488.

94. Ehrlich, *Fundamental Principles of the Sociology of Law*, 63–64.

95. Nelken, "Law in Action or Living Law?" 163.

96. B. Z. Tamanaha, "An Analytical Map of Social Scientific Approaches to the Concept of Law," *Oxford Journal of Legal Studies* 15, no. 4 (1995): 505.

97. Ehrlich, *Fundamental Principles of the Sociology of Law*, 164–65.

98. See e.g., M. Hertogh, "From 'Men of Files' to 'Men of the Senses': A Brief Characterization of Eugen Ehrlich's Sociology of Law," in *Living Law. Reconsidering Eugen Ehrlich*, ed. M. Hertogh (Oxford and Portland, OR: Hart, 2009), 1–17; S. Vogl, "Eugen Ehrlich's Linking of Sociology and Jurisprudence and the Reception of his Work in Japan," in *Living Law*, ed. Hertogh, 95–123.

99. Ehrlich, *Fundamental Principles of the Sociology of Law*, 167.

100. See also B. van Klink, "Facts and Norms: The Unfinished Debate between Eugen Ehrlich and Hans Kelsen," in *Living Law*, ed. Hertogh, 127–56.

101. M. Rheinstein, "Sociology of Law. Apropos Moll's Translation of Eugen Ehrlich's *Grundlegung der Soziologie des Rechts*," *International Journal of Ethics* 48, no. 2 (1938): 235.

CHAPTER TWO

1. See e.g., M. Galizia, "Profili storico-comparativi della scienza del diritto costituzionale," *Archivio giuridico Serafini* (1963): 3–110; S. Cassese, *Cultura e politica del diritto amministrativo* (Bologna: il Mulino, 1971); M. S. Giannini, "Profili storici della scienza del diritto amministrativo," *Quaderni Fiorentini per la storia del pensiero giuridico moderno* 2 (1973): 179–274.

2. Politically Romano was certainly a conservative, but he did not espouse the Fascist ideology with enthusiasm. It is likely that he regarded Mussolini's regime as a solution to the limits of nineteenth-century liberal constitutionalism. Be this as it may, he became member of the Fascist Party in 1928—"quite late," Aldo Sandulli (2009: 30) points out, and only to be able to take up the appointment: see A. Sandulli, "Santi Romano and the Perception of the Public Law Complexity," *Italian Journal of Public Law* 1 (2009): 1–38. In short, the relationship between Romano and Fascism is nuanced, as he never stood up against it in any significant way, but on the other hand he never allowed the "Fascistization" of the Council of State: see G. Melis, "Il Consiglio di Stato ai tempi di Santi Romano," in *La giustizia amministrativa ai tempi di Santi Romano presidente del Consiglio di Stato* (Turin: Giappichelli, 2004), 39–58.

3. Highly detailed bio-bibliographical notes are offered in A. Romano, "Nota bio-bibliografica," in id. (ed.), *L'"ultimo" Santi Romano*, ed. A. Romano (Milan: Giuffrè, 2013), 843–85, and Sandulli, "Santi Romano and the Perception of the Public Law Complexity." For a general outline of Romano's theory see F. Fontanelli, "Santi Romano and *L'ordinamento giuridico*: The Relevance of a Forgotten Masterpiece for Contemporary International, Transnational and Global Legal Relations," *Transnational Legal Theory* 2, no. 1 (2011): 67–117. For a recent reappraisal of Romano's theorizing also see M. Loughlin, *Political Jurisprudence* (Oxford: Oxford University Press, 2017); M. de Wilde, "The Dark Side of Institutionalism: Carl Schmitt Reading Santi Romano," *Ethics & Global Politics* 11, no. 2 (2018): 12–24; A. Salvatore, "A Counter-Mine that Explodes Silently: Romano and Schmitt on the Unity of the Legal Order," *Ethics & Global Politics*, 11, no. 2 (2018): 50–59; L. Vinx, "Santi Romano against the State?," *Ethics & Global Politics* 11, no. 2 (2018): 35–36.

4. S. Romano, *The Legal Order* (Abingdon, UK: Routledge, 2017)—the original Italian version is *L'ordinamento giuridico* (Florence: Sansoni, 1946, 2nd revised and enlarged edition).

5. Other remarkable Romano's writings are, among others, *Corso di diritto amministrativo* (Padua: CEDAM, 1937); S. Romano, *Corso di diritto internazionale* (Padua: CEDAM, 1939, 4th ed.); *Principii di diritto costituzionale generale* (Milan: Giuffrè, 1945).

6. See e.g., S. Cassese, "Ipotesi sulla formazione de 'L'ordinamento giuridico' di Santi Romano," *Quaderni fiorentini* 1 (1972): 248.

7. See e.g., A. Morrone, "Per il metodo del costituzionalista: riflettendo su 'Lo Stato moderno e la sua crisi' di Santi Romano," *Quaderni costituzionali* 32 (2012): 377–78.

8. Cassese, "Ipotesi sulla formazione de 'L'ordinamento giuridico' di Santi Romano," 276.

9. See D. Runciman, *Pluralism and the Personality of the State* (Cambridge: Cambridge University Press, 1997).

10. S. Romano, "Lo Stato moderno e la sua crisi," in *Lo Stato moderno e la sua crisi. Saggi di diritto costituzionale* (Milan: Giuffrè, 1969), 8.

11. Romano, "Lo Stato moderno e la sua crisi," 7.

12. Romano, "Lo Stato moderno e la sua crisi," 13.

13. Romano, "Lo Stato moderno e la sua crisi," 14; see also P. Grossi, *A History of European Law* (Malden, MA: Wiley-Blackwell, 2010), 138–39.

14. Romano, "Lo Stato moderno e la sua crisi," 12.

15. Romano, *The Legal Order*, 53.

16. Romano, "Lo Stato moderno e la sua crisi," 5.

17. Romano, "Lo Stato moderno e la sua crisi," 6.

18. Romano, "Lo Stato moderno e la sua crisi," 22.

19. Romano, "Lo Stato moderno e la sua crisi," 22.

20. For the idea of Romano's theory as a "complex self-description of society," see G. Teubner, *Constitutional Fragments: Societal Constitutionalism and Globalization* (Oxford: Oxford University Press, 2012), 21.

21. The work was initially divided into two parts that were published in two separate issues of the journal *Annali delle Università Toscane* in 1917 and 1918. The two were then published together in book form in 1918.

22. J. Paulsson, "Arbitration in Three Dimensions," *International and Comparative Law Quarterly* 60, no. 2 (2011): 291–323.

23. M. Loughlin, "Romano and the Institutional Theory of Law," in Romano, *The Legal Order*, xi.

24. Romano, *The Legal Order*, 1.

25. Romano, *The Legal Order*, 5.

26. H. L. A. Hart, *The Concept of Law*, 1st ed. in Hart, *The Concept of Law*, 2nd ed., edited by P. A. Bulloch and J. Raz (Oxford: Oxford University Press, 1994), 85. On the uncertainties that beset Hart's distinction between primary and secondary norms, see M. Bayles, *Hart's Legal Philosophy. An Examination* (Dordrecht:

Kluwer, 1992); S. Perry, "Hart's Methodological Positivism," in *Hart's Postscript: Essays on the Postscript to the Concept of Law*, ed. J. l. Coleman (Oxford: Oxford University Press, 2001), 311–54.

27. The reasons why Hart revised the scope of his analysis of social rules are abundantly discussed in Coleman, *Hart's Postscript.*

28. Romano, *The Legal Order*, 10.

29. Romano, *The Legal Order*, 10–11.

30. Romano, *The Legal Order*, 11.

31. Romano, *The Legal Order*, 11.

32. M. Hauriou, *Cours de science sociale. La science sociale traditionnelle* (Paris: Larose, 1896); M. Hauriou, *Principes de droit public* (Paris: Sirey, 1910); M. Hauriou, *Précis de droit constitutionnel* (Paris: Sirey, 1923); M. Hauriou, "La théorie de l'institution et de la fondation. Essai de vitalisme social," *Cahiers de la Nouvelle Journée* 4 (1925) (La cité moderne et les transformations du droit): 2–45.

33. A. Broderick (ed.), *The French Institutionalists: Maurice Hauriou, Georges Renard, Joseph T. Delos, Cambridge* (Boston, MA: Harvard University Press, 1970), 99.

34. Romano, *The Legal Order*, 16.

35. Romano, *The Legal Order*, 16.

36. On the relation between Hauriou's and Romano's theories also see J. Stone, *Social Dimensions of Law and Justice* (Stanford, CA: Stanford University Press, 1966), 516–28.

37. Romano, *The Legal Order*, 19–20.

38. Romano, *The Legal Order*, 21.

39. Romano, *The Legal Order*, 12.

40. Romano, *The Legal Order*, 13.

41. Romano, *The Legal Order*, 22.

42. Romano, *The Legal Order*, 20.

43. Romano, *The Legal Order*, 22.

44. M. Galanter, "Justice in Many Rooms: Courts, Private Ordering, and Indigenous Law," *Journal of Legal Pluralism and Unofficial Law* 19 (1981): 19.

45. Galanter, "Justice in Many Rooms," 19.

46. Galanter, "Justice in Many Rooms," 19.

47. Romano, *The Legal Order*, 51.

48. Romano, *The Legal Order*, 51.

49. Cesarini Sforza's original term is "giuridico," which in English is generally translated as "legal." However, he uses this word in a way that recalls Hohfeld's in *Fundamental Legal Conceptions as Applied in Judicial Reasoning* (New Haven, CT: Yale University Press, 1919). For an instructive account of "jural relations" in this sense, see H. Ross, *Law as a Social Institution* (Oxford: Hart, 2001), chapter 7. See also Roscoe Pound's preface to the English translation of G. Gurvitch, *Sociology of Law* (London: Kegan Paul, 1949).

50. W. Cesarini Sforza, *Il diritto dei privati* (Milan: Giuffrè, 1963), 11.

51. Romano, *The Legal Order*, 17.

52. Romano, *The Legal Order*, 17.

53. Romano, *The Legal Order*, 32.

54. Romano, *The Legal Order*, 33.

55. C. Schmitt, *On the Three Types of Juristic Thought* (Westport, CT: Praeger, 2004), 57.

56. Romano, *The Legal Order*, 26

57. Romano, *The Legal Order*, 5.

58. Romano, *The Legal Order*, 12.

59. S. Romano, *Frammenti di un dizionario giuridico* (Milan: Giuffrè, 1983), 141.

60. Romano, *Frammenti*, 45.

61. Romano, *Frammenti*, 205.

62. Romano, *Frammenti*, 205.

63. Romano, *Frammenti*, 81.

64. Romano, *Frammenti*, 83.

65. See W. Twining, "A Post-Westphalian Conception of Law," *Law and Society Review* 37, no. 1 (2003), 199–258; W. Twining, *General Jurisprudence. Understanding Law from a Global Perspective* (Cambridge: Cambridge University Press, 2009).

66. K. N. Llewellyn, "Law and the Social Sciences," *American Sociological Review* 14, no. 4 (1949): 454.

67. Llewellyn, "Law and the Social Sciences," 455.

68. K. N. Llewellyn, "The Normative, the Legal and the Law-Jobs: The Problem of Juristic Method," *Yale Law Journal* 49, no. 8 (1940): 1357.

69. Llewellyn, "The Normative, the Legal and the Law-Jobs," 1374.

70. On this, see W. Twining, "The Idea of Juristic Method: A Tribute to Karl Llewellyn," *University of Miami Law Review* 48 (1993): 119–58.

71. Llewellyn, "The Normative, the Legal and the Law-Jobs," 1359.

72. Cesarini Sforza, *Il diritto dei privati*, 16–17.

73. Llewellyn, "The Normative, the Legal and the Law-Jobs," 1355.

74. Cesarini Sforza, *Il diritto dei privati*, 17.

75. Cesarini Sforza, *Il diritto dei privati*, 17.

76. Cesarini Sforza, *Il diritto dei privati*, 29.

77. Romano, *The Legal Order*, 32.

78. Stone, *Social Dimensions of Law and Justice*, 529.

79. Romano, *The Legal Order*, 69.

80. Stone, *Social Dimensions of Law and Justice*, 530.

81. Twining, *General Jurisprudence*, 369.

82. See B. Malinowski, *Crime and Custom in Savage Society. An Anthropological Study of Savagery* (London, Routledge & Kegan Paul, 1926).

83. Malinowski, *Crime and Custom in Savage Society*, 58.

84. On the conceptual problems affecting Malinowski's definition of law, see above all B. Z. Tamanaha, "The Folly of the 'Social Scientific' Concept of Legal Pluralism," *Journal of Law and Society* 20, no. 2 (1993): 192–217.

85. See S. F. Moore, "Law and Social Change: The Semi-autonomous Social Field as an Appropriate Subject of Study," *Law & Society Review* 7, no. 4 (1973): 719–46.

86. Moore, "Law and Social Change," 721.

87. More recently this view has been compellingly advanced by Gordon Woodman—see e.g., G. R. Woodman, "Ideological Combat and Social Observation. Recent Debate about Legal Pluralism," *Journal of Legal Pluralism* 42 (1998): 21–59; G. R. Woodman, "The Idea of Legal Pluralism," in *Legal Pluralism in the Arab World*, ed. B. Dupret (The Hague: Kluwer Law International, 1999), 3–19.

88. See for example E. Melissaris and M. Croce, "A Pluralism of Legal Pluralisms," *Oxford Handbooks Online* (2017), DOI: 10.1093/oxfordhb/9780199935352.013.22.

89. See J. Griffiths, "What Is Legal Pluralism?" *Journal of Legal Pluralism and Unofficial Law* 24 (1986): 1–55.

90. See Woodman, "Ideological Combat and Social Observation."

91. Griffiths, "What Is Legal Pluralism?" 5.

92. E. Ehrlich, *Fundamental Principles of the Sociology of Law* (New Brunswick, NJ: Transaction, 2009), 37.

93. This was particularly flagrant in the Austro-Hungarian Empire, and especially the context of Czernowitz where Ehrlich spent most of his life.

94. Ehrlich, *Fundamental Principles of the Sociology of Law*, 85.

95. Ehrlich, *Fundamental Principles of the Sociology of Law*, 63–64.

96. See W. Twining, "Normative and Legal Pluralism: A Global Perspective," *Duke Journal of Comparative and International Law* 20 (2010): 473–517.

97. Llewellyn, "The Normative, the Legal and the Law-Jobs," 1399.

98. Romano, *Frammenti*, 224.

99. Romano, *Frammenti*, 224.

100. Romano, *Frammenti*, 232.

CHAPTER THREE

1. For recent, influential works that in a way or another take issue with Schmitt's seminal contribution to the study of the state of exception and emergency powers, see G. Agamben, *State of Exception* (Chicago: University of Chicago, 2005); D. Dyzenhaus, *The Constitution of Law: Legality in a Time of Emergency* (Cambridge: Cambridge University Press, 2006); C. Fatovic, *Outside the Law: Emergency and Executive Power* (Baltimore, MD: John Hopkins University Press, 2009); N. C. Lazar, *States of Emergency in Liberal Democracies* (Cambridge: Cambridge University Press, 2009). See also A. W. Neal, *Exceptionalism and the Politics of Counter-Terrorism: Liberty, Security and the War on Terror* (Abingdon, UK: Routledge, 2010), chapter 3.

2. See e.g., G. Balakrishnan, *The Enemy: An Intellectual Portrait of Carl Schmitt* (London: Verso, 2000), 15–16.

3. A. Salvatore, "Normalità e prassi giudiziale. Per una rilettura delle opere giovanili di Carl Schmitt (1910–1914)," *Politica & Società* 1 (2018): 131–52.

4. S. Korioth, "The Shattering of Methods in Late Wilhelmine Germany. Introduction," in *Weimar: A Jurisprudence of Crisis*, ed. A. J. Jacobson and B. Schlink (Berkeley: University of California Press, 2000), 48.

5. C. Schmitt, *Statute and Judgment*, in Jacobson and Schlink, *Weimar: A Jurisprudence of Crisis*, 64.

6. See e.g., D. Bates, "Political Theology and the Nazi State: Carl Schmitt's Concept of the Institution," *Modern Intellectual History* 3, no. 3 (2006): 415–42; L. Brännström, "Carl Schmitt's Definition of Sovereignty as Authorized Leadership," in *The Contemporary Relevance of Carl Schmitt: Law, Politics, Theology*, ed. M. Arvidsson, L. Brännström, and P. Minkkinen (Abingdon, UK: Routledge, 2016), 19–33; M. Croce, "Does Legal Institutionalism Rule Out Legal Pluralism? Schmitt's Institutional Theory and the Problem of the Concrete Order," *Utrecht Law Review* 7 (2001): 42–59; M. Croce, "The Enemy as the Unthinkable: A Concretist Reading of Carl Schmitt's Conception of the Political," *History of European Ideas* 43, no. 8 (2017): 1016–28; M. Croce and A. Salvatore, *The Legal Theory of Carl Schmitt* (Abingdon, UK: Routledge, 2013); M. Croce and A. Salvatore, "After Exception: Carl Schmitt's Legal Institutionalism and the Repudiation of Exceptionalism," *Ratio Juris* 29, no. 3 (2016): 410–26; J. Meierhenrich, "Fearing the Disorder of Things," in *The Oxford Handbook of Carl Schmitt*, ed. J. Meierhenrich and O. Simons (New York: Oxford University Press, 2016), 171–216; M. Loughlin, "Politonomy," in Meierhenrich and Simons, *The Oxford Handbook of Carl Schmitt*.

7. Kelsen's celebrated book on pure theory (H. Kelsen, *Introduction to the Problems of Legal Theory. A Translation of the First Edition of the Reine Rechtslehre or Pure Theory of Law* [Oxford: Oxford University Press]) was written in 1934, but his conception of law was making deep inroads into the contemporary debate well before the 1930s—two highly influential works of his prior to 1934 are *Hauptprobleme der Staatsrechtslehre* (Tübingen: Mohr, 1911) and *Allgemeine Staatslehre* (Berlin: Julius Springer, 1925). His ongoing polemic with Schmitt concerned key issues such as sovereignty and the constitution. See e.g., the recent translation of the Kelsen-Schmitt debate on the guardian of the constitution, with a most helpful introduction by the translator: L. Vinx, *The Guardian of the Constitution: Hans Kelsen and Carl Schmitt on the Limits of Constitutional Law* (Cambridge: Cambridge University Press, 2015).

8. C. Schmitt, *Political Theology: Four Chapters on the Concept of Sovereignty* (Chicago: University of Chicago Press, 2005), 12.

9. Schmitt, *Political Theology*, 30.

10. As we will explain in more detail below, it is important to underline that this process is not only "polemical," that is to say, thoroughly contingent upon

there being a conflict between two parties, but also "polemogenic," in that envisaging the existential conflict between friend and enemy, or better, considering it as a practical possibility, is enough to ignite the political mechanism that brings the friend into life.

11. Schmitt, *Political Theology*, 36.

12. C. Schmitt, *The Concept of the Political* (Chicago: University of Chicago Press, 2007), 26.

13. Schmitt, *The Concept of the Political*, 26.

14. Schmitt, *The Concept of the Political*, 38.

15. This important theory was developed by David Bloor with reference to the late Ludwig Wittgenstein and Barry Barnes's bootstrapping paradigm (see B. Barnes, "Social Life as Bootstrapped Induction," *Sociology* 17, no. 4 (1983): 524–45). Bloor argues that standards to understand and criticize practices emerge out of a self-referring activity, that is, an activity of citing whereby a given performance becoming a standard is determined by one's "commenting on the performances of others, and of one's self" (D. Bloor, *Wittgenstein, Rules and Institutions* [London: Routledge, 1997], 33). Such a creational activity is thoroughly resolved into the practice itself when people draw their attention to a given performance and provide it with a stable, objectified, and transmissible description of it.

16. As Loughlin suggests, the concept of the political is constituted by the criteria that enable us to identify a group as a group, as an organized political entity (see Loughlin, "Politonomy").

17. Vinx, *The Guardian of the Constitution*, 15.

18. See e.g., Brännström, "Carl Schmitt's Definition of Sovereignty as Authorized Leadership"; Meierhenrich, "Fearing the Disorder of Things"; S. Weber, *Targets of Opportunity: On the Militarization of Thinking* (New York: Fordham University Press, 2005).

19. Brännström, "Carl Schmitt's Definition of Sovereignty as Authorized Leadership," 21.

20. C. Schmitt, *Roman Catholicism and Political Form* (Westport, CT: Greenwood, 1996), 8. On this issue, see J. P. McCormick, *Carl Schmitt's Critique of Liberalism. Against Politics as Technology* (Cambridge: Cambridge University Press, 1997), chapter 4.

21. C. Schmitt, *Der Begriff des Politischen. Text von 1932 mit einem Vorwort und drei Corollarien* (Berlin: Duncker & Humblot, 1963), 15. Authors' translation.

22. Schmitt, *Der Begriff des Politischen*, 65.

23. Schmitt, *The Concept of the Political*, 19.

24. E.-W. Böckenförde, "The Concept of the Political: A Key to Understanding Carl Schmitt's Constitutional Theory," *Canadian Journal of Law & Jurisprudence* 10, no. 5 (1997): 5–19.

25. Schmitt, *The Concept of the Political*, 7.

26. Schmitt, *The Concept of the Political*, 9.

27. Schmitt, *The Concept of the Political*, 40.

28. Schmitt, *The Concept of the Political*, 44.

29. The analysis here draws from the argument put forward in Croce and Salvatore, *The Legal Theory of Carl Schmitt.*

30. C. Schmitt, "State Ethics and the Pluralist State," in Jacobson and Schlink, *Weimar: A Jurisprudence of Crisis*, 306.

31. Schmitt, "State Ethics and the Pluralist State," 301.

32. Schmitt, "State Ethics and the Pluralist State," 307.

33. Schmitt, "State Ethics and the Pluralist State," 307.

34. Schmitt, "State Ethics and the Pluralist State," 308.

35. Contrary to this reading of Schmitt's essay, see B. A. Schupmann, *Carl Schmitt's State and Constitutional Theory. A Critical Analysis* (Oxford: Oxford University Press, 2017).

36. Schmitt, *Political Theology*, 2–3.

37. C. Schmitt, "Un giurista davanti a se stesso. Intervista a Carl Schmitt," in Schmitt, *Un giurista davanti a se stesso. Saggi e interviste* (Vicenza: Neri Pozza, 2005), 166–67.

38. See Loughlin, *Political Jurisprudence*, 112–14.

39. A. Broderick (ed.), *The French Institutionalists: Maurice Hauriou, Georges Renard, Joseph T. Delos* (Cambridge, MA: Harvard University Press, 1970).

40. See e.g., I. Maus, "The 1933 'Break' in Carl Schmitt's Theory," *Canadian Journal of Law and Jurisprudence* 10 (1997): 125–40.

41. Bates, "Political Theology and the Nazi State," 416.

42. C. Schmitt, *On the Three Types of Juristic Thought* (Westport, CT: Praeger, 2004), 89.

43. Schmitt, *Political Theology*, 3.

44. Bates, "Political Theology and the Nazi State," 423.

45. Schmitt, *On the Three Types of Juristic Thought*, 49–51.

46. S. Romano, *The Legal Order* (Abingdon, UK: Routledge, 2017), 7.

47. On the relation between Schmitt and Romano, see Croce and Salvatore, *The Legal Theory of Carl Schmitt*, 109–24; M. de Wilde, "The Dark Side of Institutionalism: Carl Schmitt Reading Santi Romano," *Ethics & Global Politics* 11 (2018): 12–24; A. Salvatore, "A Counter-mine that Explodes Silently: Romano and Schmitt on the Unity of the Legal Order," *Ethics & Global Politics* 11 (2018): 50–59.

48. Schmitt, *On the Three Types of Juristic Thought*, 53.

49. Romano, *The Legal Order*, 11.

50. Schmitt, *On the Three Types of Juristic Thought*, 55.

51. Schmitt, *On the Three Types of Juristic Thought*, 56.

52. Schmitt, *On the Three Types of Juristic Thought*, 55.

53. Schmitt, *On the Three Types of Juristic Thought*, 54.

54. Schmitt, *On the Three Types of Juristic Thought*, 90.

55. T. Krebs, *Restitution at the Crossroads: A Comparative Study* (London: Cavendish, 2001), 20.

56. C. Schmitt, *State, Movement, People: The Triadic Structure of the Political Unity* (Corvallis, OR: Plutarch, 2001), 50.

57. Schmitt, *On the Three Types of Juristic Thought*, 50.

58. Schmitt, *On the Three Types of Juristic Thought*, 52.

59. Schmitt, *On the Three Types of Juristic Thought*, 48.

CHAPTER FOUR

1. It is common to refer to a speech given by Mussolini to the House of Representatives on January 3, 1925, as the formal beginning of the process of transformation that included new competences and prerogatives for the head of government (statute 2263/1925), the enactment of laws to forbid political associations, strikes, freedom of expression, and strong limitation of the freedom of information, the abolition of the election of the mayors, a new charter for labor, and the attribution (with statute 2693/1928) of constitutional functions to an organ (the Great Council of Fascism) that was the direct emanation of the Fascist movement. For a historical analysis, see G. Sabbatucci and V. Vidotto, *Storia contemporanea* (Rome: Laterza, 2019), 66–87; U. Allegretti, *Storia costituzionale d'Italia* (Bologna: il Mulino, 2014), chapter 7–9; C. Ghisalberti, *Storia costituzionale d'Italia* (Rome: Laterza, 2002), chapter 4.

2. During the 1920s Mortati worked at the Corte dei Conti (Italian Court of Auditors) for a few years, as mentioned by F. Lanchester, *Pensare l'Italia: I giuspubblicisti nell'Italia unitaria* (Rome: Laterza, 2004), 97.

3. Ilse Staff has noted that two of the main concerns of Mortati's legal thought were formed within the horizon of prominent legal issues at the time of the Fascist regime. She mentions, in particular, the questions of the nature of the government and of the political party: "Verfassungtheoretische Probleme in der demokratischen Republik Italien. Ein Beitrag zur Staatstheorie Constantino Mortatis," *Der Staat* 2 (1996): 272.

4. The first three (key) monographs by Mortati were published over one decade: *L'ordinamento del governo* (1931) (Milan: Giuffrè, 2000): *La volontà e la causa nell'atto amministrativo e nella legge* (1935), in *Raccolta di scritti*, Vol. II (Milan: Giuffrè, 1972), 471–614; and *La costituzione in senso materiale* (1940) (Milan: Giuffrè, 1998) (an English translation is forthcoming in 2021).

5. The red biennium (1919–1920) denotes a couple of years marked by intensive conflict both in the industrial and agriculture sectors. For a classic reconstruction see A. Tasca, *Nascita e avvento del fascismo* (1938) (Rome: Laterza, 1978, 8th ed.). On the red biennium: P. Spriano, *L'occupazione delle fabbriche* (Turin: Einaudi, 1968).

6. As we have seen in the previous chapter, this is a concern that Mortati shared with Schmitt.

7. See M. S. Giannini, *Il pubblico potere. Stati e amministrazioni pubbliche* (Bologna: il Mulino, 1986), chapter 3.

8. R. Smend, *Handwörterbuch der Sozialwissenschaften* (Stuttgart: Fisher, 1959), 301fn (quoted by S. Korioth, "Rudolf Smend," in *A Jurisprudence of Crisis*, ed. A. Jacobson and B. Schlink [Berkeley: University of California Press, 2002], 210).

9. H. Heller, "Political Democracy and Social Homogeneity," in Jacobson and Schlink, *A Jurisprudence of Crisis*, 257.

10. Heller, "Political Democracy and Social Homogeneity," 258.

11. Heller, "Political Democracy and Social Homogeneity," 260.

12. See the reconstruction of Heller's political and legal thought by D. Dyzenhaus, *Legality and Legitimacy* (Oxford: Oxford University Press, 1996), chapter 4. More recently, Dyzenhaus has edited and written a long preface to the English translation of H. Heller, *Sovereignty* (Oxford: Oxford University Press, 2019).

13. See, for example, the positive evaluation of the role of articulated organized groups for the functioning of modern parliamentarianism in "Parlamento e democrazia," *Raccolta di scritti*, Vol. IV (Milan: Giuffrè, 1972), 13. Paolo Grossi has also noted that Mortati had always scorned the idea of a state legal order detached from society and emphasized his related support for intermediary institutions: P. Grossi, *La scienza giuridica italiana. Un profilo storico, 1860–1950* (Milan: Giuffrè, 2000), 292.

14. For an argument in support of the genetic connection between the Fascist regime and Mortati's theory see M. La Torre, "The German Impact on Fascist Public Law Doctrine: Costantino Mortati's Material Constitution," in *Dark Legacies of Europe*, ed. C. Joerges and N. Singh Galeigh (Oxford: Hart, 2003), 305–25. The other chapter, in the same volume, puts forward a less negative view on Mortati's thought: G. Della Cananea, "Mortati and the Science of Public Law: A Comment on La Torre," 326ff.

15. For a recent summary of the different interpretations, see I. Stolzi, "Fascismo e cultura giuridica: persistenze e trasformazioni della storiografia," *Rivista Italiana di Storia del Diritto* 83 (2014): 257–85: See, also, from the same author: *L'ordine corporativo. Poteri organizzati e organizzazione dei poteri nella cultura giuridica dell'Italia Fascista* (Milan: Giuffrè, 2007).

16. On Mortati's participation to the Constituent Assembly see F. Bruno, "Costantino Mortati e la Costituente," in *Costantino Mortati. Costituzionalista calabrese*, ed. F. Lanchester (Naples: Edizioni Scientifiche Italiane, 1989), 135–56.

17. More reflections about the potential Fascist imprint of Mortati's thought will be presented in different parts of the chapter.

18. For a solid argument in favor of discontinuity see M. Brigaglia, *La teoria del diritto di Costantino Mortati* (Milan: Giuffrè, 2006).

19. Recently, there seems to be a renewed interest in this notion: see C. Jouin (ed.), *La constitution matérielle de l'Europe* (Paris: Pedone, 2019); J. Colón-Ríos, *Constituent Power and the Law* (Oxford: Oxford University Press, 2020), chapter 8.

20. As we will see later, this is partly under the influence of the Italian tradition of political studies whose founding fathers were Gaetano Mosca and Vilfredo Pareto.

21. Mortati clarifies that legal rules operate like insurance-type devices. In a preventive way, they provide standards that will allow the consociates to figure out the negative effects attached to disobedience; *ex post*, they make possible to formulate judgments on the conformity of social behaviour to the norms and hence to assess the consequences of the violation: *Istituzioni di diritto pubblico* (Padua: Cedam, 1958), 3.

22. This variety is documented, for example, in the essays collected in Coleman, *Hart's Postscript: Essays on the Postscript to 'The Concept of Law.*

23. C. Mortati, "Costituzione," (1962) now republished in *Una e indivisibile* (Milan: Giuffrè, 2007), 128.

24. In Italy, see also the work of A. Levi, *Contributo ad una teoria filosofica dell'ordine giuridico* (Genoa: Formiggini, 1914, often quoted approvingly by Mortati).

25. Mortati, *Istituzioni di diritto pubblico (I)*, 5–6.

26. To these characters, Mortati adds another possible, but not essential trait: "abstractness" or "generality," which are important for regulating future behaviour and ensuring legal certainty: *Istituzioni di diritto pubblico (I)*, 20–22.

27. Mortati speaks of a synthesis of is and ought: see "Realismo e certezza del diritto nel pensiero di Carlo Esposito," *Raccolta di scritti*, vol. IV, 251–62.

28. Another important distinction for classifying legal orders is the one between those which are voluntary and those necessary or where belonging is not a choice of the subject.

29. Mortati mentions two examples of these original legal orders: the international community and the state: *Istituzioni di diritto pubblico (I)*, 46.

30. Mortati's conception of sovereignty will be examined in the following section.

31. The ordering principle is embedded in the part of the legal order that Mortati defines as the constitution in the material sense. For an analysis of this crucial concept, see the following section.

32. Mortati, *Costituzione in senso materiale*, 46.

33. Most of Mortati's legal theory and his dialogue with other versions of institutionalism are contained in two works: *La costituzione in senso materiale* and *Costituzione.* It is important to note that, despite some differences, in both works the main tenets of his legal institutionalism are presented in the same way.

34. See F. Lafaiffe, "La notion de constitution en sens matériel chez Costantino Mortati," *Jus Politicum* 7 (2012): 7.

35. A. Ross, *Theorie der Rechtsquellen* (Leipzig: Deuticke, 1929).

36. Mortati, *La costituzione in senso materiale*, 41.

37. This is left in the singular, but it should be noted that Mortati thought there could be more (and usually there are more) than one basic norms. What was foundational for him, as for other institutionalists as well, was the idea of legal or-

der, which precedes the idea of the legal norm. The unity of the legal order, which plays a major role in his theory, can be secured without referring to a final norm. But it should be clear that for Mortati there is a final closure in every legal order.

38. Mortati, "Costituzione," 88.

39. Mortati, "Costituzione," 89. Mortati quotes G. Gurvitch, *L'expérience juridique et la philosophie pluraliste du droit* (Paris: Pedone, 1935).

40. For a recent reconstruction, see M. Hailbronner, *Traditions and Transformations: The Rise of German Constitutionalism* (Oxford: Oxford University Press, 2015).

41. At the same time, it has been noted that Mortati's effort is the most productive and serious engagement with Schmitt in Italy during the interwar years: C. Galli, "Carl Schmitt nella cultura italiana (1924–1978). Storia, prospettive, bilancio di una presenza problematica," *Materiali per una storia della cultura giuridica* 1 (1979): 81–160 (especially 124).

42. For an insightful analysis of the relation between these two authors see M. Croce and A. Salvatore, *The Legal Theory of Carl Schmitt* (Abingdon, UK: Routledge, 2013), 124–39; A. Catania, "Mortati e Schmitt," in *La costituzione materiale. Percorsi culturali e attualità di un'idea*, ed. A. Catelani and S. Labriola (Milan: Giuffrè, 2001), 109–28. On the differences between Schmitt's constitutional doctrine and Mortati's, see the next section.

43. It should be noted that Mortati never seriously engaged with the works published by Schmitt post–*Three Types of Juridical Thought*. For example, *Nomos of the Earth* is never discussed, even in Mortati's late works.

44. Mortati, *La costituzione in senso materiale*, 45.

45. See the partial translation of R. Smend, *Verfassung und Verfassungsrecht* (Berlin: Duncker & Humblot, 2014 [1928]) as *Constitution and Constitutional Law*, collected in *Weimar: A Jurisprudence of Crisis*, ed. A. J. Jacobson and B. Schlink (Berkeley: University of California Press, 2000).

46. Loughlin has also remarked the differences between Mortati, on one hand, and Smend and Schmitt on the other, on the point of stability: "He [Mortati] criticizes both the decisionist theory of Schmitt and the communitarian theory of Smend, in each case claiming that such theories are unable to maintain stability: the former because it highlights the necessity of decision without institutional constraint, and the latter because 'the people' as an existential entity are riven by conflict and can never form a homogeneous group": M. Loughlin, *Foundations of Public Law* (Oxford: Oxford University Press, 2010), 397.

47. Mortati, *La costituzione in senso materiale*, 40–41.

48. R. Carré de Malberg, *Contribution à la théorie générale de l'Etat* (Paris: Sirey, 1922). For a study of Malberg's approach to state theory see E. Maulin, *La théorie de l'Etat de Carré de Malberg* (Paris: PUF, 2003).

49. Accordingly, Mortati sees in Malberg another version of the doctrine of the social contract.

50. See M. Hauriou, *Principes de droit public* (Paris: Larose, 1911); see G. Renard, *La théorie de l'institution* (Paris: Sirey, 1930).

51. Mortati, *La costituzione in senso materiale*, 50.

52. Mortati, *Costituzione*, 107n58.

53. This interpretation is partially accepted, for example, by M. Brigaglia, *La teoria del diritto di Costantino Mortati* (as previously remarked, Brigaglia puts a lot of emphasis on Mortati's development, highlighting the discontinuity of his thought after the publication of *La costituzione in senso materiale*); a different interpretation is presented by G. Bognetti, "Costantino Mortati e la scienza del diritto," *Quaderni costituzionali* 31, no. 4 (2011): 803–93.

54. M. La Torre, *Law as Institution* (Dordrecht: Springer, 2007), 35–37.

55. Mortati, *La costituzione in senso materiale*, 55.

56. Note that already in Machiavelli this is seen as the constitutive difference of politics: J. McCormick, *Machiavellian Democracy* (Cambridge: Cambridge University Press, 2011), 22–23. Gramsci as well, in his notebook on Machiavelli's Prince, seemed to concede that the distinction between rulers and ruled is unavoidable and constitutive of politics. See B. Fontana, *Hegemony and Power: On the Relation between Gramsci and Machiavelli* (Minneapolis: University of Minnesota Press, 1993); more recently, P. Anderson, *The H-Word. The Peripeteia of Hegemony* (London: Verso, 2017), 21.

57. Mortati, "Costituzione," 80–81n21. It must be added that Mortati does not address the question of what constitutes a sanction, but he provides some hints. For example, it is not necessary for the qualification of the norm as juridical that there is a systematic and explicit organization for sanctioning the transgressors. What seems to count is that certain interests of the transgressor are affected in a substantial way.

58. Mortati, "Costituzione."

59. Mortati, "Note sul potere discrezionale" (1936) in *Raccolta di scritti*, Vol. III (Milan: Giuffrè, 1972), 999–1020.

60. Mortati, "Note sul potere discrezionale," 1018.

61. This is first introduced in Mortati, *La costituzione in senso materiale*, and developed further in "Costituzione."

62. For a reconstruction of the context see M. Dogliani, *Indirizzo politico* (Naples: Jovene, 1985), 145–52; F. Lanchester, "Costantino Mortati e la dottrina degli anni Trenta," in Lanchester, *Costantino Mortati. Costituzionalista calabrese*, 89–110.

63. For a recent constitutional assessment see C. Thornhill, "The Rise and Fall of Corporatist Constitutionalism," in *Corporatism and Fascism: The Corporatist Wave*, ed. A. Costa Pinto (Abingdon, UK: Routledge, 2017), 79–100.

64. Even in this case, the literature abounds. An exemplary criticism of parliamentary politics is C. Schmitt, *The Crisis of Parliamentary Democracy* (Boston: MIT Press, 1986 [1926]).

65. V. E. Orlando, *La giustizia amministrativa*, Vol. III (Milan: Giuffrè, 1901), 907. It should be noted that what moved this inquiry into the nature of the gov-

erning function was the jurisdictional issue related to the justiciability of the acts of the government, an issue widely disputed during that epoch.

66. An important representative of this view was also O. Ranelletti, *Principii di diritto amministrativo* (Naples: Pierro, 1912), 332. Santi Romano, despite his adhesion to the Fascist regime, also shared the same approach toward administrative law. He would not speak of a governing function, but only of a "reorganized and enhanced executive power, finally restated in that prominent position required for the safety of the State": S. Romano, "Discorso per l'insediamento a Presidente del Consiglio di Stato," *Il Foro amministrativo* 6 (1929) (quoted in Fioravanti, *La scienza del diritto pubblico*, 701). In his textbook of constitutional law, Romano recognizes the principle of unity by highlighting the need of coordination among the different state functions. He speaks indeed of a category of governing acts (*atti di governo*), which are those that "the Crown performs for the coordination of the three fundamental powers of the State:" S. Romano, *Corso di diritto costituzionale* (Padua: CEDAM, 1926), 312.

67. Some of the most important works of the twentieth century on the separation of powers would indeed address this issue only marginally: see M. Vile, *Constitutionalism and Separation of Powers* (Oxford: Clarendon Press, 1967); M. Troper, *La séparation des pouvoirs en France* (Paris: PUF, 1973); G. Bognetti, *La divisione dei poteri* (Milan: Giuffrè, 2001). For a recent engagement (more aware of the potential issues) with the topic see C. Möllers, *The Three Branches: A Comparative Model of Separation of Powers* (Oxford: Oxford University Press, 2013).

68. Mortati, *L'ordinamento del governo*, chapter 1.

69. Mortati, *L'ordinamento del governo*, 68. It should be noted that it is not clear what "constitutional law" means in this quote, but certainly it is not a reference to a statute having constitutional relevance. Possibly, Mortati wants to signal the fact that the "absolute discretion" is in reality mitigated by the internal limits imposed by the constitutional structure of the modern state.

70. Actually, parts of the monograph are devoted to the comparison of other forms of government.

71. Mortati himself recognizes his debt toward Smend (and Otto Mayer before him) in *L'ordinamento del governo*, 14n1.

72. S. Panunzio, *Il sentimento dello Stato* (Rome: Editore del Littorio, 1927). Panunzio was initially a supporter of national syndicalism, but during the Fascist regime became the main theorist of corporatism. See G. Cavallari, "Pluralismo e gerarchia nel pensiero filosofico-politico di Sergio Panunzio," in *I giuristi e la crisi dello Stato liberale in Italia tra Otto e Novecento*, ed. A. Mazzacane (Naples: Liguori, 1986), 413–28.

73. R. Smend, *Die Politische Gewalt im Verfassungstaat und das Problem der Staatsform*, in *Festgabe der Berliner Juristischen Fakultat fur W. Kahl* (Tübingen: Mohr, 1923), 15–20.

74. Smend, *Constitution and Constitutional Law* (105 of the German original).

75. Panunzio, *Il sentimento dello Stato*, 168.

76. A. Gramsci, *Quaderni dal carcere*, Vol. III, notebook XV (Turin: Einaudi, 1975), 1807–9. However, Gramsci's judgement was not positive: "A curious point [in Panunzio's work] is made when Panunzio writes that the functions of the state are not only three, 'as it was according to the old little figures [*figurini*, in the original, a debasing word, n.a.]' . . . but to those another one should be added, that is, the supreme one even in parliamentary regimes, the fundamental governing function which steers the political direction of the State." A few paragraphs below, Gramsci accuses Panunzio of formalism: "In reality, Panunzio thinks formalistically, even worse than old constitutionalists. In order to explain his thesis, he should explain how the detachment between government and parliament happened in a way that the unity of these two institutions cannot produce a unitary political trajectory any longer. However, this phenomenon cannot be explained with logical schemes, but only by referring to the political structure of the country, which means, realistically, with a historical-political analysis."

77. Mortati, *L'ordinamento del governo*, 14–15.

78. Mortati, *L'ordinamento del governo*, 68.

79. Mortati, *La costituzione in senso materiale*, 146n57. This is part of a debate internal to the nature of the Italian Fascist regime. The question was which institution or organ is supreme in this order. There is no need to investigate further this question.

80. The role of the party cannot be underestimated and it will be properly analyzed in the following subsection.

81. See R. Cover, "Nomos and Narrative," *Harvard Law Review* 94 (1983): 44–45.

82. Mortati, *La costituzione in senso materiale*, 74.

83. Mortati juxtaposes explicitly his approach to those that draws a rigid distinction between the political and the legal dimensions of constitutional law.

84. J. Murkens, *From Empire to Union* (Oxford: Oxford University Press, 2015), 61.

85. Mortati, *La costituzione in senso materiale*, 109.

86. This is one of the lasting original contributions of the Italian constitutional tradition to European scholarship. There are no real equivalents of the expression *indirizzo politico* in Anglophone constitutional traditions and for this reason it is difficult to capture its meaning with an accurate translation. At times, *indirizzo politico* is translated as general policy, but we believe that this solution does not capture the sense of permanence of the fundamental political aims of a polity. For a reconstruction of this debate see E. Cheli, *Atto politico e indirizzo politico* (Milan: Giuffrè, 1961); Dogliani, *Indirizzo politico*; P. Ciarlo, *Mitologie dell'indirizzo politico* (Naples: Liguori, 1991).

87. A first seminal occurrence of this distinction, albeit in a different context, is by C. Lavagna, *Contributo per la determinazione dei rapporti fra Capo del governo e ministri* (Rome: Edizioni Universitarie, 1942). Lavagna suggests keeping

separate the general policy making of the government from the fundamental political aims of the state, a solution that will find some form of expression when the Great Council decided to dethrone Mussolini on July 25, 1943.

88. Mortati, *La costituzione in senso materiale*, 109.

89. Mortati, *La volontà e la causa nell'atto amministrativo e nella legge*, 150.

90. Mortati, *La costituzione in senso materiale*, 106. For a contemporary use of the tradition of political law (or *droit politique*) see M. Loughlin, *The Idea of Public Law* (Oxford: Oxford University Press, 2003); O. Beaud, *Puissance de l'Etat* (Paris: PUF, 1994). See, also, the journal *Jus Politicum: Revue de droit politique* (available online at www.juspoliticum.com).

91. Mortati, *La costituzione in senso materiale*, 110.

92. This seems to be identified as the main law of cyclical constitutional change: Mortati, *Lezioni sulle forme di governo*, 8.

93. Loughlin, *The Idea of Public Law*, 5. Unlike Mortati, Loughlin understands governing as a practice rather than as a function: "What I want to argue is that public law—the law relating to the activity of governing—must be conceived as an assemblage of rules, principles, canons, maxims, customs, usages, and manners that condition and sustain the activity of governing:" 30.

94. C. Mortati, "Brevi note su costituzione e politica nel pensiero di Carl Schmitt,"' *Quaderni fiorentini per la storia del pensiero giuridico moderno* 2 (1973): 511–23.

95. An exhaustive analysis of the role of the party in Mortati and its difference with Schmitt is available in L. Rubinelli, "Costantino Mortati and the Idea of the Material Constitution," *History of Political Thought* 40 (2019): 515–46.

96. Fiovaranti, *La scienza del diritto pubblico in Italia*, 770 (italics in the original).

97. Indirectly, one can assume an influence of Gramsci's notion of hegemony. This is, for example, the argument proposed by G. Volpe, *Il costituzionalismo del Novecento* (Rome: Laterza, 2000), 122–27. Obviously, Mortati did not have the chance to read the *Notebooks* before writing and publishing the *Constitution in the Material Sense*. Yet, both Gramsci and Mortati move from a series of assumptions that Roberto Esposito has recently found present in what he defines as "Italian thought": *Living Thought* (Stanford, CA: Stanford University Press, 2012).

98. See the scattered references contained in *Il lavoro nella costituzione* (1954), in *Costantino Mortati e il lavoro nella costituzione: una rilettura*, ed. L. Gaeta (Milan: Giuffrè, 2005), 7–101.

99. Mortati, *La costituzione in senso materiale*, 71. As we will see, this is one of the most outdated aspects of Mortati's reflection.

100. It should be noted that this point explains why certain institutions cannot be political according to Mortati. For example, while Romano contended the Mafia possessed a legal order of its own, Mortati did not.

101. Mortati, *La costituzione in senso materiale*, 73. On the following page, Mortati notes that "in the modern state, the party is the subject from whom the fundamental constitution emanates."

102. C. Mortati, "Sulla posizione del partito nello Stato" (1941), in *Raccolta di scritti*, Vol. IV, 497ff.

103. Mortati, *La Costituente* (1945), in *Raccolta di scritti*, Vol. I, 65.

104. Some scholars have proposed to see the relations among the ruling political forces as an "arch" (echoing a famous expression used to describe the Italian constitutional system: *arco costituzionale*), whose existence is supported by the friction among all its constitutive blocks: M. Dogliani and I. Massa Pinto, *Elementi di diritto costituzionale* (Turin: Giappichelli, 2015), 129.

105. An iconic example of the importance of the hegemonic political forces for constitutional law is provided by one of Mortati's famous interventions at the Constituent Assembly. In a debate with the doyen of Italian public law, Vittorio Emanuele Orlando, on the constitutionalization of norms concerning the family, arts, sciences, education, and health, he stated (against Orlando, who wanted to exclude these subjects from the constitution) that "there are no issues that are in themselves absolutely legislative and issues that are absolutely constitutional, because these are evaluations to be left to the political forces that, in a specific moment, decide for the constitutional or legislative relevance of these issues": *Raccolta di scritti*, Vol. I, 575.

106. C. Mortati, *Istituzioni di diritto pubblico*, 5th ed. (Padua: Cedam, 1960), 69.

107. Later, Mortati defines the ruling class "in a wide sense, including the individuals and the groups who have various positions capable of securing their predominance (ownership of weapons, of land, or of what could be defined as spiritual capital, comprised of religious and cultural values)": "Costituzione," 114.

108. M. Dogliani, *Introduzione al diritto costituzionale* (Bologna: il Mulino, 1995), 337–38; see also M. Dogliani, "Diritto costituzionale e scrittura," *Ars Interpretandi* 2 (1997): 103–36.

109. In Mortati's words: "The theory that sees the condition of validity (or of the positive status) of the norm's juridical nature in its awareness is based on the technical needs of explaining the juridical phenomenon, of determining its own constitutive element and . . . it does not have any connection with contractualist or neocontractualist theories, because the latter tend to provide more a justification of the law than an explanation": 'Il problema della fonte del potere costituente," in *Raccolta di scritti*, Vol. I, 357n4.

110. David Hume provides a first example of a conventionalist political philosophy: see his essays "On the Origin of Government" and "Of the Original Contract," in *Political Essays* (Cambridge: Cambridge University Press, 1994), chapters 4 and 21.

111. A clarification is in order. As highlighted by Marmor, the fact that conventional rules are arbitrary does not mean that they are indifferent. There are

always reasons behind one rule or another. But the arbitrariness of conventional rules is still something different from the arbitrariness of the material constitution because the normativity of the principles and rules of the latter is not separable from their content. This is not the case with conventional constitutive rules, as is made clear by the two conditions of arbitrariness that Marmor sketches out: "First, a rule is arbitrary if it has a conceivable alternative. . . . The second aspect of arbitrariness concerns the nature of reasons for following a convention. The reason for following a rule that is a convention depends on the fact that others follow it too"; see A. Marmor, *Social Conventions* (Princeton, NJ: Princeton University Press, 2008), 9–10.

112. Marmor, *Social Conventions*, 157–62. See also K. Lagerspetz, *Opposite Mirrors* (Dordrecht: Springer, 1995) chapters 3–5. For a discussion of the main tenets of legal conventionalism, see F. J. Arena, *El convencionalismo jurídico* (Madrid: Marcial Pons, 2014). See the recent volume by L. Ramirez-Ludeña and J. Vilajosana (eds.), *Legal Conventionalism* (Dordrecht: Springer, 2019).

113. Following Marmor's scheme, one might note that the surface convention that is instantiated in the material constitution would be grounded in an underlying deeper convention, which would constitute the background legal culture based on reasons for having law in the first place: "There are deep conventions that determine ways of organizing a legal order, its main building blocks, as it were, and those deep conventions are instantiated by the surface conventions of recognition that are specific to particular legal systems": *Social Conventions*, 175.

114. Mortati, *La Costituente*, 304.

115. Notoriously, legal conventionalists tend to resort to the example of games (like chess) for explaining the role of constitutive conventions, but they often do not explain away whether conventionalism provides the reasons for participation to the game in the first place.

116. C. Mortati, "La fonte del potere costituente" (1945), in *Raccolta di scritti*, Vol. I, 356.

117. Mortati, *La Costituente*, 297.

118. For a completely opposite reading, that is, that the failure was caused by the capture of political institutions by fragmented social interests, see C. Thornhill, *A Sociology of Transnational Constitutions* (Cambridge: Cambridge University Press, 2015), 154–58.

119. C. Mortati, *Costituzione di Weimar* (1946), in *Raccolta di Scritti*, Vol. IV, 349–50.

120. Mortati, "Costituzione," 126.

121. This is the famous expression used by Pietro Scoppola to describe the first phase of the Italian Republic: *La repubblica dei partiti* (Turin: Einaudi, 1996).

122. For a reconstruction of late eighteenth- and nineteenth-century doctrines of constituent power, see the old but insightful volume by E. Zweig, *Zum Lehre vom Pouvoir Constituant* (Tübingen: Mohr, 1909). More recent analysis

of conceptions of constituent power are offered in C. Klein, *Théorie et pratique du pouvoir constituant* (Paris: PUF, 1996); A. Negri, *Insurgencies: Constituent Power and the Modern State* (Minneapolis: University of Minnesota Press, 1999); M. Loughlin and N. Walker (eds.), *The Paradox of Constitutionalism* (Oxford: Oxford University Press, 2007); E. W. Böckenforde, *Constitutional and Political Theory* (Oxford: Oxford University Press, 2017), chapter 7.

123. H. Kelsen, *Introduction to the Problems of Legal Theory. A Translation of the First Edition of the Reine Rechtslehre or Pure Theory of Law* (Oxford: Oxford University Press), 65–68.

124. Negri, *Insurgencies: Constituent Power and the Modern State*, 18–19.

125. Mortati, *La Costituente*, 13.

126. A. Barbera, "Intervento," in Catelani and Labriola, *La costituzione materiale*, 52 (where it is noted that constituent power "by producing law realizes itself by subjecting to the same norms that it has enacted").

127. Mortati, *La Costituente*, 14.

128. Mortati, *La Costituente*, 12.

129. This is what distinguishes sharply Mortati's conception of constituent power from those based on social normativity (and Negri's is one of them) or legal pluralism (think, for example, at Robert Cover's idea of jurisgenesis as put forward in *Nomos and Narrative*, 12–18).

130. Mortati, *La costituzione in senso materiale*, 191.

131. C. Mortati, "Commentario all'articolo 1 Costituzione Italiana," in *Commentario alla costituzione italiana*, ed. G. Branca (Bologna: Zanichelli, 1975), 21.

132. The source of uncertainty about the autonomy of the political system is given by the distinction of the hegemonic class into the ruling class (the social basis of political power) and the "political class," which is mostly composed of professional politicians. Mortati draws this distinction, but he is not adamant about the relation between these two subgroups: see "Costituzione," 115–16.

133. Croce and Salvatore, *The Legal Theory of Carl Schmitt*, 130.

134. C. Mortati, *Persona, Stato e comunità intermedia* (Rome: Eri, 1971) (this is a transcript of a series of lessons given on the radio to a general public).

135. Mortati, *Persona, Stato e comunità intermedia*, 8.

136. C. Mortati, "La repubblica presidenziale," *Politica d'oggi* 5 (1945): 214.

137. G. Zagrebelsky, "Costantino Mortati: Founding Father of the Italian Constitution," in *Italian Studies in Law*, ed. A. Pizzorusso (Dordrecht: Springer, 1994), 38.

138. Here we follow the illuminating reconstruction offered by F. Bruno, "I giuristi alla costituente: l'opera di Costantino Mortati," in *Scelte della Costituente e cultura giuridica*, ed. U. De Siervo (Bologna: il Mulino, 1980), 94–107.

139. See V. Cocozza, "Mortati e l'autonomia regionale," in Lanchester, *Costantino Mortati. Costituzionalista calabrese*, 245–77.

140. See the otherwise quite liberal concern for some subjective rights as expressed in his last writing: C. Mortati, "Note introduttive ad uno studio sulle garanzie dei diritti dei singoli nelle formazioni sociali," in *Scritti in onore di S. Pugliatti*, ed. AAVV (Milan: Giuffrè, 1977), 1563ff.

141. Notoriously, during the constituent assembly, Mortati proposed a different composition of the parliamentary bicameral system in order to encompass corporatist elements and the creation of an Economic Council (inspired by article 165 of the Weimar constitution), which would have to ratify collective agreements. For an accurate reconstruction of this proposal see E. Balboni, "Note introduttive allo studio delle formazioni sociali nel pensiero di Mortati," in Lanchester, *Costantino Mortati. Costituzionalista calabrese*, 157–84.

142. See his reflections on the link between these liminal figures and constitutional guarantees in C. Mortati, *La costituzione dello Stato e le garanzie costituzionali* (Milan: Giuffrè, 1965), 88ff.

143. In the constituent assembly, Mortati proposed to introduce a loose regulation of the domestic state of emergency (the proposal was ultimately rejected): see G. de Vergottini, "Necessità, costituzione materiale e disciplina dell'emergenza. In margine al pensiero di Costantino Mortati," in *Forme di governo e forme di stato: nuovi studi sul pensiero di Costantino Mortati*, ed. M. Galizia (Milan: Giuffrè, 2007), 481–82.

144. Mortati, "Costituzione," 192.

145. Mortati, "Brevi note sul rapporto fra costituzione e politica," 528.

146. Croce and Salvatore, *The Legal Theory of Carl Schmitt*, 136.

147. Mortati, "Costituzione," 114. On the limits of this new identification of the dominant forces see G. Azzariti, "La costituzione materiale e le forze politiche dominanti," in Catelani and Labriola, *La costituzione in senso materiale*, 298–301.

148. Two of these instruments were the use of referendums and of electoral laws. See A. Barbera and A. Morrone, "La lenta conversione maggioritaria di Mortati," *Quaderni costituzionali* 15 (1995): 67–94.

CHAPTER FIVE

1. A line pursuing this enterprise can be traced from Kelsen to Shapiro via Hart and Raz. For an account of this stream of normative thought see A. Marmor, *Philosophy of Law* (Princeton, NJ: Princeton University Press, 2011).

2. For an attempt at tackling pluralism from the point of view of legal positivism see N. Roughan, *Authorities* (Oxford: Oxford University Press, 2013). For a recent collection gathering contributions from different traditions, see A. Halpin and N. Roughan (eds.), *In Pursuit of Pluralist Jurisprudence* (Oxford: Oxford University Press, 2018).

3. More detailed accounts of this transition are offered in R. van Caenegem, *Judges, Legislators, and Professors. Chapters in European Legal History* (Cambridge:

Cambridge University Press, 1987); P. Grossi, *A History of European Law* (Malden, MA: Blackwell, 2010); L. Benton and R. Ross, *Legal Pluralism and Empires, 1500–1850* (New York: New York University Press, 2013).

4. J. Austin, *The Province of Jurisprudence Determined* (Cambridge: Cambridge University Press, 1995 [1832]), 11.

5. H. Kelsen, *Pure Theory of Law* (Clark, NJ: Lawbook Exchange, 1995), 355.

6. H. Kelsen, *Introduction to the Problems of Legal Theory. A Translation of the First Edition of the Reine Rechtslehre or Pure Theory of Law* (Oxford: Oxford University Press), 7.

7. S. Romano, *Principii di diritto costituzionale generale* (Milan: Giuffrè, 1945), 22.

8. N. Luhmann, *Law as a Social System* (Oxford: Oxford University Press, 2004). Contemporary updates of Luhmann's systemic thinking have taken up pluralist and nonpluralist versions. For the former case, see A. Fischer-Lescano and G. Teubner, "Regime-Collisions: The Vain Search for Legal Unity in the Fragmentation of Global Law," *Michigan Journal of International Law* 25, no. 4 (2004): 999–1046.

9. This is not always the case for legal institutionalists. Hauriou had in mind a mix of subjective will and objective ideas, while Cesarini Sforza openly criticized Romano's objectivism. See M. Hauriou, *Précis de droit constitutionnel* (Paris: Sirey, 1929), 5; W. Cesarini Sforza, *Il diritto dei privati* (Milan: Giuffrè, 1963), 14–15.

10. S. Romano, *The Legal Order* (Abingdon, UK: Routledge, 2017), 18. In the subsequent page, Romano argues that the institution is a self-standing body whose identity is not determined by its members, patrimony, means. Furthermore, the identity of the institution is never determined by those who are comprised within it.

11. For systems theorists this is the cause of a foundational paradox affecting all modern systems. But as a paradox it should be conceived in a productive way. This is the case because the paradox is what enables the law to be operative by remaining cognitively open to the environment. For an overview of this theme, see O. Perez and G. Teubner, *Paradoxes and Inconsistencies in the Law* (Oxford: Hart, 2005). It should be added that Romano did not share the same concern for the paradoxical foundation of legal orders.

12. Under this aspect we can detect a further common trait with systems theory and, more recently, societal constitutionalism. Although it should be noted that the function of law as a system is more specific in Luhmann's theory: law manages the temporal dimension of normative expectations by solving conflicts. See Luhmann, *Law as a Social System*, chapter 1. As we will mention shortly, Romano would certainly concur that one of law's chief concerns is to solve social conflicts.

13. N. Luhmann, "Operational Closure and Structural Coupling: The Differentiation of the Legal System," *Cardozo Law Review* 13 (1991): 1431.

14. This distinction echoes the difference between imperial and insular nomoi originally introduced by R. Cover, "Nomos and Narrative," *Harvard Law Review* 94 (1983): 12–16.

15. See the remarks by D. Grimm, *Constitutionalism: Past, Present, Future* (Oxford: Oxford University Press, 2016), 143–46; see E. W. Böckenforde, *Constitutional and Political Theory* (Oxford: Oxford University Press, 2017), chapters 10 and 11.

16. Though, again, Schmitt would not concede that the political aims of the state would be value-based: C. Schmitt, *The Tyranny of Values* (Washington, DC: Plutarch, 1996). The problem is that a value-based constitutional order entails that there are limits to integration and these have to be patrolled. Theoretically, it is possible to date back this idea to the notion of a militant order, as introduced already in the 1930s by Karl Loewenstein. His work on the need for a democratic order to protect itself from those who have the serious intention to subvert it will become a standard guideline in the construction of the new constitutional orders out of previous authoritarian regimes. See K. Löewenstein, "Militant Democracy and Fundamental Rights I," *American Political Science Review* 31 (1937): 417–32; K. Löewenstein, "Militant Democracy and Fundamental Rights II," *American Political Science Review* 31 (1937): 638–58.

17. C. Thornhill, *A Sociology of Transnational Constitutions* (Cambridge: Cambridge University Press, 2014), chapter 2.

CONCLUSION

1. We have discussed across the chapters of this volume a number of other figures that might be included in the constellation of legal institutionalism. For example, this is the case for Gierke, Hauriou, Heller, Smend, and Cesarini Sforza. We also believe that some legal theorists coming from anglophone contexts might share fundamental assumptions with legal institutionalists: Karl Llewellyn and Harold Laski.

2. See E. Traverso, *Fire and Blood: The European Civil War 1914–1945* (London: Verso, 2016).

3. T. Judt, *Postwar* (London: Penguin, 2005); J.-W. Müller, *Contesting Democracy: Political Ideas in Twentieth-Century Europe* (New Haven, CT: Yale University Press, 2013).

4. See the reconstruction in Teubner, G., *Constitutional Fragments. Societal Constitutionalism and Globalization* (Oxford: Oxford University Press, 2012).

5. N. Krisch, *Beyond Constitutionalism: The Pluralist Structure of Postnational Law* (Oxford: Oxford University Press, 2012); A. Somek, *The Cosmopolitan Constitution* (Oxford: Oxford University Press, 2015), chapter 6.

6. For theoretical reflections on the consequences of this proliferation of legal sites (and with no intention of being exhaustive), see W. Twining, *Globalisation and Legal Theory* (Cambridge: Cambridge University Press, 2008); N. Walker,

Intimations of Global Law (Cambridge: Cambridge University Press, 2015); H. Lindahl, *Authority and the Globalisation of Inclusion and Exclusion* (Cambridge: Cambridge University Press, 2018).

7. See B. Kingsbury, N. Krisch, and R. Stewart, "The Emergence of Global Administrative Law," *Law and Contemporary Problems* 68 (2005): 15–61; N. Krisch, "Global Administrative Law and the Constitutional Ambition," in *The Twilight of Constitutionalism*, ed. P. Dubner and M. Loughlin (Oxford: Oxford University Press, 2010), 245–66; B. Kingsbury, "The Concept of 'Law' in Global Administrative Law," *European Journal of International Law* 20 (2009): 23–57.

8. For an overview see R. Michaels, "Global Legal Pluralism," *Annual Review of Law and Social Sciences* 5 (2009): 243–62; P. Schiff Berman, *Global Legal Pluralism: A Jurisprudence of Law Beyond Borders* (Cambridge: Cambridge University Press, 2012).

9. Societal constitutionalism, as put forward by Teubner and Thornhill, represents one exception: P. Blokker and C. Thornhill (eds.), *Sociological Constitutionalism* (Cambridge: Cambridge University Press, 2017). Another legal theoretical work whose awareness of the lesson of legal institutionalism institutionalism is noticeable is H. Lindhal, *Fault Lines of Globalisation* (Oxford: Oxford University Press, 2013).

10. We put forward a critique of such new pluralist streams in M. Croce and M. Goldoni, "A Sense of Self-Suspicion: Global Legal Pluralism and the Authority of Law," *Ethics & Global Politics* 8 (2016): 1–20.

Index

Jurists: Profiles in Legal Theory

General Editor
WILLIAM TWINING

STEPHEN GUEST, *Ronald Dworkin*, Third Edition

MARTIN KRYGIER, *Philip Selznick: Ideals in the World*

HUGH BAXTER, *Habermas: The Discourse Theory of Law and Democracy*

THOMAS GARDEN BARNES, edited and with an introduction by Allen D. Boyer, *Shaping the Common Law: From Glanvill to Hale, 1188–1688*

WILLIAM E. CONKLIN, *Hegel's Laws: The Legitimacy of a Modern Legal Order*

NEIL MACCORMICK, *H. L. A. Hart*, Second Edition

WOUTER DE BEEN, *Legal Realism Regained: Saving Realism from Critical Acclaim*

JOHN DINWIDDY, edited by William Twining, *Bentham: Selected Writings of John Dinwiddy*

ALLEN D. BOYER, *Sir Edward Coke and the Elizabethan Age*

COLIN IMBER, *Ebu's-su 'ud: The Islamic Legal Tradition*

ROBERT W. GORDON, editor, *The Legacy of Oliver Wendell Holmes, Jr.*

FSC
www.fsc.org
MIX
Papier | Fördert gute Waldnutzung
FSC® C083411

Kolibri 360 GmbH
Ferdinand-Jühlke-Straße 7
99095 Erfurt, Deutschland
produktsicherheit@kolibri360.de

FSC
www.fsc.org
MIX
Papier | Fördert gute Waldnutzung
FSC® C083411

Kolibri 360 GmbH
Ferdinand-Jühlke-Straße 7
99095 Erfurt, Deutschland
produktsicherheit@kolibri360.de